PUBLIC POLICY IN GIFTED EDUCATION

ESSENTIAL READINGS IN GIFTED EDUCATION

SERIES EDITOR

SALLY M. REIS

James J. Gallagher

EDITOR

PUBLIC POLICY IN
GIFTED EDUCATION

A Joint Publication of Corwin Press and the National Association for Gifted Children

ESSENTIAL READINGS IN GIFTED EDUCATION
Sally M. Reis, SERIES EDITOR

CORWIN PRESS
A Sage Publications Company
Thousand Oaks, California

For information:

Corwin Press
A Sage Publications Company
2455 Teller Road
Thousand Oaks, California 91320
www.corwinpress.com

Sage Publications Ltd
1 Oliver's Yard
55 City Road
London EC1Y 1SP
United Kingdom

Sage Publications India Pvt. Ltd.
B-42, Panchsheel Enclave
Post Box 4109
New Delhi 110 017 India

Printed in the United States of America

Library of Congress Cataloging-in-Publication Data

A catalog record for this book is available from the Library of Congress.

ISBN 1-4129-0437-4

This book is printed on acid-free paper.

04 05 06 07 08 10 9 8 7 6 5 4 3 2 1

Acquisitions Editor:	Kylee Liegl
Editorial Assistant:	Jaime Cuvier
Production Editor:	Sanford Robinson
Typesetter:	C&M Digitals (P) Ltd.
Cover Designer:	Tracy E. Miller
NAGC Publications Coordinator:	Jane Clarenbach

Contents

About the Editors

Sally M. Reis is a professor and the department head of the Educational Psychology Department at the University of Connecticut where she also serves as principal investigator of the National Research Center on the Gifted and Talented. She was a teacher for 15 years, 11 of which were spent working with gifted students on the elementary, junior high, and high school levels. She has authored more than 130 articles, 9 books, 40 book chapters, and numerous monographs and technical reports.

Her research interests are related to special populations of gifted and talented students, including: students with learning disabilities, gifted females and diverse groups of talented students. She is also interested in extensions of the Schoolwide Enrichment Model for both gifted and talented students and as a way to expand offerings and provide general enrichment to identify talents and potentials in students who have not been previously identified as gifted.

She has traveled extensively conducting workshops and providing professional development for school districts on gifted education, enrichment programs, and talent development programs. She is co-author of *The Schoolwide Enrichment Model, The Secondary Triad Model, Dilemmas in Talent Development in the Middle Years*, and a book published in 1998 about women's talent development titled *Work Left Undone: Choices and Compromises of Talented Females*. Sally serves on several editorial boards, including the *Gifted Child Quarterly*, and is a past president of the National Association for Gifted Children.

James J. Gallagher is a senior investigator at the Frank Porter Graham Child Development Institute at the University of North Carolina at Chapel Hill. He has worked in the field of education of exceptional children for over 40 years.

Dr. Gallagher has served as the president of the World Council for Gifted and Talented, president of the Council for Exceptional Children (CEC), and is past president of the National Association for Gifted Children (NAGC). In addition, he is coauthor of a leading textbook, *Educating Exceptional Children*, with Samuel Kirk and Nick Anastasiow, and coauthor with his daughter, Dr. Shelagh Gallagher, of the book *Teaching the Gifted Child*.

Series Introduction

Sally M. Reis

The accomplishments of the last 50 years in the education of gifted students should not be underestimated: the field of education of the gifted and talented has emerged as strong and visible. In many states, a policy or position statement from the state board of education supports the education of the gifted and talented, and specific legislation generally recognizes the special needs of this group. Growth in our field has not been constant, however, and researchers and scholars have discussed the various high and low points of national interest and commitment to educating the gifted and talented (Gallagher, 1979; Renzulli, 1980; Tannenbaum, 1983). Gallagher described the struggle between support and apathy for special programs for gifted and talented students as having roots in historical tradition—the battle between an aristocratic elite and our concomitant belief in egalitarianism. Tannenbaum suggested the existence of two peak periods of interest in the gifted as the five years following *Sputnik* in 1957 and the last half of the decade of the 1970s, describing a valley of neglect between the peaks in which the public focused its attention on the disadvantaged and the handicapped. "The cyclical nature of interest in the gifted is probably unique in American education. No other special group of children has been alternately embraced and repelled with so much vigor by educators and laypersons alike" (Tannenbaum, 1983, p. 16). Many wonder if the cyclical nature to which Tannenbaum referred is not somewhat prophetic, as it appears that our field may be experiencing another downward spiral in interest as a result of current governmental initiatives and an increasing emphasis on testing and standardization of curriculum. Tannenbaum's description of a valley of neglect may describe current conditions. During the late 1980s, programming flourished during a peak of interest and a textbook on systems and models for gifted programs included 15 models for elementary and secondary programs (Renzulli, 1986). The Jacob Javits Gifted and Talented Students Education Act passed by Congress in 1988 resulted in the creation of the National Research Center on the Gifted and Talented, and dozens of model programs were added to the collective knowledge in the field in areas related to underrepresented populations and successful practices. In the 1990s, reduction or elimination of gifted programs occurred, as budget pressures exacerbated by the lingering recession in the late 1990s resulted in the reduction of services mandated by fewer than half of the states in our country.

Even during times in which more activity focused on the needs of gifted and talented students, concerns were still raised about the limited services provided to these students. In the second federal report on the status of education for our nation's most talented students entitled *National Excellence: A Case for Developing America's Talent* (Ross, 1993), "a quiet crisis" was described in the absence of attention paid to this population: "Despite sporadic attention over the years to the needs of bright students, most of them continue to spend time in school working well below their capabilities. The belief espoused in school reform that children from all economic and cultural backgrounds must reach their full potential has not been extended to America's most talented students. They are under-challenged and therefore underachieve" (p. 5). The report further indicates that our nation's gifted and talented students have a less rigorous curriculum, read fewer demanding books, and are less prepared for work or postsecondary education than the most talented students in many other industrialized countries. Talented children who come from economically disadvantaged homes or are members of minority groups are especially neglected, the report also indicates, and many of them will not realize their potential without some type of intervention.

In this anniversary series of volumes celebrating the evolution of our field, noted scholars introduce a collection of the most frequently cited articles from the premiere journal in our field, *Gifted Child Quarterly*. Each volume includes a collection of thoughtful, and in some cases, provocative articles that honor our past, acknowledge the challenges we face in the present, and provide hopeful guidance for the future as we seek the optimal educational experiences for all talented students. These influential articles, published after a rigorous peer review, were selected because they are frequently cited and considered seminal in our field. Considered in their entirety, the articles show that we have learned a great deal from the volume of work represented by this series. Our knowledge has expanded over several decades of work, and progress has been made toward reaching consensus about what is known. As several of the noted scholars who introduce separate areas explain in their introductions, this series helps us to understand that some questions have been answered, while others remain. While we still search for these answers, we are now better prepared to ask questions that continue and evolve. The seminal articles in this series help us to resolve some issues, while they highlight other questions that simply refuse to go away. Finally, the articles help us to identify new challenges that continue to emerge in our field. Carol Tomlinson suggests, for example, that the area of curriculum differentiation in the field of gifted education is, in her words, an issue born in the field of gifted education, and one that continues to experience rebirth.

Some of the earliest questions in our field have been answered and time has enabled those answers to be considered part of our common core of knowledge. For example, it is widely acknowledged that both school and home experiences can help to develop giftedness in persons with high potential and that a continuum of services in and out of school can provide the greatest likelihood that this development will occur. Debates over other "hot" issues such as grouping and acceleration that took place in the gifted education community 30 years ago are now largely unnecessary, as Linda Brody points out in her introduction to a series of articles in this area. General agreement seems to have been reached, for example, that grouping, enrichment and acceleration are all necessary to provide appropriate educational opportunities for gifted and talented learners. These healthy debates of the past helped to strengthen our field but visionary and reflective work remains to be done. In this series, section editors summarize what has been learned and raise provocative questions about the future. The questions alone are some of the most thoughtful in our field, providing enough research opportunities for scholars for the next decade. The brief introductions below provide some highlights about the series.

DEFINITIONS OF GIFTEDNESS (VOLUME 1)

In Volume 1, Robert Sternberg introduces us to seminal articles about definitions of giftedness and the types of talents and gifts exhibited by children and youth. The most widely used definitions of gifts and talents utilized by educators generally follow those proposed in federal reports. For example, the Marland Report (Marland, 1972) commissioned by the Congress included the first federal definition of giftedness, which was widely adopted or adapted by the states.

The selection of a definition of giftedness has been and continues to be the major policy decision made at state and local levels. It is interesting to note that policy decisions are often either unrelated or marginally related to actual procedures or to research findings about a definition of giftedness or identification of the gifted, a fact well documented by the many ineffective, incorrect, and downright ridiculous methods of identification used to find students who meet the criteria in the federal definition. This gap between policy and practice may be caused by many variables. Unfortunately, although the federal definition was written to be inclusive, it is, instead, rather vague, and problems caused by this definition have been recognized by experts in the field (Renzulli, 1978). In the most recent federal report on the status of gifted and talented programs entitled *National Excellence* (Ross, 1993), a newer federal definition is proposed based on new insights provided by neuroscience and cognitive psychology. Arguing that the term *gifted* connotes a mature power rather than a developing ability and, therefore, is antithetic to recent research findings about children, the new definition "reflects today's knowledge and thinking" (p. 26) by emphasizing talent development, stating that gifted and talented children are children and youth with outstanding talent performance or show the potential for performing at remarkably high levels of accomplishment when compared with others of their age, experience, or environment. These children and youth exhibit high performance capability in intellectual, creative, and/or artistic areas, possess an unusual leadership capacity, or excel in specific academic fields. They require services or activities not ordinarily provided by the schools. Outstanding talents are present in children and youth from all cultural groups, across all economic strata, and in all areas of human endeavor. (p. 26)

Fair identification systems use a variety of multiple assessment measures that respect diversity, accommodate students who develop at different rates, and identify potential as well as demonstrated talent. In the introduction to the volume, Sternberg admits, that just as people have bad habits, so do academic fields, explaining, "a bad habit of much of the gifted field is to do research on giftedness, or worse, identify children as gifted or not gifted, without having a clear conception of what it means to be gifted." Sternberg summarizes major themes from the seminal articles about definitions by asking key questions about the nature of giftedness and talent, the ways in which we should study giftedness, whether we should expand conventional notions of giftedness, and if so, how that can be accomplished; whether differences exist between giftedness and talent; the validity of available assessments; and perhaps most importantly, how do we and can we develop giftedness and talent. Sternberg succinctly summarizes points of broad agreement from the many scholars who have contributed to this section, concluding that giftedness involves more than just high IQ, that it has noncognitive and cognitive components, that the environment is crucial in terms of whether potentials for gifted performance will be realized, and that giftedness is not a single thing. He further cautions that the ways we conceptualize giftedness greatly influences who will have opportunities to develop their gifts and reminds readers of our responsibilities as educators. He also asks one of the most critical questions in our field: whether gifted and talented individuals will use their knowledge to benefit or harm our world.

IDENTIFICATION OF HIGH-ABILITY STUDENTS (VOLUME 2)

In Volume 2, Joseph Renzulli introduces what is perhaps the most critical question still facing practitioners and researchers in our field, that is how, when, and why should we identify gifted and talented students. Renzulli believes that conceptions of giftedness exist along a continuum ranging from a very conservative or restricted view of giftedness to a more flexible or multidimensional approach. What many seem not to understand is that the first step in identification should always be to ask: identification for what? For what type of program or experience is the youngster being identified? If, for example, an arts program is being developed for talented artists, the resulting identification system must be structured to identify youngsters with either demonstrated or potential talent in art.

Renzulli's introductory chapter summarizes seminal articles about identification, and summarizes emerging consensus. For example, most suggest, that while intelligence tests and other cognitive ability tests provide one very important form of information about one dimension of a young person's potential, mainly in the areas of verbal and analytic skills, they do not tell us all that we need to know about who should be identified. These authors do not argue that cognitive ability tests should be dropped from the identification process. Rather, most believe that (a) other indicators of potential should be used for identification, (b) these indicators should be given equal consideration when it comes to making final decisions about which students will be candidates for special services, and (c) in the final analysis, it is the thoughtful judgment of knowledgeable professionals rather than instruments and cutoff scores that should guide selection decisions.

Another issue addressed by the authors of the seminal articles about identification is what has been referred to as the distinction between (a) convergent and divergent thinking (Guilford, 1967; Torrance, 1984), (b) entrenchment and non-entrenchment (Sternberg, 1982), and (c) schoolhouse giftedness versus creative/productive giftedness (Renzulli, 1982; Renzulli & Delcourt, 1986). It is easier to identify schoolhouse giftedness than it is to identify students with the potential for creative productive giftedness. Renzulli believes that progress has been made in the identification of gifted students, especially during the past quarter century, and that new approaches address the equity issue, policies, and practices that respect new theories about human potential and conceptions of giftedness. He also believes, however, that continuous commitment to research-based identification practices is still needed, for "it is important to keep in mind that some of the characteristics that have led to the recognition of history's most gifted contributors are not always as measurable as others. We need to continue our search for those elusive things that are left over after everything explainable has been explained, to realize that giftedness is culturally and contextually imbedded in all human activity, and most of all, to value the value of even those things that we cannot yet explain."

ACCELERATION AND GROUPING, CURRICULUM, AND CURRICULUM DIFFERENTIATION (VOLUMES 3, 4, 5)

Three volumes in this series address curricular and grouping issues in gifted programs, and it is in this area, perhaps, that some of the most promising practices have been implemented for gifted and talented students. Grouping and curriculum interact with each other, as various forms of grouping patterns have enabled students to work on advanced curricular opportunities with other talented students. And, as is commonly known now about instructional and ability grouping, it is not the way students are grouped that matters most, but rather, it is what happens within the groups that makes the most difference.

In too many school settings, little differentiation of curriculum and instruction for gifted students is provided during the school day, and minimal opportunities are offered. Occasionally, after-school enrichment programs or Saturday programs offered by museums, science centers, or local universities take the place of comprehensive school programs, and too many academically talented students attend school in classrooms across the country in which they are bored, unmotivated, and unchallenged. Acceleration, once a frequently used educational practice in our country, is often dismissed by teachers and administrators as an inappropriate practice for a variety of reasons, including scheduling problems, concerns about the social effects of grade skipping, and others. Various forms of acceleration, including enabling precocious students to enter kindergarten or first grade early, grade skipping, and early entrance to college are not commonly used by most school districts.

Unfortunately, major alternative grouping strategies involve the reorganization of school structures, and these have been too slow in coming, perhaps due to the difficulty of making major educational changes, because of scheduling, finances, and other issues that have caused schools to substantially delay major change patterns. Because of this delay, gifted students too often fail to receive classroom instruction based on their unique needs that place them far ahead of their chronological peers in basic skills and verbal abilities and enable them to learn much more rapidly and tackle much more complex materials than their peers. Our most able students need appropriately paced, rich and challenging instruction, and curriculum that varies significantly from what is being taught in regular classrooms across America. Too often, academically talented students are "left behind" in school.

Linda Brody introduces the question of how to group students optimally for instructional purposes and pays particular concern to the degree to which the typical age-in-grade instructional program can meet the needs of gifted students—those students with advanced cognitive abilities and achievement that may already have mastered the curriculum designed for their age peers. The articles about grouping emphasize the importance of responding to the learning needs of individual students with curricular flexibility, the need for educators to be flexible when assigning students to instructional groups, and the need to modify those groups when necessary. Brody's introduction points out that the debate about grouping gifted and talented learners together was one area that brought the field together, as every researcher in the field supports some type of grouping option, and few would disagree with the need to use grouping and accelerated learning as tools that allow us to differentiate content for students with different learning needs. When utilized as a way to offer a more advanced educational program to students with advanced cognitive abilities and achievement levels, these practices can help achieve the goal of an appropriate education for all students.

Joyce VanTassel-Baska introduces the seminal articles in curriculum, by explaining that they represent several big ideas that emphasize the values and relevant factors of a curriculum for the gifted, the technology of curriculum development, aspects of differentiation of a curriculum for the gifted within core subject areas and without, and the research-based efficacy of such curriculum and related instructional pedagogy in use. She also reminds readers of Harry Passow's concerns about curriculum balance, suggesting that an imbalance exists, as little evidence suggests that the affective development of gifted students is occurring through special curricula for the gifted. Moreover, interdisciplinary efforts at curriculum frequently exclude the arts and foreign language. Only through acknowledging and applying curriculum balance in these areas are we likely to be producing the type of humane individual Passow envisioned. To achieve balance, VanTassel-Baska recommends a full set of curriculum options across domains, as well as the need to nurture the social-emotional needs of diverse gifted and talented learners.

Carol Tomlinson introduces the critical area of differentiation in the field of gifted education that has only emerged in the last 13 years. She believes the diverse nature of the articles and their relatively recent publication suggests that this area is indeed, in her words, "an issue born in the field of gifted education, and one that continues to experience rebirth." She suggests that one helpful way of thinking about the articles in this volume is that their approach varies, as some approach the topic of differentiation of curriculum with a greater emphasis on the distinctive mission of gifted education. Others look at differentiation with a greater emphasis on the goals, issues, and missions shared between general education and gifted education. Drawing from an analogy with anthropology, Tomlinson suggests that "splitters" in that field focus on differences among cultures while "lumpers" have a greater interest in what cultures share in common. Splitters ask the question of what happens for high-ability students in mixed-ability settings, while lumpers question what common issues and solutions exist for multiple populations in mixed-ability settings.

Tomlinson suggests that the most compelling feature of the collection of articles in this section—and certainly its key unifying feature—is the linkage between the two areas of educational practice in attempting to address an issue likely to be seminal to the success of both over the coming quarter century and beyond, and this collection may serve as a catalyst for next steps in those directions for the field of gifted education as it continues collaboration with general education and other educational specialties while simultaneously addressing those missions uniquely its own.

UNDERREPRESENTED AND TWICE-EXCEPTIONAL POPULATIONS AND SOCIAL AND EMOTIONAL ISSUES (VOLUMES 6, 7, 8)

The majority of young people participating in gifted and talented programs across the country continue to represent the majority culture in our society. Few doubts exist regarding the reasons that economically disadvantaged, twice-exceptional, and culturally diverse students are underrepresented in gifted programs. One reason may be the ineffective and inappropriate identification and selection procedures used for the identification of these young people that limits referrals and nominations and eventual placement. Research summarized in this series indicates that groups that have been traditionally underrepresented in gifted programs could be better served if some of the following elements are considered: new constructs of giftedness, attention to cultural and contextual variability, the use of more varied and authentic assessments, performance-based identification, and identification opportunities through rich and varied learning opportunities.

Alexinia Baldwin discusses the lower participation of culturally diverse and underserved populations in programs for the gifted as a major concern that has forged dialogues and discussion in *Gifted Child Quarterly* over the past five decades. She classifies these concerns in three major themes: *identification/selection, programming,* and *staff assignment and development.* Calling the first theme **Identification/Selection**, she indicates that it has always been the Achilles' heel of educators' efforts to ensure that giftedness can be expressed in many ways through broad identification techniques. Citing favorable early work by Renzulli and Hartman (1971) and Baldwin (1977) that expanded options for identification, Baldwin cautions that much remains to be done. The second theme, **Programming**, recognizes the abilities of students who are culturally diverse but often forces them to exist in programs designed "for one size fits all." Her third theme relates to **Staffing and Research,** as she voices concerns about the diversity of teachers in these programs as well as the attitudes or mindsets of researchers who develop theories and conduct the research that addresses these concerns.

Susan Baum traces the historical roots of gifted and talented individuals with special needs, summarizing Terman's early work that suggested the gifted were healthier, more popular, and better adjusted than their less able peers. More importantly, gifted individuals were regarded as those who could perform at high levels in all areas with little or no support. Baum suggests that acceptance of these stereotypical characteristics diminished the possibility that there could be special populations of gifted students with special needs. Baum believes that the seminal articles in this collection address one or more of the critical issues that face gifted students at risk and suggest strategies for overcoming the barriers that prevent them from realizing their promise. The articles focus on three populations of students: twice-exceptional students—gifted students who are at risk for poor development due to difficulties in learning and attention;

gifted students who face gender issues that inhibit their ability to achieve or develop socially and emotionally, and students who are economically disadvantaged and at risk for dropping out of school. Baum summarizes research indicating that each of these groups of youngsters is affected by one or more barriers to development, and the most poignant of these barriers are identification strategies, lack of awareness of consequences of co-morbidity, deficit thinking in program design, and lack of appropriate social and emotional support. She ends her introduction with a series of thoughtful questions focusing on future directions in this critical area.

Sidney Moon introduces the seminal articles on the social and emotional development of and counseling for gifted children by acknowledging the contributions of the National Association for Gifted Children's task forces that have examined social/emotional issues. The first task force, formed in 2000 and called the Social and Emotional Issues Task Force, completed its work in 2002 by publishing an edited book, *The Social and Emotional Development of Gifted Children: What Do We Know?* This volume provides an extensive review of the literature on the social and emotional development of gifted children (Neihart, Reis, Robinson, & Moon, 2002). Moon believes that the seminal studies in the area of the social and emotional development and counseling illustrate both the strengths and the weaknesses of the current literature on social and emotional issues in the field of gifted education. These articles bring increased attention to the affective needs of special populations of gifted students, such as underachievers, who are at risk for failure to achieve their potential, but also point to the need for more empirical studies on "what works" with these students, both in terms of preventative strategies and more intensive interventions. She acknowledges that although good counseling models have been developed, they need to be rigorously evaluated to determine their effectiveness under disparate conditions, and calls for additional research on the affective and counseling interventions with specific subtypes of gifted students such as Asian Americans, African Americans, and twice-exceptional students. Moon also strongly encourages researchers in the field of gifted education to collaborate with researchers from affective fields such as personal and social psychology, counseling psychology, family therapy, and psychiatry to learn to intervene most effectively with gifted individuals with problems and to learn better how to help all gifted persons achieve optimal social, emotional, and personal development.

ARTISTICALLY AND CREATIVELY TALENTED STUDENTS (VOLUMES 9, 10)

Enid Zimmerman introduces the volume on talent development in the visual and performing arts with a summary of articles about students who are talented in music, dance, visual arts, and spatial, kinesthetic, and expressive areas. Major themes that appear in the articles include perceptions by parents, students, and teachers that often focus on concerns related to nature versus nurture in arts talent development; research about the crystallizing experiences of artistically talented students; collaboration between school and community members about identification of talented art students from diverse backgrounds; and leadership issues related to empowering teachers of talented arts students. They all are concerned to some extent with teacher, parent, and student views about educating artistically talented students. Included also are discussions about identification of talented students from urban, suburban, and rural environments. Zimmerman believes that in this particular area, a critical need exists for research about the impact of educational opportunities, educational settings, and the role of art teachers on the development of artistically talented students. The impact of the standards and testing movement and its relationship to the education of talented students in the visual and performing arts is an area greatly in need of investigation. Research also is needed about students' backgrounds, personalities, gender orientations, skill development, and cognitive and affective abilities as well as cross-cultural contexts and the impact of global and popular culture on the education of artistically talented students. The compelling case study with which she introduces this volume sets the stage for the need for this research.

Donald Treffinger introduces reflections on articles about creativity by discussing the following five core themes that express the collective efforts of researchers to grasp common conceptual and theoretical challenges associated with creativity. The themes include **Definitions** (how we define giftedness, talent, or creativity), **Characteristics** (the indicators of giftedness and creativity in people), **Justification** (Why is creativity important in education?), **Assessment** of creativity, and the ways we **Nurture** creativity. Treffinger also discusses the expansion of knowledge, the changes that have occurred, the search for answers, and the questions that still remain. In the early years of interest of creativity research, Treffinger believed that considerable discussion existed about whether it was possible to foster creativity through training or instruction. He reports that over the last 50 years, educators have learned that deliberate efforts to nurture creativity are possible (e.g., Torrance, 1987), and further extends this line of inquiry by asking the key question, "What works best, for whom, and under what conditions?" Treffinger summarizes the challenges faced by educators who try to nurture the development of creativity through effective teaching and to ask which experiences will have the greatest impact, as these will help to determine our ongoing lines of research, development, and training initiatives.

EVALUATION AND PUBLIC POLICY (VOLUMES 11, 12)

Carolyn Callahan introduces the seminal articles on evaluation and suggests that this important component neglected by experts in the field of gifted education for at least the last three decades can be a plea for important work by both evaluators and practitioners. She divides the seminal literature on evaluation, and in particular the literature on the evaluation of gifted programs into four categories, those which (a) provide theory and/or practical guidelines, (b) describe or report on specific program evaluations, (c) provide stimuli for the discussion of issues surrounding the evaluation process, and (d) suggest new research on the evaluation process. Callahan concludes with a challenge indicating work to be done and the opportunity for experts to make valuable contributions to increased effectiveness and efficiency of programs for the gifted.

James Gallagher provides a call-to-arms in the seminal articles he introduces on public policy by raising some of the most challenging questions in the field. Gallagher suggests that as a field, we need to come to some consensus about stronger interventions and consider how we react to accusations of elitism. He believes that our field could be doing a great deal more with additional targeted resources supporting the general education teacher and the development of specialists in gifted education, and summarizes that our failure to fight in the public arena for scarce resources may raise again the question posed two decades ago by Renzulli (1980), looking toward 1990: "Will the gifted child movement be alive and well in 2010?"

CONCLUSION

What can we learn from an examination of our field and the seminal articles that have emerged over the last few decades? First, we must **respect the past** by acknowledging the times in which articles were written and the shoulders of those persons upon whom we stand as we continue to create and develop our field. An old proverb tells us that when we drink from the well, we must remember to acknowledge those who dug the well, and in our field the early articles represent the seeds that grew our field. Next, we must **celebrate the present** and the exciting work and new directions in our field and the knowledge that is now accepted as a common core. Last, we must **embrace the future** by understanding that there is no finished product when it comes to research on gifted and talented children and how we are best able to meet their unique needs. Opportunities abound in the work reported in this series, but many questions remain. A few things seem clear. Action in the future should be based on both qualitative and quantitative research as well as longitudinal studies, and what we have completed only scratches the surface regarding the many variables and issues that still need to be explored. Research is needed that suggests positive changes that will lead to more inclusive programs that recognize the talents and gifts of diverse students in our country. When this occurs, future teachers and researchers in gifted education will find answers that can be embraced by educators, communities, and families, and the needs of all talented and gifted students will be more effectively met in their classrooms by teachers who have been trained to develop their students' gifts and talents.

We also need to consider carefully how we work with the field of education in general. As technology emerges and improves, new opportunities will become available to us. Soon, all students should be able to have their curricular needs preassessed before they begin any new curriculum unit. Soon, the issue of keeping students on grade-level material when they are many grades ahead should disappear as technology enables us to pinpoint students' strengths. Will chronological grades be eliminated? The choices we have when technology enables us to learn better what students already know presents exciting scenarios for the future, and it is imperative that we advocate carefully for multiple opportunities for these students, based on their strengths and interests, as well as a challenging core curriculum. Parents, educators, and professionals who care about these special populations need to become politically active to draw attention to the unique needs of these students, and researchers need to conduct the experimental studies that can prove the efficacy of providing talent development options as well as opportunities for healthy social and emotional growth.

For any field to continue to be vibrant and to grow, new voices must be heard, and new players sought. A great opportunity is available in our field; for as we continue to advocate for gifted and talented students, we can also play important roles in the changing educational reform movement. We can continue to work to achieve more challenging opportunities for all students while we fight to maintain gifted, talented, and enrichment programs. We can continue our advocacy for differentiation through acceleration, individual curriculum opportunities, and a continuum of advanced curriculum and personal support opportunities. The questions answered and those raised in this volume of seminal articles can help us to move forward as a field. We hope those who read the series will join us in this exciting journey.

REFERENCES

Baldwin, A.Y. (1977). Tests do underpredict: A case study. *Phi Delta Kappan, 58,* 620-621.

Gallagher, J. J. (1979). Issues in education for the gifted. In A. H. Passow (Ed.), *The gifted and the talented: Their education and development* (pp. 28-44). Chicago: University of Chicago Press.

Guilford, J. E. (1967). *The nature of human intelligence.* New York: McGraw-Hill.

Marland, S. P., Jr. (1972). *Education of the gifted and talented: Vol. 1. Report to the Congress of the United States by the U.S. Commissioner of Education.* Washington, DC: U.S. Government Printing Office.

Neihart, M., Reis, S., Robinson, N., & Moon, S. M. (Eds.). (2002). *The social and emotional development of gifted children: What do we know?* Waco, TX: Prufrock.

Renzulli, J. S. (1978). What makes giftedness? Reexamining a definition. *Phi Delta Kappan, 60*(5), 180-184.

Renzulli, J. S. (1980). Will the gifted child movement be alive and well in 1990? *Gifted Child Quarterly, 24*(1), 3-9. **[See Vol. 12.]**

Renzulli, J. (1982). Dear Mr. and Mrs. Copernicus: We regret to inform you . . . *Gifted Child Quarterly, 26*(1), 11-14. **[See Vol. 2.]**

Renzulli, J. S. (Ed.). (1986). *Systems and models for developing programs for the gifted and talented.* Mansfield Center, CT: Creative Learning Press.

Renzulli, J. S., & Delcourt, M. A. B. (1986). The legacy and logic of research on the identification of gifted persons. *Gifted Child Quarterly, 30*(1), 20-23. **[See Vol. 2.]**

Renzulli J., & Hartman, R. (1971). Scale for rating behavioral characteristics of superior students. *Exceptional Children, 38,* 243-248.

Ross, P. (1993). *National excellence: A case for developing America's talent.* Washington, DC: U.S. Department of Education, Government Printing Office.

Sternberg, R. J. (1982). Nonentrenchment in the assessment of intellectual giftedness. *Gifted Child Quarterly, 26*(2), 63-67. **[See Vol. 2.]**

Tannenbaum, A. J. (1983). *Gifted children: Psychological and educational perspectives.* New York: Macmillan.

Torrance, E. P. (1984). The role of creativity in identification of the gifted and talented. *Gifted Child Quarterly, 28*(4), 153-156. **[See Vols. 2 and 10.]**

Torrance, E. P. (1987). Recent trends in teaching children and adults to think creatively. In S. G. Isaksen (Ed.), *Frontiers of creativity research: Beyond the basics* (pp. 204-215). Buffalo, NY: Bearly Limited.

Introduction to Public Policy in Gifted Education

James J. Gallagher

University of North Carolina at Chapel Hill

I t is an honor to participate in the impressive *Gifted Child Quarterly* seminal article series. An attempt to summarize various dimensions of our profession at the fiftieth anniversary of the National Association for Gifted Children is an impressive effort. The reader should be aware that although this project focuses on the contributions made to the field through *GCQ*, there are many fine and relevant contributions made on this topic in two other journals focusing on gifted children, *Roeper Review* and *Journal for the Education of the Gifted*, as well as relevant articles in more general journals such as *American Psychologist*, and *Exceptional Children*, among others.

The selection of articles in this section on educational policy does represent many of the major issues to face educators of gifted students, and those concerned about them, over several decades. After all this time we can still marvel at the basic questions with which we are still struggling. Who are the gifted students? Indeed, are there such persons as gifted students? What should be done differently with them in the educational system? Should the teachers of these children receive special instruction?

But what are the questions that are *not* being asked in this collection of articles? Questions such as, "Do we have the necessary tools to do our job well?" "If the tools are not there, (e.g. curriculum differentiation, personnel preparation) can we create them, and can we convince public decision makers to help us create them?" These are policy issues of some consequence to our future as a profession. Is it any wonder that we have been unable to impact the major engines of change in our society: *legislation, court decisions, administrative rule making,* and *professional initiatives?* (Gallagher, 2002). The articles in this section speak eloquently to the uncertainty with which we present the image of our profession to public decision makers and to educational leaders.

Let us take, for example, the central issue of who "gifted students" are, or should we even say "gifted students" at all? Renzulli and Reis (1991) lay out one of the clear issues of our field. Are we dealing with gifted individuals *or* gifted behaviors? Well, special education is about people, not constructs such as giftedness or creativity. It is the business of public decision makers to care for people, not abstractions. Can we imagine a parent's day at the National Association for Gifted Behaviors? No, for good or ill, we are dealing with human beings with certain characteristics and their fate in our educational system.

Are they a homogeneous group? Of course not, any more than children with mental retardation or learning disabilities or shortstops form a homogeneous group, but the gifted students' advanced ability to think well beyond their age level does create a *common* problem for the educational system and policy makers.

INEQUITY AND GIFTEDNESS

This author would like to suggest that we are periodically embarrassed by the obvious inequality among students of differing classes, ethnic backgrounds, etc. It is as though the phrase, "All men (women) are created equal," is supposed to refer to their personal characteristics and talents rather than their status before the law. Renzulli and Reis (1991) suggest, "Many people have been led to believe that certain individuals have been endowed with a golden chromosome that makes him or her a gifted person."

As Gallagher (2000) points out, the field of behavioral genetics has made it overwhelmingly clear that there are such things as 'golden chromosomes.' If we would pay attention to something as monumental as the Human Genome Project we should conclude that there *are* some youngsters who are born with the capacity to learn faster than others those ideas or concepts that modern societies value in children and adults (Gallagher, p. 6). Are we ready to believe the statement by Coleman, Sanders, and Cross (1997) that it makes sense that some people are more able than others in certain areas at certain times in their lives, and that program options for the development of different paths for different people, from talent to talent, and from time to time, should be sought out? (p. 107) These authors point out that there is no universal gifted child, only children who are more able than others in some areas of life. However, there are still clusters of these students waiting for someone to challenge their special talents.

THE COST OF INDECISION

The consequences of the inability of the professional gifted community to present a strong case to influence the engines of change can be seen in what can happen when these engines *are* energized. The education of children with disabilities, with its own many problems of definition, has made remarkable progress because of public decision makers who were convinced by professionals and parents of the need for special education. The Individuals with Disabilities Education Act (IDEA) is a powerful piece of *legislation,* which provides for a Free and Appropriate Public Education (FAPE) for all children. *Court decisions* have confirmed the rights of children to this Free and Appropriate Public Education. *Administrative rule making* also sharpens the requirements for inclusion of children with disabilities with general education. Together, with strong public initiative, these public actions have created a climate of acceptance for these children in the educational enterprise. But if we sound an uncertain trumpet, who will follow? Why are we so tentative in our actions?

The Unfairness of It All

After many years, this author has reached a conclusion that there is a thread of hidden values that lie behind the opposition to gifted education that has even made educators and parents of gifted students hesitant in espousing their cause. This was dramatically illustrated by an angry woman who approached the author after he had given a talk on gifted students and said, "God wouldn't do that." Puzzled, I asked her to explain. She continued, "God wouldn't make a world where some children (gifted students) had so much and other children had so little."

Just so. The appearance of the unfairness of it all has bothered many people and influenced more of the discussion of the issues related to gifted students than we would like to believe. For example, if we can attribute the cognitive differences that we can clearly observe between students to unfair environments rather than unfair genetics then the differences are manmade and more acceptable to us. Perhaps these "gifted behaviors" are solely due to a favorable environment? It is easier to blame unhappy social conditions than an inequitable universe.

The clear differences observed in the attitudes of middle school teachers and teachers of cooperative learning from the attitudes of teachers of gifted students reported by Gallagher, Coleman, and Nelson (1995) also showed the tendency in general education to *minimize* the differences between gifted students and the general run of students. In the view of these general education teachers, nothing special need be done for gifted students; the reforms of cooperative learning and the middle school movement should suffice. Teachers of gifted students clearly differed on that point, accepting a difference between general and gifted students that called for different educational approaches.

The article by Purcell (1993) clearly demonstrates what would happen when gifted programs are eliminated and gifted students are put back into the general education program. They would resume the same program as all the other students, and no special notice would be taken of them, at least in that setting. Even the article by Jackson (1988) reporting that "[p]recocious reading ability is associated with general intelligence but not all precocious readers have high IQ and not all children with high IQs learn to read early" (p. 204) seems to downplay the differences.

Obviously some children with high IQs will not be early readers for a variety of environmental reasons, but the fact that some (many?) of these students can read three or more grades beyond their life age would seem to catch our attention and require some differentiated education. By admitting that such students require some differentiated education, we confirm that there are meaningful differences between gifted students and average students—a difference that has made us nervous in the first place.

We concern ourselves with differences between racial and ethnic groups on ability measures, but the significant point is that there is an extraordinary range of measured ability *within* each group, with students scoring at the highest level of ability in whatever group you choose. Until we can accept the fact that inherent differences between students are a natural part of life and, indeed, can be seen as creating persons who through their superior intellect can creatively play a significant role in solving many of mankind's continuing problems (war, plague, poverty, injustice, etc.), we may continue to apologize for putting effort and resources into providing special education for gifted students and gifted programs.

The Contributions of Gifted Education

Should gifted education be a pilot experimental program designed to improve general education? Tomlinson and Callahan (1992) point out in their article the many real and potential contributions that gifted education has made to general education. These include the emphasis on advanced thinking processes (such as problem solving and problem finding), and metacognitive processes (such as planning and strategies for attacking ill-defined problems).

In addition, the emphasis in gifted education on multiple modes of instruction (inquiry learning, curriculum differentiation, compacting, etc.) and holding to standards of excellence in content fields, seeking hidden talent through unconventional methods (such as portfolio analysis, product review, etc.) beyond standard testing, have all been helpful to general education in its continual search for a more effective education. Such contributions could hardly be made without separation of those gifted students for special instruction. Treffinger (1991) also notes the important role played by gifted educators as catalysts to bring to the students and other staff skills and resources to reach their own instructional goals.

Certainly, encouraging cross communication between general education and special education through journals, conferences, conventions, etc. as suggested by Tomlinson and Callahan (1992) can be one method of enriching both areas and facilitating the transmission of ideas from one group to another.

How to blend gifted education with general education has been a question decades old. Two decades ago, Treffinger (1982) proposed a blended program as follows:

1. Gifted programming leads to a wide range of services that are considered valuable by the staff of the schools. . . .

2. These services cannot be provided effectively by various teachers in the regular program.

3. Gifted education staff provides resources and consultation to nurture and enhance the performance of all staff members. . . .

4. The efforts of the gifted program are integrated with . . . the other components of the school program.

Treffinger's proposals still seem appropriate but leave some questions unanswered. Who is going to train the gifted specialists? From whence comes differentiated curriculum? Where will the research come from to undergird the special program? How will these *support features* be paid for? The answers to these questions will not emerge naturally out of current programs, as we must plan and fight for them to occur.

DO WE NEED SPECIALISTS IN GIFTED EDUCATION?

A part of the establishment of a specialty in education is the employment of teachers who have received special preparation. One half of the fifty states have certification requirements for teachers of gifted students in specialized programs but, of course, this means that half of the states do not. Renzulli (1985) reports on a court case in Massachusetts using the issue of whether there is indeed a specialty in this area where a teacher of the gifted was hired over a teacher of more general experience. Gallagher (2000) raises the issue again as to whether there truly is a personnel preparation program for professionals while pointing out that the Board of Professional Teaching Standards still does not recognize a teacher of the gifted as a specialty. Coleman's perceptive case study (1994) of a teacher at work with gifted students typifies what we would hope all teachers can become. Coleman did a detailed observation and interview of a teacher whose sensitivity and commitment to high student performance made you wish he could be cloned.

It is time that the profession collectively answers the questions that it continually asks itself. Until it does so, it shall have few hopes that public decision makers will divert scarce resources in their direction. To the question, "Are there such persons as gifted students?" the answer is, "Yes, there are, and their abilities are partly genetic and partly the result of rich opportunities." The difference in prevalence of measured giftedness in ethnic groups is due to the wide variation of social and educational opportunities available to them, and the call for special efforts to find and nurture hidden talent in less environmentally favored groups is now being encouraged in the federal Javits program.

Do we need teachers who are specially trained? Yes, we do. Their training should include helping students to understanding the special nature of gifted individuals, teaching them research techniques to seek knowledge, how to organize knowledge, and how to be an active learner. Should all students be taught these things? Yes, but the level of conceptual understanding of gifted students should require them to go into more depth since they will likely go on to graduate and professional training. Programs like the International Baccalaureate in middle and secondary schools, or strong Advanced Placement courses, can bring desired rigor to the content subjects they are taking.

Does our work have relevance to general education? Yes, it does. We can be a pilot study for new educational techniques but we should remember educational separation is part of the training of gifted musicians and athletes. We also need separation and special training.

Are we a support system for general education, or a separate entity unto ourselves? We are certainly part of a potential support system for general education, but we also should have a degree of separation that helps develop students who will be the top rank of their professions and fields of interest. Cooper (1998) aims higher, for a curriculum of conscience that helps students establish an ethical or moral base for their lives; but who will pay for the differentiated curriculum development to bring such goals to life?

The engines of educational change: *legislation, court decisions, administrative rule making* and *professional initiatives* have only lightly touched the education of gifted students (Gallagher, 2002). Most of the discussions in this section have focused upon differences between professional viewpoints about definition, identification, differentiation, etc.

There have been few major initiatives to place into public codes (legislation, court decisions, rule making, etc.) special programs for gifted education for personnel preparation, for development of differentiated curricula, for research and program evaluation, or technical assistance. Those support system elements help to bring quality education to students of all levels of ability. Yet, it is only by establishing these special support programs and related public support that quality education for gifted students can be attained and maintained.

In another profession, the physician treating a patient will often start with the weakest treatment available and then progress to stronger treatments once the first attempt has been seen to have little effect. We seem to have been following that approach in educating gifted students by prescribing a minimal treatment (one might even say a nontherapeutic dose) designed hopefully to do some good without upsetting other people, perhaps because of the inequity issues noted earlier.

As a profession, we need to come to some consensus that we need stronger treatments. Should we diminish our requests for needed assistance if we are accused of elitism or racism? Or should we respond that we are doing work important to our community and our country, and we need the tools to do the job well? What we are doing for these students is worth doing, but we could be doing a great deal more with additional targeted resources supporting the general education teacher and the development of specialists in gifted education. The failure to fight in the public arena for such scarce resources will raise again the question posed two decades ago by Renzulli (1980), looking toward 1990. "Will the gifted child movement be alive and well in 2010?"

REFERENCES

Coleman, L. J. (1994). "Being a teacher": Emotions and optimal experience while teaching gifted children. *Gifted Child Quarterly, 38*(3), 146-152. **[See Vol. 12, p. 131.]**

Coleman, L. J., Sanders, M. D., & Cross, T. L. (1997). Perennial debates and tacit assumptions in the education of gifted children. *Gifted Child Quarterly, 41*(3), 105-111. **[See Vol. 12, p. 35.]**

Cooper, C. R. (1998). For the good of humankind: Matching the budding talent with a curriculum of conscience. *Gifted Child Quarterly, 42*(4), 238-244. **[See Vol. 12, p. 147.]**

Gallagher, J. J., Coleman, M. R., & Nelson, S. (1995). Perceptions of educational reform by educators representing middle schools, cooperative learning, and gifted education. *Gifted Child Quarterly, 39*(2), 66-76. **[See Vol. 12, p. 49.]**

Gallagher, J. J. (2002). Society's role in educating gifted students: The role of public policy. Storrs, CT: The National Research Center on the Gifted and Talented.

Gallagher, J. J. (2000). Unthinkable thoughts: Education of gifted students. *Gifted Child Quarterly, 44*(1), 5-12. **[See Vol. 12, p. 21.]**

Jackson N. E. (1988). Precocious reading ability: What does it mean? *Gifted Child Quarterly, 32*(1), 200-204. **[See Vol. 12, p. 95.]**

Purcell, J. H. (1993). The effects of the elimination of gifted and talented programs on participating students and their parents. *Gifted Child Quarterly, 37*(4), 177-187. **[See Vol. 12, p. 71.]**

Renzulli, J. S. (1985). Are teachers of the gifted specialists? A landmark decision on employment practices in special education for the gifted. *Gifted Child Quarterly, 29*(1) 24-28. **[See Vol. 12, p. 121.]**

Renzulli, J. S. (1980). Will the gifted child movement be alive and well in 1990? *Gifted Child Quarterly, 24*(1), 3-9. **[See Vol. 12, p. 1.]**

Renzulli, J. S., & Reis, S. M. (1991). The reform movement and the quiet crises in gifted education. *Gifted Child Quarterly, 35*(1), 26-35 **[See Vol. 12, p. 159.]**

Tomlinson, C. A., & Callahan, C. M. (1992). Contributions of gifted education to general education in a time of change. *Gifted Child Quarterly, 36*(4), 183-189. **[See Vol. 12, p. 107.]**

Treffinger, D. J. (1982). Demythologizing gifted education: An editorial essay. *Gifted Child Quarterly, 26*(1), 3-10.

Treffinger, D. J. (1991). School reform and gifted education-opportunities and issues. *Gifted Child Quarterly, 35*(1), 6-11.

1

The Reform Movement and the Quiet Crisis in Gifted Education

Joseph S. Renzulli and Sally M. Reis

The University of Connecticut

The reform movement in education appears to focus on the ways in which schools are organized and managed rather than on the interaction that takes place among teachers, students, and the material to be learned. In the process of designing reform to encourage our most promising students and also to meet the needs of at-risk students, we need to examine the types of changes currently being advocated. An examination of the various reform efforts and the effect that they are having on gifted education is provided in this article. Rather than allowing all reform movements to affect our students without our consent (especially those that call for the elimination of grouping), we need to address the impact of gifted education programs and practices and how they might influence the reform effort. We must also be concerned with continued advocacy for gifted

Editor's Note: From Renzulli, J. S., & Reis, S. M. (1991). The reform movement and the *quiet crisis in gifted education. Gifted Child Quarterly, 35*(1), 26-35. © 1991 National Association for Gifted Children. Reprinted with permission.

programming, creating and maintaining exemplary programs and practices that can serve as models of what can be accomplished for high ability students. Simply to allow high ability students to be placed in classrooms in which no provisions will be made for their special needs is an enormous step backwards for our field. To lose our quest for excellence in the current move to guarantee equity will undoubtedly result in a disappointing, if not disastrous, education for our most potentially able children.

Nobody believes in action any more, so words have become a substitute, all the way up to the top, a substitute for the truth nobody wants to hear because they can't change it, or they'll lose their jobs if they change it, or maybe they simply don't know how to change it.

John Le Carré, *The Russia House*

Although a crisis is something that usually follows in the aftermath of a natural disaster or political upheaval, there is also a kind of crisis that sneaks up on us and takes its toll before we even know that a problem has been simmering beneath the surface of a seemingly stable environment. This type of "quiet crisis" often knocks off its victims one at a time and therefore prevents the kind of mobilization that might be possible if the nature of the crisis was more sensational. We believe that the field of education for the gifted and talented is currently facing a quiet crisis and that in many ways this crisis is directly related to the educational reform movement in America. In our opinion, the major focus of the reform movement is on cosmetic administrative changes in the ways in which schools are organized and managed rather than on the essential three-way interaction that takes place among teachers, students, and the material to be learned. In short, the grand designs of restructuring seem to be focusing on everything but the heart of the learning process.

We also believe that this quiet crisis is the direct result of the conflict that exists between two noble goals of American education, both of which have given rise to the reform movement but have not been able to live in harmony with one another. In the sections that follow, we will discuss these goals, but before doing so, we want to point out that both goals are important, and we do not believe that because one of the goals relates to serving gifted and talented youth, it should be pursued at the expense of the other goal, which focuses on general education and the education of at-risk youngsters. In the final section, we will make some recommendations that might provide a plan for achieving a resolution between the two seemingly incompatible goals.

Noble Goal #1: *To provide the best possible education to our most promising students so that we can reassert America's prominence in the intellectual, artistic, and moral leadership of the world.*

For reasons that are discussed in the following paragraphs, Noble Goal #1 has finally made it to the "front burner" of American education. Up to this point in our history, the goal was less important because the economy and the society at large could only absorb a certain amount of high level talent. The gigantic filtration system known as the public schools delivered to colleges and universities a fairly good supply of the nation's best and brightest—if, of course, they had the ability to pay the costs of higher education or were fortunate enough to obtain some of the limited available financial assistance. With the help of the immigration process, industry was able to fill both its top level and blue collar needs, and industry was not unhappy about the availability of a large labor force with strong backs and willing hands. The fact that this filtration system excluded vast numbers of the ethnic poor, females, and nontraditional learners did not seem to bother social planners because our nation was leading the world in agriculture, scientific development, and industrial productivity. But "the times they are a-changing," and as we enter what economists have called the postindustrial age, we must re-examine the ways in which our educational system has dealt with this change.

Whether we are willing to admit it or not, America is rapidly becoming a second-rate nation in all of the areas on which we prided ourselves in the past. Not only has assembly line productivity fallen behind competition from Asian and Western European nations, but we are also losing the knowledge and the creativity races—areas that traditionally have been viewed as the turf of special educational efforts for gifted and talented students. Japan now produces almost twice the number of scientists and engineers per 10,000 people as the U.S., and Korea has the highest number of PhDs per capita in the world (Naisbitt & Aburdene, 1990). While America once viewed itself as a place where we designed and invented what other nations manufactured, Naisbitt and Aburdene (1990) report that the Japanese are now playing a leading role in fashion design, the arts, and almost all other areas of industrial, commercial, and domestic design (pp. 181–182). According to the *New York Times* (in Doyle, 1989), Japan's annual share of American patents grew over the last 15 years from 4% to 19%, while our own share dropped 20% over the same period. *Statistical Abstracts of the United States, 1988* reported that 47% of all patents issued by the U.S. Patent Office were to foreign companies or individuals, and that only 2 of the 10 companies with the most patents were American. Like the colonies of the seventeen and eighteen hundreds, we are exporting more and more of our raw materials and importing larger amounts of high technology from abroad.

Although the reasons for our declining leadership and productivity are obviously complex and diverse, our nation's schools have been cited as a major cause of our inability to meet the challenge from abroad. Reports such as *A Nation at Risk* and books such as Alan Bloom's *The Closing of the American Mind* (1987) all point to an educational system that is indeed in need of reform at all levels. SAT scores, which fell precipitously in the sixties and seventies have rebounded by only 16 points—still 90 points below their historic highs. The number of high scores (650 or higher out of 800) on both the verbal and mathematical portions of the SAT remain lower than in the 1950s (Doyle, 1989, p. E14). At one time we rationalized declining SAT scores by pointing out that more students were taking the tests and therefore dragging down the national averages, but a recent report by the International Association of Educational Achievement (1988) has presented some shocking statistics with regard to our most gifted students.

> The most able U.S. students scored the lowest of all these countries [Hungary, Scotland, Canada, Finland, Sweden, New Zealand, Japan, Belgium, England, and Israel]. *Average* Japanese students achieved higher than the top 5% of the U.S. students in college preparatory mathematics . . . The U.S. came out the lowest of any country for which data were available. That is to say, the algebra achievement of our most able students (the top 1%) was lower than the top 1% of any other country . . . and our top 5% was lower than any other country except Israel . . . In the upper grades of secondary school, advanced science students in the U.S. were last in biology and behind most students in chemistry and physics . . . What's more, it is not that children in other countries are just a bunch of grinds who do better on their tests because they memorize reams of information by rote. Instead, it turns out that, the more complex and advanced the concepts being tested, the worse the American students do in the comparisons. (p. 12)

Consider the following two mathematics problems reported by Kie Ho (1990), a research scientist who is the parent of Asian-American children attending school in California.

1. Five girls and three boys reached the top of Hurricane Mountain. How many children reached the top of the mountain together?

2. Mark, Theo, and Jack are brothers. Theo was born second. Mark is the youngest. Who is the oldest?

In an unscientific survey, I passed these problems to 15 children, all under 8 years old; two were kindergartners. To no one's surprise, they solved them handily.

These problems, however, did not come from 1st- or 2nd-grade textbooks; they appeared in a mathematics textbook for fifth graders in one of the most prestigious public schools in California . . . I was saddened to discover that what is taught to 14-year-olds in the Netherlands and Indonesia—the solution of quadratic equations—was given at the college level here . . . In Taiwan, a 5th-grader has already started studying motion problems ("At what time will the two cars meet?"). In the Dutch system, multiplication and division are considered finished by the third grade level. When I took a peek at a Japanese 5th grade level math book, I felt sad, embarrassed, and outraged. Who made the decision that our 5th graders, even in classes for the gifted, are not qualified to learn elementary algebra (negative numbers and first degree equations) and geometry (Pythagorean theorem) like their counterparts in Asia?

I shudder to think that if this is happening in schools that are nationally ranked in the 90th percentile, what is being taught to our children in the inner cities? (p. 20)

The upshot of all this for both our most promising young people and for our nation's future role in world affairs is apparent. While the quiet crisis has produced a firestorm of rhetoric about the need for reform, we must examine the degree to which such rhetoric has promoted real and lasting change, and we must also examine the types of changes that are being advocated. If Noble Goal #1 is to develop a plan that will promote challenge and excellence for high potential youth, then a good starting point might be to take a look at the history of previous reform efforts, and especially the discrepancy between the ideal and the reality of making even small changes in places called schools. Almost every major effort to reform American education has been met with limited and temporary success. Progressive education, programmed instruction, discovery learning, open education, and a host of other "innovations" lie battered and broken on the roadside of educational reform. Goodlad (1983), Cuban (1982), and other analysts tell us that in spite of massive efforts and billions of dollars expended to bring about significant changes in the education process, present-day schools bear a striking resemblance to the structure of education at the turn of the century. Whole group instruction, prescribed and didactic curriculum, and an emphasis on standardized achievement and minimum competence have turned our schools into dreary places that can't begin to compete with nonschool interests, extracurricular activities, and endless hours in front of the television set.

Noble Goal #2: To improve the education of at-risk students [and especially those students in inner city schools and rural poor areas] who, if they don't drop out, often graduate from high school without the ability to read, write, or do basic arithmetic.

This second goal has unquestionably been the driving force in American education since the reform movement began in the early 1960s. A concern for at-risk students led to the first major federal support for general education through the Head Start program; and since that time, literally billions of federal and state dollars have been appropriated to help overcome limited achievement on the part of children and youth from disadvantaged backgrounds. It would be nothing short of immoral to question the value of this goal, and even to hint that it has drawn support away from services to gifted and talented students would conjure up all of the social and political criticisms about elitism that our field has judiciously sought to avoid. But the nobility of the goal should not prevent us from questioning the wisdom and the quality of means used to achieve it, nor should it preclude an examination of the side effects of these actions on all aspects of education. Such an examination is even more consequential when we consider the undeniable fact that, at best, most of these actions have had limited impact. Each year, 700,000 functionally illiterate students graduate from U.S. high schools, dropout rates hover around 25%, and they exceed 50% in many of the nation's urban centers (Doyle, 1989, pp. El4, 22).

Not only is there a problem at the elementary and secondary school levels, but the colleges in which our most able students matriculate are also experiencing severe problems. In a report issued by the National Science Foundation's Disciplinary Workshops on undergraduate education (April, 1989), several problems in the sciences were cited. "Undergraduate education in science and engineering in the United States is in a state of crisis . . ." (Chemistry Workshop, p. 3), and "inadequate precollege instruction, declining enrollments, deteriorating instructional facilities and lack of funding for research efforts involving students are particularly evident" (Geosciences Workshop, p. 3). To be certain, isolated examples of success have emerged from the multitude of programs and projects that have attempted to improve education for at-risk students. But for the vast majority, nothing of any consequence has taken place. Achievement continues to decline or remain at low levels, the dropout rate continues to climb, and related problems such as unemployability, teenage pregnancy, drug and alcohol addiction, suicide, crime, and despair on the part of young people are increasing.

The nobility of the second goal and our failure to achieve it has resulted in nothing short of desperate acts of decision making on the part of policy makers. Standardized achievement testing and minimum competence have become the trademarks of the effectiveness movement, and the concept of "excellence" has in many instances been interpreted as "getting the scores up" a few points higher than last year! *Minimum* competence has become the goal rather than the starting point, and the mentality of a test-driven education system has even caused schools with generally good reputations to eliminate or reduce enrichment programs in order to save a few dollars that might be spent to gain a few points' advantage over the next town on the statewide competency tests. And in times of tight budgets, the let's-get-rid-of-the-frills argument has great appeal to anxious taxpayers.

Failure to achieve Noble Goal #2 is undoubtedly the strongest motivation behind the reform movement. And, as is always the case when frustration turns to desperation, peremptory solutions are sought, solutions that seldom have any basis in research and sometimes even less basis in logic or common sense. Our schools have been subjected to an ever-growing list of regulations and a test-driven curriculum that is unprecedented in the history of central planning. The motives for these actions on the part of policy makers are certainly high minded, but as Atkin (1990) points out, the results often produce unintended uniformity and discourage local initiative and imagination:

> State policy makers and school officers must think not simply about one school or community, but many. Pockets of initiative and imagination may be fine, but public policies are usually directed toward improvement of the entire system. *And there's the rub.* Time and again, existing patterns of state-level policy making—with their emphasis on standardization, compulsion and regulation—militate against local variation, whether it be helpful or harmful. And though prescription and regulation may help insure against unsound practice, they are not likely to motivate the most gifted people in a school or in a community. (p. 36) (italics added)

We can better understand "the rub" when we translate it into actual practice. How did some educators jump from the Carnegie Commission's criticism of grouping to doing away with honors classes or replacing entire programs for the gifted with cooperative learning? How do required statewide proficiency examinations translate into every student working on the exact same page and text on any given day of the year? How does the adoption of a policy for school-based management result in turning all curricular decisions over to the union or to an inexperienced parent group? How does Benjamin Bloom's concept of mastery learning result in successful students marking time until less successful students are retaught and retested? And how do a few insubstantial and even trivial studies on grouping (mainly dealing with the social aspects) result in all of the nation's governors calling for an end to any kind of special grouping arrangements?

THE CRUEL TRICKS GAME

Our inability to make any important gains in overcoming the plight of at-risk students has resulted in a short but devastating list of "cruel tricks" that have been used in attempts to explain our failures and lead at-risk youth and their parents to believe that sincere efforts are being made on their behalf. Early rationalizations were embedded in the heredity and environment controversy. Thus, the first explanation was that nonmajority youth were genetically inferior and therefore simply unable to learn at rates and levels commensurate with the majority population. Although this notion has been disproven, the environmentalists have not been much help in offering solutions. Simply stating (or even proving) that poverty, discrimination, and *de facto* segregation are major contributors to school failure only serves to highlight societal problems that will take generations to overcome. But it is a cruel trick to lead people to believe that ineffective schools are the cause rather than the result of such problems. And it is an even crueler trick to lead people to believe that one or another quick-fix restructuring scheme will overcome the accumulated effects of poverty, discrimination, and segregation. The environmentalists also added their own contribution to the cruel tricks game by blaming the families and community backgrounds. Maintaining that the families of at-risk groups failed to prepare their children for school and support them in educational pursuits was yet another rationalization to justify labeling, tracking, and generally lowering expectations for large segments of the population.

Another wave of rationalizations for poor schools attempted to lay the blame on the teaching profession and teacher education, the perennial whipping boy for almost all educational dilemmas. This explanation resulted in a new surge of regimented teaching formulas and a proliferation of so-called teacher-proof materials. These formulas and materials, with their emphasis on prescription, control, and the standardization of the learning process, effectively factored out the intelligence, understanding, and creativity that teachers might otherwise bring to bear on situations that require imagination, individualization, and enjoyment in learning.

Blaming the tests came next in the cruel tricks game, and so we progressed through a period of giving new names to the same old procedures for assessment; but by now the tests had become the dominant decision maker for almost all educational activity. In rapid succession, achievement tests became criterion-referenced tests, minimum competency tests, and now there is a movement afoot to rename them curriculum-referenced tests. Although there is a good deal of rhetoric about alternative forms of assessment through procedures such as product evaluation and student portfolios, serious efforts in these directions are almost always clobbered to death by state regulators and basic skills advocates who say, "Yes, but . . ."and then wrap themselves in the flags of reliability, validity, and objectivity. Tests of general intelligence are indeed being deemphasized, mainly as a result of new theories such as Gardner's work on multiple intelligences (Gardner, 1983). But the testing establishment's obsession with metric measurement has mainly resulted in replacing a general metric (i.e., the IQ) with a broader range of specific scores. The overpowering influence of metric measurement on the curriculum penalizes teachers who want to move away from the "drill and kill" routines that are supposed to pump up test scores. Even the emerging trend toward introducing more thinking skills into the curriculum has largely been relegated to formula-driven practices and prescriptive exercises that can easily be assessed by marking the preferred response on a multiple choice answer sheet. So now, instead of publishing the district-by-district achievement test scores on the front pages of the states' leading newspapers, we will play the same old game with thinking skills test results and pretend that we have something that is a true reform or major act of restructuring.

And when the renamed tests fail once again to explain the gap that exists between advantaged and disadvantaged communities, the testing lobby will offer its tedious and time-worn cliche: "The problems associated with standardized tests are not inherent in the tests themselves, but rather in the ways in which they are used."

NEW TRICKS ON THE BLOCK

Since none of these earlier tricks has explained discrepancies in learning, much less enabled us to do anything about them, the search for additional excuses to stem the dramatic increase in dissatisfaction with the schools continues; and with each new rationalization come recommendations for yet another unexamined panacea. But now, policy makers are really getting desperate because the public *and larger and larger numbers of teachers and administrators* are calling for actions that could be the first steps in dismantling public education. Voucher systems and tax rebates for private schools, issues that were only talked about a decade ago, have become realities in some states and are under consideration in others.

The newest trick on the block is a simple but potentially devastating one for almost all students. By dragging the nation's entire school achievement level down so low that group differences are minimized, it will *appear* as if at-risk students are closing the gap with their higher scoring peers. If this accusation seems to border on the fanatical, consider the following two practices that are already underway in our schools.

The Dumbing Down of the Curriculum

A study conducted by the Education Products Information Exchange Institute (1979), a nonprofit educational consumer agency, revealed that 60% of the fourth graders in certain school districts' studies were able to achieve a score of 80% or higher on a test of the content of their math texts before they had opened their books in September. Similar findings were reported in content tests with fourth and tenth grade science texts and with tenth grade social studies texts.

In a more recent study dealing with average and above-average readers, Taylor and Frye (1988) found that 78 to 88% of fifth and sixth grade average readers could pass pretests on basal comprehension skills *before* they were covered by the basal reader. The average students were performing at approximately 92% accuracy and the better readers were performing at 93% on comprehension skills pretests.

One reason that so many average and above-average students can demonstrate mastery of the regular curriculum in this way is that contemporary textbooks are so much easier than they were only decades ago. Former Secretary of Education Terrel Bell labeled this practice the "dumbing down" of textbooks and criticized the publishing industry for their textbook content as well as the policies and procedures of textbook adoption committees across the country.

Textbooks have dropped two grade levels in difficulty over the past 10 to 15 years. Kirst (1982) reports: "When Californians tried to reserve two slots on the statewide adoption list for textbooks that would challenge the top one-third of students, no publisher had a book to present. They could only suggest reissuing textbooks from the late sixties (now unacceptable because of their inaccurate portrayals of women and minorities) or writing new ones, a three to five year project" (p. 7). The lack of challenge in textbooks has been cited by every major content group in our country. In a national report on the future of mathematics, Lynn Arthur Steen, a professor of mathematics at St. Olaf College, aptly summarizes the problems associated with the lack of challenge in mathematics: "In fact if not in law, we have a national course of study in mathematics. It is an 'underachieving' curriculum that follows a spiral of constant radius, each year reviewing so much of the past that little new learning takes place" (1989, p. 2).

Harriet T. Bernstein (1985), who has written extensively on the politics of textbook adoption and the mandated use of readability formulas, believes that publishers have been impelled to change textbooks to meet state or local readability formulas. She believes that these formulas have resulted in textbooks that flit from topic to topic and result in what textbook researchers call "mentioning." Bernstein aptly summarizes the particular problem that current textbooks pose for gifted and talented students: "Even if there were good rules of thumb about the touchy subject of the difficulty of textbooks, the issue becomes moot when a school district buys only one textbook, usually at "grade level," for all students in a subject or grade. Such a purchasing policy pressures adoption committees to buy books that the least-able students can read. As a result, the needs of more advanced students are sacrificed" (p. 465). Imagine, for example, the frustration faced by a precocious reader entering kindergarten or first grade. When a six-year-old who loves to read and is accustomed to reading several books a day encounters the typical basal reading system, the beginning of the end of a love affair with reading may result. As Brown and Rogan (1983) have stated, "For primary level gifted children who have already begun to read, modification toward the mean represents a serious regression" (p. 6). Savage (1983) believes that basals may not be the best way to promote reading interest and ability: "Very capable readers often find the story content uninteresting, the reading level unchallenging, and the tedious inevitability of the follow-up workbook pages an anathema. Children with considerable reading ability can be held back by rigidly marching page by page through a basal program" (p. 9).

In our field tests of curriculum modification through curriculum compacting (Renzulli, Reis, & Smith, 1981) during the last decade, we have found that most elementary classroom teachers can eliminate as much as 50% of the basal regular curriculum for students who qualify for admission into programs based on the Enrichment Triad Model, or approximately 10–15% of students in the general population. In basal language arts and mathematics programs, it is not unusual for extremely bright youngsters to be able to have 80% of their regular curriculum eliminated. Our field tests of compacting at the middle school level have demonstrated that in classes where students can be grouped by their prior knowledge *of* the subject and interest *in* the subject, approximately 50% of the regular curriculum can be eliminated. In fact, many content area teachers who have worked with bright students in self-contained classes indicate that they cover the regular curriculum in two days a week, leaving the majority of time for alternate work.

Because of the change in textbooks and because repetition is built into all curricular approaches to reinforce learning, many gifted students spend much of their time in school practicing skills and reading content they already know. This is documented by the widespread dissatisfaction expressed by so many school personnel about the use of basal textbooks for high ability students. Despite research by Kulik & Kulik (1984), Slavin (1984), Slavin (1986), Slavin, Karweit, & Madden (1989), and others indicating that students learn skills and concepts at a faster rate when grouping and individualization take place, teachers still utilize whole-group instruction (Cuban, 1982; Goodlad, 1983, 1984).

The Elimination of Grouping

The second practice that will undoubtedly result in dragging down achievement throughout the entire country is the current trend of eliminating most forms of grouping. Before discussing some of the issues related to grouping, we want to emphasize that a distinction is made between grouping and tracking. We view tracking as the general and usually permanent assignment of students to classes that are taught at a certain level, and that usually are taught using a whole-group instructional model. Grouping, on the other hand, is viewed as the more flexible (i.e., less permanent) arrangement of students that takes into consideration factors *in addition to* ability, and sometimes in place of ability. These factors might include motivation, specific interests, complementary skills (e.g., an artist who might illustrate the short stories of students in a creative writing group), career aspirations, and even friendships that might help to promote self-concept, self-efficacy, or group harmony. The major criteria for group effectiveness are commonality of purpose, mutual respect and harmony, group and individual progress toward goals, and individual enjoyment and satisfaction.

The argument over grouping has been a long and passionate one, and every faction rattles off its cache of research studies, while simultaneously pointing out the shortcomings of research presented by the opposition. And like armies who are convinced that God is on *their* side, adversaries even lay claim to the same study by adding their own surplus interpretation or procedure for reanalyzing the data. For the sake of argument, we will take the neutral position that there is no conclusive evidence to support or refute the effects of ability grouping on achievement.[1] But let us examine how a few studies that reported negative social and attitudinal effects of grouping have been blown out of proportion in the popular press and in nonresearch journals. In an article in *The Middle School Journal* entitled "Tracking and Grouping: Which Way for the Middle School?" (1988), George uses the results of a questionnaire to draw conclusions that are clearly not justified by the data. But the most manipulative practice was carried out by the journal's editors who selected out takes (large type, bold print quotes) that unanimously favored the antigrouping position and that were in agreement with their own position as set forth in an editor's note preceding the article. A subsequent report sponsored by the National Association of Secondary School Principals (Toepfer, 1989) draws upon the earlier article in a fashion that would lead the casual reader to believe that it is more powerful research than is the case; and then the report proceeds to highlight yet another string of antigrouping statements. What has clearly happened is that commentators are using "the research" to support a political issue rather than an educational issue, and "the research" has become little more than a pawn that is being used for political expediency. The best way to substantiate this accusation about political interpretation of research is to assume for a minute that the research on grouping is inconclusive or neutral and then examine conclusions drawn from grouping studies. Whenever average or below-average students fail to show growth in achievement from grouping studies, the almost universal conclusion is that it is the fault of grouping. But note how some writers use another set of logic when positive growth occurs.

> Gifted and special education programs may be conceived of as one form of ability grouping, but they also involve many other changes in curriculum, class size, resources, and goals that make them fundamentally different from comprehensive ability grouping plans . . . Studies of special programs for the gifted tend to find achievement benefits for the gifted students . . . and others, would give the impression that ability grouping is beneficial for high achievers and detrimental for low achievers. *However, it is likely that characteristics of special accelerated programs for the gifted account for the effects of gifted programs, not the fact of separate grouping per se. . . .* (Slavin, 1984, p. 307) (italics added)

We have attempted to point out this exercise in illogic (see Figure 1) by contrasting the conclusions of a typical research paradigm that might be used to study the effects of grouping. If the research is inconsistent and far from overwhelming in either direction, then we are at least obligated to apply the same set of logic to the interpretation of those studies that are available. *You can't have it both ways!* If positive growth is the result of curriculum adaptations, class size, resources, and goals, why then cannot we apply the same explanation to cases in which growth is not shown and then use this finding as a rationale for exploring ways to promote better performance in lower achieving students?

A popular item that is currently receiving front page attention in the national press and almost universal coverage in the professional literature is the list of national goals for the year 2000 (National Governors' Association, 1990).

Figure 1   Research Paradigm on the Effects of Grouping

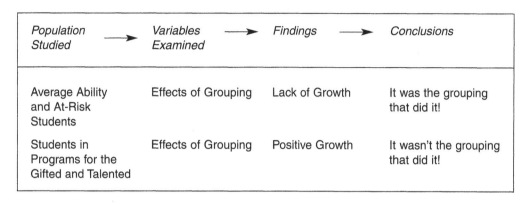

High on this list is a goal that states, "Challenge educators to eliminate ability grouping and tracking." This "headline" item has already provided a rationale for some administrators and policy makers to eliminate or severely water down programs for high potential students. Persons who use these headlines ordinarily do not "read the small print," but if they did, they would find within the context of the same report, the following disclaimer:

> Eliminating these practices does not require ending special opportunities for students, such as gifted and talented or Advanced Placement courses. Nor does it mean abandoning special education or remedial programs for those who need additional services or assistance. (p. 17)

SURVIVING THE QUIET CRISIS

The results of Noble Goal #2 have already had a major impact on gifted education. As Bernstein has pointed out, when districts select textbooks that the majority of students can read, the inevitable outcome is a declining level of challenge for higher ability students. The result of the dumbing down of the curriculum and the proliferation of basic skills practice material may result in the creation of the largest percentage of high ability underachievers in the history of public schools in America. Many of these bright students will learn at a very early age that if they do their best in school, they will be rewarded by endless pages of more of the same kind of practice materials. These same young people may also learn that if they display their abilities in a heterogeneous classroom, the result may be ridicule from peers and the attainment of one of a multitude of nicknames, including brain, nerd, dweeb, and/or others. Consider the following quotation written by a high school student in support of homogeneous grouping and gifted programs for high ability students:

In my 12 years in Torrington Schools, I have been placed in many "average" classes—especially up until the junior high school level—in which I have been spit on, ostracized, and verbally abused for doing my homework on a regular basis, for raising my hand in class, and particularly for receiving outstanding grades, (Peters, 1990)

Sharing the Technology

Perhaps one way that we can achieve resolution between the two national goals discussed in this article is through extending the technology that has been developed in gifted and talented programs to a broader spectrum of general education (Renzulli & Reis, 1985). Our field's technology admittedly will not provide quick-fix solutions to the organizational questions raised by the reform movement, but it can offer numerous creative alternatives regarding instruction and curriculum. In our relatively short history we have achieved a rather impressive menu of exciting curricular adaptations, thinking skills applications, methods for teaching independent study, and numerous other innovations. For example, specialists in the area of education of the gifted have concentrated on identifying student interests and learning styles and providing relevant and challenging curricular experiences to *individual* students instead of identical experiences to 30 students in a classroom without consideration of their previous knowledge or background.

Specialists in the area of gifted education have also gained expertise in adjusting the regular curriculum to meet the needs of advanced students in a variety of ways, including accelerating content, incorporating a thematic approach, and substituting more challenging textbooks or assignments. As depicted in Figure 2, the present range of instructional techniques used in most classrooms observed by Goodlad (1984) and his colleagues is vastly different from what is recommended in many gifted programs today. The flexibility in grouping that is encouraged in many gifted programs might also be helpful in other types of educational settings.

We can, therefore, make every attempt to share with other educators the technology we have gained in teaching students process skills, modifying the regular curriculum, and helping students become producers of knowledge (Renzulli, 1977). We can extend enrichment activities and provide staff development in the many principles that guide our programming models. Yet without the changes at the local, state, and national policy-making levels that will alter the current emphasis on raising test scores and purchasing unchallenging, flat, and downright sterile textbooks, our efforts may be insignificant.

Maintaining Our Identity

Until the reform movement has produced a sufficient impact on current educational policy, we cannot afford to channel the majority of our efforts into providing staff development and technical assistance to classroom teachers to

Figure 2   Provisions for Gifted Students in Regular Classroom Settings

Present Reality of Activities for Students in Upper Elementary Classrooms	Percent	Observable Provisions Suggested for Gifted Students in Classroom Settings
Written Work	30.4	Differentiated Curriculum—Higher Level
Listening to Explanations/Lectures	20.1	Content
Preparation for Assignments	11.5	Curriculum Compacting or Modification
Discussion	7.7	Adaptation of Classwork for Individual
Reading	5.5	Learning Styles
Practice/Performing-Physical	5.3	Assignment of More Challenging Written
Use of AV Equipment	4.9	Work or Reading Material
Student Nontask Behavior—No		Independent or Small Group Work on
Assignment	4.8	Assigned Topics
Practice/Performance-Verbal	4.4	Learning Centers
Taking Tests	3.3	Small Group Work on Self-Selected Interests
Watching Demonstrations	1.0	Use of Contracts or Management Plans to
Simulation/Role Play	0.4	Facilitate Independent Study
Being Disciplined	0.3	Use of Instructional Grouping to Facilitate
		Individual Needs
		Self-Directed Learning/Decision-Making
		Opportunities for Students
		Provision for Open-Ended Thinking
		and Problem Solving
(Goodlad, 1984, p. 107)		(Renzulli, 1986)

meet the needs of gifted students in regular classroom settings. Because of fiscal constraints, more and more gifted programs are being eliminated and fewer students are being challenged by these programs. Consider the following correspondence received from a classroom teacher with 10 years of experience and a graduate degree in education of the gifted and talented.

> My frustration at not being able to adequately challenge the gifted students in my heterogeneous classroom grows each year. With 28 students of varying levels and abilities and special needs, I often find the most neglected are the brightest. Even though I know *what* to do for these youngsters, I simply do not have the time to provide the differentiated instruction they need and deserve. Instead, my attention shifts, as it has in the past, to the students in my class with special learning problems who are already terribly behind in second grade, (P. C. Morgan, personal communication, September 10, 1990)

While sharing our technology is, indeed, one of our own noble goals, we must continue to create and maintain exemplary programs and practices that serve as models of what *can be* accomplished for high ability students. Through our professional organizations we must continue to advocate the different needs of high ability students. We must argue logically and forcefully to maintain the programs, the equitable grouping practices, and the differentiated learning experiences that the students we represent so desperately need. Simply to allow these youngsters to be placed in classrooms in which no provisions will be made for their special needs is an enormous step backwards for our field. To lose our quest for excellence in the current move to guarantee equity will undoubtedly result in a disappointing, if not disastrous, education for our most potentially able children.

A Change in Direction: From Being Gifted to the Development of Gifted Behaviors

While we believe it is imperative to maintain our identity through our programs and professional organizations, we advocate, as we have in the past (Renzulli, 1980), a slight change in our labeling processes. Up to this time, the general approach to the study of gifted persons could easily lead the casual reader to believe that giftedness is an absolute condition that is magically bestowed upon a person in much the same way that nature endows us with blue eyes, red hair, or a dark complexion. This position is not supported by the research. For too many years we have pretended that we can identify gifted children in an absolute and unequivocal fashion. Many people have been led to believe that certain individuals have been endowed with a golden chromosome that makes him or her "a gifted person." This belief has further led to the mistaken idea that all we need to do is find the right combination of factors that prove the existence of this "gift." The further use of terms such as "the truly gifted," "the highly gifted," "the moderately gifted," and "the borderline gifted" only serve to confound the issue because they invariably hearken back to a conception of giftedness that equates the concept with test scores. The misuse of the concept of giftedness has given rise to a great deal of criticism and confusion about both identification and programming, and the result has been that so many mixed messages have been sent to educators and the public at large that both groups now have a justifiable skepticism about the credibility of the gifted education establishment and our ability to offer services that are qualitatively different from general education.

Most of the confusion and controversy surrounding the definitions of giftedness that have been offered by various writers can be placed into proper perspective if we examine a few key questions. Is giftedness an absolute or a relative concept? That is, is a person either gifted or not gifted (the absolute view), or can varying degrees of gifted behavior be developed in certain people, at certain times, and under certain circumstances (the relative view)? Is gifted a static concept (i.e., you have or you don't have it) or is it a dynamic concept (i.e., it varies within persons and learning/performance situations)?

These questions have led us to advocate a fundamental change in the ways the concept of giftedness should be viewed in the future. Except for certain functional purposes related mainly to professional focal points (i.e., research, training, legislation) and to ease of expression, we believe that labeling students as "the gifted" is counterproductive to the educational efforts aimed at providing supplementary educational experiences for certain students in the general school population. We believe that our field should shift its emphasis from a traditional concept of "being gifted" (or not being gifted) to a concern about the *development of gifted behaviors* in those youngsters who have the highest potential for benefiting from special educational services. This slight shift in terminology might appear to be an exercise in heuristic hair splitting, but we believe that it has significant implications for the entire way that we think about the concept of giftedness and the ways in which we should structure our identification and programming endeavors. This change in terminology may also provide the flexibility in both identification and programming endeavors that will encourage the inclusion of at-risk and underachieving students in our programs. If that occurs, not only will we be giving these high potential youngsters an opportunity to participate, we will also help to eliminate the charges of elitism and bias in grouping that are sometimes legitimately directed at some gifted programs.

Reform, restructuring, and innovation are not just the catchwords of the 1990s. Efforts to change and improve education have been around for decades, if not centuries; and they will undoubtedly be around as long as thoughtful people have the courage, creativity, and vision to look for better ways of solving the endless array of problems that a changing culture and society places on the doorsteps of the school. But amidst all of the restructuring efforts, there are some things that constantly must be brought to the attention of reformers.

You don't develop the potential of a budding young concert pianist or composer by providing him or her with ordinary music classes for one or two hours a week. You don't produce future Thomas Edisons or Marie Curies by forcing them to spend large amounts of their science and mathematics classes tutoring students who don't understand the material. A student who is tutoring others in a cooperative learning situation in mathematics may refine some of his or her basic skill processes, but this type of situation does not provide the level of challenge necessary for the most advanced types of involvement in the subject.

You don't prepare a young man or woman to become a world class athlete by keeping him or her in regular gym classes and by not allowing him or her to compete against other youngsters who can provide appropriate levels of challenge. When a high school tennis player is fighting it out with an opponent in practice or in a championship game, he or she is competing like hell, but s/he is also refining his/her skills and pushing his/her talent to the upper limit of its potential.

You don't develop world leaders such as Martin Luther King, Golda Meir, and Mahatma Gandhi by having them practice basic skills over and over again or by reiterating mundane concepts that they can undoubtedly learn faster than all of their schoolmates and, in some cases, even many of their teachers.

Talent development is the "business" of our field, and we must never lose sight of this goal, regardless of the direction that reform efforts may take.

NOTE

1. Actually, the research on grouping has the strongest and clearest effects for high ability students. See especially Rogers (in press), Kulik & Kulik (1982); Kulik & Kulik (1984); and Kulik & Kulik (1987).

REFERENCES

Atkin, J. M. (1990, April). On 'alliances' and science education. *Education Week,* *9*(29), 36.

Bell, T. (1984, February). Speech before American Association of School Administrators.

Bernstein, H. T. (1985). The new politics of textbook adoption. *Phi Delta Kappan, 66*(7), 463–466.

Bloom, A. (1987). The closing of the American mind. New York: Simon & Schuster

Brown, W., & Rogan, J. (1983). Reading and young gifted children. *Roeper Review, 5*(3), 6–9.

Cuban, L. (1982). Persistent instruction: The high school classroom 1900–1980. *Phi Delta Kappan, 64*(2), 113–118.

Doyle, D. P. (1989). Endangered species: Children of promise. [Reprint.] *Business Week.*

Education Products Information Exchange Institute (EPIE). (1979). Grant Progress Report NIE G-790083. Mimeographed. Stonybrook, NY: EPIE.

Gardner, H. (1983). Frames of mind. New York: Basic Books.

George, P. S. (1988). Tracking and ability grouping—Which way for the middle school? *The Middle School Journal,* (9), 21–28.

Glasser, W. (1989). Quality: The key to the disciplines. *Phi Kappa Phi Journal* (Winter), 36–38.

Goodlad, J. (1983). A study of schooling: Some findings and hypotheses. *Phi Delta Kappan, 64*(7), 465–470.

Goodlad, J. (1984). A place called school. New York: McGraw-Hill.

Ho, K. (1990). Parents must act to change school math. *Education Week, 9*(35), 20.

International Association for the Evaluation of Educational Achievement (IEA). (1988). Science achievement in seventeen countries: A preliminary report. Oxford: Pergamon Press.

Kirst, M. W. (1982). How to improve schools without spending more money. *Phi Delta Kappan, 64*(1), 6–8.

Kulik, C.-L. C., & Kulik, J. A (1982). Effects of ability grouping on secondary school students: A meta-analysis of evaluation findings. *American Educational Research Journal, 19*, 415–428.

Kulik, C.-L. C., & Kulik, J. A. (1984, August). Effects of ability grouping on elementary school pupils: A meta-analysis. Paper presented at the annual meeting of the American Psychological Association. Ontario, Canada. (ERIC No. ED 255 329)

Kulik, J. A., & Kulick, C. (1987). Effects of ability grouping on student achievement. *Equity & Excellence, 23*(1–2), 22–30.

Naisbitt, J., & Aburdene, P. (1990) Megatrends 2000: Ten new directions for the 1990s. New York: William Morrow.

National Commission on Excellence in Education. (1983, April). A nation at risk: The imperative for educational reform. (Stock No. 065-000-00177-2). Washington, DC: U.S. Government Printing Office.

National Governors' Association. (1990) Education America: State strategies for achieving the national educational goals. Report of the task force on education.

National Science Foundation, (1989, April). Report on disciplinary workshops on undergraduate education.

Peters, P. (1990, July). TAG student defends programs against critic. [Letter to the editor]. *The Register Citizen* (Torrington, CT), p. 10.

Renzulli, J. S. (1977). The enrichment triad model: A guide for developing defensible programs for the gifted and talented. Mansfield Center, CT: Creative Learning Press.

Renzulli, J. S. (1980). Will the gifted child movement be alive and well in 1990? *Gifted Child Quarterly, 24,* 3–9.

Renzulli, J. S. (Ed.). (1986). Systems and models for developing programs for the gifted and talented. Mansfield Center, CT: Creative Learning Press.

Renzulli, J. S., & Reis, S. M. (1985). The schoolwide enrichment model: A comprehensive plan for educational excellence. Mansfield Center, CT: Creative Learning Press.

Renzulli, J. S., Reis, S. M., & Smith, L. H. (1981). The revolving door identification model. Mansfield Center, CT: Creative Learning Press.

Rogers, K. B. (in press). A research synthesis on the effects of ability grouping. University of Connecticut. Storrs, CT: National Research Center on the Gifted and Talented Monograph Series.

Savage, J. F. (1983). Reading guides: Effective tools for teaching the gift ed. *Roeper Review, 5*(3), 9–11.

Slavin, R. E. (1984). Meta-analysis in education: How has it been used? *Educational Researcher, 13*(8), 24–27.

Slavin, R. E. (1986). Best-evidence synthesis: An alternative to meta-analytic and traditional reviews. *Educational Researcher, 15*(9), 5–11.

Slavin, R. E. (1987). Ability grouping and student achievement in elementary schools: A best evidence synthesis. *Review of Educational Research, 57,* 293–336.

Slavin, R. E., Karweit, N. L., & Madden, N. A. (1989). Effective programs for students at risk. Needham Heights, MA: Allyn & Bacon.

Statistical abstracts of the United States. (1988).

Steen, L. A. (1989). Everybody counts: A report to the nation on the future of mathematics education. Washington, DC: National Research Council of the National Academy of Sciences.

Taylor, B. M., & Frye, B. J. (1988). Pretesting: Minimize time spent on skill work for intermediate readers. *The Reading Teacher, 42*(2), 100–103.

Toepfer, C. F. (1989, May). Planning gifted/talented middle level programs: Issues and guidelines. [Report.] National Association of Secondary School Principals.

2

Unthinkable Thoughts: Education of Gifted Students

James J. Gallagher

The University of North Carolina at Chapel Hill

The advent of a new millennium is an appropriate time to consider some "unthinkable thoughts," those thoughts that make us so uncomfortable that most professionals prefer to ignore them. Yet, if progress is to be made, such challenges to our professional roles must be confronted. Four such ugly questions are considered for gifted education, together with suggested actions to cope with them.

1. Is there really such an entity as a gifted child?

2. Is there such an entity as gifted education?

3. Is there such an entity as special personnel preparation for teachers of gifted students?

Editor's Note: From Gallagher, J. J. (2000). Unthinkable thoughts: Education of gifted students. *Gifted Child Quarterly, 44*(1), 5-12. © 2000 National Association for Gifted Children. Reprinted with permission.

4. Is the application of special services for gifted students sufficient in scope and intensity to make a difference in the classroom?

We should recognize that, however we choose to cope with these issues, our status quo, business as usual, is hardly a viable choice for the 21st century.

The beginning of a new millennium is an excellent time to take stock and review where we are in this professional field of education of gifted students and where we should be going. One of the ways to engage ourselves is to consider a few *unthinkable thoughts,* those questions that are so painful for professionals to consider that there is often a conspiracy of silence about them, an unspoken agreement that we would not, as professionals in the field, bring these questions up in polite company (Gallagher, 1984). While it is understandable that we would wish to avoid painful questions, it is not in the best interest of our special field to do so.

This paper is an attempt to confront some major and significant questions regarding the core beliefs within the field of educating gifted students. We will consider four major questions that are indeed unthinkable thoughts to most of us in the education of gifted students, together with what the author believes should be the actions to follow.

First of all, we should recognize that if the answer to question number one is "no," then the rest of the discussion is rather meaningless. Similarly, if the answer to question number two is "no," then points three and four lose their meaning. So, it becomes of some significance to confront each of these questions, which have been posed by a variety of critics and friends, in turn.

IS THERE SUCH AN ENTITY AS A GIFTED CHILD?

The Question

One of the first questions is whether high intelligence is the property of the individual, or merely the favorable confluence of circumstances that allows one youngster to make full use of his or her talents while other youngsters are stunted in their true potential. Renzulli and Reis (1997) prefer, for example, to discuss "gifted behaviors" rather than gifted individuals. Their Schoolwide Enrichment Model is designed to stimulate the problem solving and thinking skills of all students, and they reject "giftedness as a state of being" (p. 140) instead preferring to use *gifted* as an adjective, rather than a noun.

Putting the Research to Use

Classroom teachers of gifted students have been beset recently in this field by a variety of contradictory arguments from "Is there such a thing as a gifted child?" to "Should we have inclusion for gifted students in the general classroom?" This paper tries to reassure teachers that there are such children and they deserve competent educational services and experiences.

If teachers believe that many gifted students are being short-changed in terms of the intensity or relevance of their current experiences as noted in this article, then they might consider joining hands with their professional colleagues for some collective action through their professional associations. Such collective action to set standards may be the best chance we have for an appropriate set of services for gifted students.

Critics such as Sapon-Shevin (1996) and Oakes (1985) have made the point that "giftedness" is a *social construct* and not a separate entity of nature. One can be gifted in Sweden, but not in Botswana. Yes, the gifted child is a social construct of the West. But, so are constructs such as "learning disabilities," "social competency," "athletic ability," and so forth. They, too, were all created for some meaningful social or educational purpose. Actually, it is not the social construct aspect of this term that bothers many critics, but whether the social construct is educationally useful or not (Borland, 1997).

Are there youngsters who, at birth, have a neurological constitution that allows them to learn faster, remember more, process information more effectively, and generate more new and unusual ideas than their age peers? These are important features in the information age. There are two major lines of evidence here. The first lies in twin studies and the close relationship of the abilities of adoptive children to the abilities of their natural parents (Plomin, 1997). The studies of identical and fraternal twins clearly indicate a powerful genetic influence in intelligence. Even when identical twins are reared apart (Bouchard, Lykken, McGue, Segal, & Tellegen, 1990), their IQ correlations are in the .70 to .75 range. At the same time, adoption studies also indicate the important role that nurturing plays (Bouchard & McGue, 1981). The second line of evidence for the existence of constitutional giftedness lies in the undeniable presence of prodigies (Morelock & Feldman, 1997), youngsters who do remarkable things before the age of 10 at the level of an adult professional (i.e., an eight-year-old playing competitive chess with adults). Although families play a role in enhancing this early ability it is impossible to assign such remarkable gifts solely to environmental factors (Gallagher & Gallagher, 1994).

So, we can conclude there is evidence to support the following statement: There are some youngsters who are born with the capability to learn faster than others those ideas or concepts that modern societies value in children and adults. Such youngsters and their abilities are subject to many social influences and must interact with their environmental context. Therefore, it often becomes difficult to find students with these special talents in a multicultural society (Baldwin, 1994; Frasier, 1991).

The real objection to the term *gifted* is not that it is a social construct, but that it is a social construct designed with what are perceived as nefarious purposes, in particular, favoring already economically favored children and families. The consequence of this advantage might be suppressing or limiting the capabilities of youngsters from less socially favored circumstances (Margolin, 1996; Oakes & Lipton, 1992). One consequence of the use of intelligence test results in identification is that there is a disproportion in membership in the special programs for gifted students that reflects this "unfairness," with fewer Black and Hispanic students enrolled than their proportions in the population, but also with an excess of Asian students in programs for gifted to their proportions in the population (Gallagher & Gallagher, 1994). Such findings call into question our current procedures and have stimulated a search for alternative identification policies (Frasier, 1997).

One of the major initiatives in the field of gifted education has been attempts to discover and nurture hidden talent (Baldwin, 1994; Patton, 1992). The federal Javits legislation has spurred these efforts. In addition, states like Illinois, Ohio, Texas, North Carolina, and Georgia have made major changes in their identification procedures and policies designed to discover the talented child from cultural backgrounds different from the American mainstream (Coleman, Gallagher, & Foster, 1994).

The obvious gradations in the construct of intelligence and its multiple dimensions in students cause many critics to complain about the "all-or-nothing" aspect of being in "a gifted program" and the unfairness of failing to take into account these gradations of ability or multiple abilities (Pendarvis & Howley, 1996). This objection ignores the fact that many educational decisions are also of a similar all-or-nothing nature. You are either on the basketball team or you are not, despite obvious gradations in athletic ability and skill. You are either in a music program at Julliard or you are not, despite obvious gradations in musical talent. You are either accepted into a special school of math and science or you are not, despite gradations in student interest and ability.

Actions Based on Current Knowledge

The process of the identification of gifted students in educational programs was originally for the purpose of establishing eligibility for special programs and obtaining financial reimbursement for local districts from the state. Now that state reimbursement for local districts has often been placed on the basis of a formula that places a cap on available state resources (e.g., 4% of average daily attendance) rather than on an individual head count of gifted students, the need for such individual identification as a gifted student has been lessened.

We need to establish rules of eligibility for specific advanced programs in content fields that take advantage of the advanced mental abilities and achievement levels of gifted students, such as an advanced math program or a problem-based learning unit in social studies, where eligibility could be determined through multiple criteria including aptitude, academic track record, and interest. Eligibility for specific services, programs, or classes has already been established as the pattern at the secondary level in Advanced Placement courses and Honors programs where eligibility standards may include general intellectual aptitude as one of a number of admission criteria. This multiple selection criteria also fits well into Howard Gardner's (Ramos-Ford & Gardner, 1997) multiple intelligences framework in that high math aptitude can place a student in the advanced math program, but not necessarily make him or her eligible for a special creative arts programs.

IS THERE SUCH AN ENTITY AS GIFTED EDUCATION?

The Question

What is the special character of programs for gifted students? Are they exciting? *Yes.* Are they boring and trivial? *Yes.* Do they discriminate against minorities? *Yes.* Do they fight discrimination? *Yes.* The truth of the matter is that any statement made about programs or services for gifted students (or anyone else) in this diverse country is partially true. What we really need to focus upon is how much truth there is in particular claims and what can be done to make the programs more positive in nature.

Are there identifiable special or differentiated programs for gifted students? The answer to this question is not nearly so clear, nor is the nature of differentiation. Differentiation can refer to changes from the basic curriculum in *content,* in *skills,* in *learning environments,* and even in *technology.* Is our differentiated program based upon content (history or math), or upon special skills (problem solving or creativity)? Surely it is not sufficient to refer to the geographic place where gifted students are (resource room, regular class, special class, etc.) as the differentiation. Presumably they are in a special place to allow for something different and distinctive to happen in the curriculum. If they sit in a different place but are given the same inappropriate curriculum as they would confront in the general classroom, why should we expect that anything of educational importance will happen (Kulik & Kulik, 1997)?

Is a differential program actually needed? The voices of the gifted students themselves provide persuasive testimony. More than 800 gifted students from nine separate school districts in North Carolina were asked to comment on whether they were being challenged by their current content courses in mathematics, science, social studies, and language arts (Gallagher, Harradine, & Coleman, 1997). Only mathematics and their special classes in gifted education were able to get over 50% approval in this regard. Student comments focused on the redundancy of the curriculum and the low level of thought required, which then triggered many statements of student boredom.

In his critique of gifted education, Margolin (1996) does not believe that the program focus is *content,* stating that a review of gifted textbooks revealed only 11% of the pages in the textbooks are concerned with the *content* of the lessons. The examples of trivial and irrelevant lessons presented by Margolin, as well as Sawyer (1988), on what goes on in gifted classes leaves one to wonder what parents in their right minds would want their child in such a program. Margolin's view is that it is not the content of the lessons that is important, but the privilege and status of the term *gifted* that drives parents to insist that their child be provided with these services or programs (and this label!).

Is it high-level thinking processes that we wish to cultivate that comprises the differentiated program? As Callahan (1996) has pointed out, this goal seems to presume that the regular classroom teacher is not concerned with the stimulation of thinking skills of her students, an obvious misrepresentation. It is certainly true that the development of thinking skills, such as problem solving, problem finding, and creativity, often play a significant role in what is "differentiated" (Treffinger & Feldhusen, 1996).

Sapon-Shevin (1996) has a different reason for attacking gifted education. It is not that it is bad education, but that it is so good! "The benefits provided by such programs—smaller classes, more enthusiastic teachers, a rich curriculum, more individualization—are all changes that would benefit all students" (p. 199). By providing that type of program to the children of the wealthy and the well-positioned in our society, Sapon-Shevin believes that we increase the gap between gifted students and the economically disadvantaged students. So, education for the gifted becomes, to her, a device to maintain these unfair cultural advantages.

We can hardly deny that there are some parents who would be willing to see the public education ship sink if their children were provided the lifeboats of a gifted program, but, to claim that this is the primary reason why thousands of parents and teachers support and work in programs for gifted students is to be extremely naive. Nevertheless, we still have the responsibility to state clearly just what we are about when we say we are "differentiating" the program for gifted students, in addition to what outcomes we expect and what outcomes we have obtained (Gallagher, 1998).

One of the important questions to raise in education of gifted students—and in all of education—is, "Are the practices that we are using beneficial, or do they just represent established practice that, through repetition, becomes the established way of doing things?" Shore and his colleagues (Shore, Cornell, Robinson, & Ward, 1991) produced a volume on *Recommended Practices in Gifted Education: A Critical Analysis* that identified 101 widely advocated practices for educating gifted students. They also did a detailed literature review to indicate which of these had research backing and which did not. As a follow-up on this effort, Shore and Delcourt (1996) included more recent studies in their analysis

Table I   Desirable Practices in Gifted and General Education

Uniquely Appropriate for Gifted Education	Effective with Gifted and General
Acceleration	Enrichment
Career education (girls)	Inquiry, discovery, problem solving,
Ability grouping	and creativity
High level curriculum	Professional end products as standards
Differential Programming	Microcomputers

Note: From "Effective curricular and program practices in gifted education and the interface with general education," by B. Shore & M. Delcourt, 1996, Journal for the Education of the Gifted, 20, pp. 138–154. Copyright 1996 by Prufrock Press. Adapted with permission.

and reached the following conclusion (summarized in Table 1) about effective education programs. Table 1 represents those policies that research indicates result in more favorable outcomes for gifted students. Although some of these (grouping, acceleration, high-level content) would seem to apply particularly to gifted students, such things as well-trained teachers, thinking processes, and microcomputers would seem to be beneficial for all students. These practices include elements of changing learning environments, content, and skills, supporting the goal of curriculum differentiation.

One of the mistakes we have made in the past has been to treat the broad spectrum of giftedness as one entity in our programming or service design. There is good reason to believe that the far high end of the distribution of intelligence requires something different than what is provided for the gifted students who are merely somewhat superior in learning ability to the average student. If we can speak of the "highly gifted," then I believe these rare students (perhaps less than 1% of the total) should be the instructional responsibility of the specialist in gifted education, rather than the general education teacher. The distance between these quite special youngsters and the average student of the same chronological age now becomes too great for the regular teacher to fold this student into the general curriculum. Whereas the "run-of-the-mill" gifted student may be dealt with by the support system we have described here, the highly gifted student needs more individual attention, perhaps by providing tutoring, acceleration, or planning individualized studies and projects.

Actions Based on Current Knowledge

The critiques leveled against the triviality and irrelevance of some of our "differentiated" programs for gifted students need to be taken seriously. General education teachers and teachers of gifted students both need models of differentiated units that stress advanced content *and* mastery of thinking processes, such as those developed by VanTassel-Baska (1997) in science and Gallagher and Stepien (1998) in social studies (see also Stepien & Gallagher, 1993), to help them challenge their students. The movement toward establishing content standards in general education requires the specialists in gifted education to add to these *standards* what would be *standards plus* that would represent differentiated content for gifted students.

For example, the National Science Education Standards (Klausner, 1996) propose that, in life science in grades 5–8, "all students should develop understanding of structure and function in living systems, reproduction and heredity, regulation and behavior, populations and ecosystems and diversity and adaptations of organisms" (p. 155). Within those broad areas there are many opportunities for scientific inquiry and individual or group projects to challenge gifted students beyond the level expected of all students. This would require a consistent application of a type of *curriculum compacting* (Reis & Renzulli, 1992) so that gifted students could demonstrate that they have met the general standards for their grade level and would then either address the standards for advanced grades or become involved in genuine enrichment adventures *based upon the general course curriculum.*

This does not mean that there should not also be continued attention given to special efforts at enhancing creativity, problem solving, problem-based learning, and the like (Treffinger & Feldhusen, 1996), but that the mastery of these skills has to relate to significant and relevant content in order to be meaningful and useful to the student.

IS THERE SUCH AN ENTITY AS SPECIAL PERSONNEL PREPARATION FOR TEACHERS OF GIFTED STUDENTS?

The Question

One of the most often-presented strategies for educational improvement for gifted students is sophisticated personnel preparation where teachers and leadership personnel, who will be dealing with children who are gifted and talented, are given special preparation for presenting and organizing services and curriculum for these students. It is this preparation, that creates the "specialist," since this preparation is most often applied on top of some general education certification at the elementary, middle, or secondary level. The unthinkable thought is that such preparation is often haphazard and superficial, consisting of a summer workshop here, a three-day conference there, hardly justifying the term *specialist.* Although rules have been suggested for extended educational experience in this area (Parker, 1996; Council for Exceptional Children [CEC], 1995), most of the state standards expect the teacher to be learning about the characteristics of gifted students, differentiating curriculum for such students, studying about intelligence and higher thinking processes, plus a supervised practicum. Whatever additional preparation the teacher of gifted students is able to find is too often strictly on her or his own (Feldhusen, 1997).

Let us first consider our role as "specialist" in the field of education. We need to answer the question: What can we do that others in education cannot, for is that not the definition of a specialist? If we are psychologists, we can give tests that no other professional can do. If we are pediatricians, we can prescribe medicine when other professionals cannot. If we are teachers of children who are deaf, we can teach American Sign Language. Or, if we are teachers of children with visual impairments, we can teach travel training and Braille. Each of these skills is more or less unique and distinguishes the specialist. Our specialty appears to rest in our energizing thinking skills and strategies for differentiating curriculum.

When we ask *where* these specialists are being prepared in gifted education, we get a discouraging diversity of experiences from higher education courses, to workshops, to staff development, to conference participation. It is this kind of haphazard record of personnel preparation that has motivated, in part, the National Board for Professional Teaching Standards to question the actual presence of a "specialty" of gifted education (J. Kelly, personal communication, 1996).

Actions Based on Current Knowledge

We need to take the critique of the National Board for Professional Teaching Standards seriously when they raise doubts about the legitimate existence of a teaching specialization in gifted education. We need to be clear on what the special knowledges and skills are that are needed by such specialists (Baldwin, 1994; Feldhusen, 1997; Gallagher & Gallagher, 1994; Parker, 1987; VanTassel-Baska, 1997).

Certainly, this specialist must have the skills to develop differentiated lessons and units that stress complex ideas and conceptual systems, and that means the specialist should have content sophistication in some content area or areas (e.g., history, math, economics, etc.). She or he should have extensive knowledge of the various ways to access information sources so that the students can search effectively for a wide range of information on their projects. He or she should also have a fundamental grasp of higher thinking processes and how these can be utilized in instruction, be able to collaborate with general education teachers in enriching the program for advanced students in the general classroom, and, finally, be able to do some individual mentoring for those extraordinary students who are clearly three or more grades in advance of their age group.

So, the key questions are, where will this personnel preparation take place and under whose guidance? Although a few higher education centers have established some basis for such training, most of this preparation will have to be executed in organized staff development programs at a state and local level. An example of this approach is illustrated in the module strategy designed by Harrison, Coleman, and Howard (1994), who transformed the North Carolina certification standards into a state-approved series of 10-hour modules that can be delivered at the local level by university and experienced school system personnel. By assembling these modules, the teachers can eventually earn certification in gifted education.

It should be the task of leaders in state departments of education and professional associations such as TAG and NAGC to set standards and help organize systematic and sequential experiences for on-the-line teachers. The Association for the Gifted (TAG) has tried to develop a statement on what teachers of students with gifts and talents should know (What Every Special Educator Must Know, *CEC*, 1995), and the National Association for Gifted Children (NAGC) has developed potential standards for graduate education, as well (Parker, 1996). Nevertheless, it will take a major effort on the part of the professional community to design and, in some fashion, produce a personnel preparation package that can be delivered at a local or regional level by qualified personnel that would lead to a form of advanced certification for teachers of gifted students.

IS THE APPLICATION OF SPECIAL SERVICES FOR GIFTED STUDENTS SUFFICIENT IN SCOPE AND INTENSITY TO MAKE A DIFFERENCE IN THE CLASSROOM?

The Question

There has been a relatively widespread practice in programs that provide special services for gifted students to set aside some instructional time for the student to interact with a specially trained teacher. While that could mean a couple of half-days a week, or an hour a day, it very often, in local systems, means less (i.e., merely an hour to an hour and a half per week) in some instances.

What can a teacher do in that hour and a half per week (probably broken into two 45 minute blocks) that can make up for 23-½ hours per week spent in a regular program with a curriculum that may not be appropriate for the student's needs? Should they ask the students to read a special book? How about a library project that lasts for a month (that would be six hours' worth)? Why do we put up with such obviously nonfunctional educational adjustments? Such assignments are "justified" in terms of limited budgets and an attempt by harried educational administrators to stretch available resources to the limit. Although one can have sympathy for the hard-pressed administrator, such limited time allocations come perilously close to educational fraud. In essence, we are promising something we cannot deliver.

Consider the following scenario in the field of medicine. A doctor prescribes 50 mg of cortisone for a student with asthma attacks. The pharmacist notes that there are many students needing asthma medicine and he is running short of cortisone, so he regretfully gives the student a 5 mg pill instead of the 50 mg pill the doctor prescribed. Would the doctor passively shrug his shoulders and say, "Well, that's the way it goes," or would you likely hear a roar of outrage that the doctor's patient was being given a *nontherapeutic dosage* contrary to his or her professional instructions?

Well, we are the doctors of education, quite literally. Should our answer be, "Well, what can you do?" or "That's the way it goes," or should we speak out against a practice, *a nontherapeutic educational dosage,* that no one can really defend as good education for gifted students, but that many of us tolerate through our silence? Should not guidelines be created for what is the "minimum" amount of contact time that one needs for any expected gain or benefit?

The answer of our specialists in gifted education often comes back: "Well, we agree this short-changing of students is terrible, but what can just one person do about such policies as the 'hour-a-week' gifted program?" Well, this one person often belongs to a large professional organization, and collectively such groups could at least consider setting minimal standards in terms of sheer contact time. Then, we could suggest such standards as necessary to get the TAG or NAGC Seal of Approval. Anything less than that minimum time commitment would be considered unprofessional. If such standards were presented in journals, such as *Parenting for High Potential,* the parents of gifted students might be interested in them.

There is a similar issue related to the amount of time that a specialist in gifted education can provide to the general education classroom teacher. The growing popularity of the policy of *inclusion* for gifted students in the regular classroom has been supported on the grounds that a gifted specialist can come into that classroom and provide some extra activities for gifted students, or for cluster groups of high-ability students. But, how much time should that specialist spend in any one classroom? Is one hour every two weeks sufficient to get some sort of meaningful gain or improvement? Maybe an hour a week?

Again, most of the policies that determine the time available for the interaction of general education teachers and specialists in gifted education are driven by economics rather than good educational practice or theory. The question is, do we collectively have an obligation to say something about these practices? Are there minimum time standards that we are ready to defend as proper professional behavior? If we do not stand up to the economic arguments of the "bottom line," then who will? Is this minimal use of special consultants just another case of educational fraud about which we stand silent? Why do we not say so?

Actions Based on Current Knowledge

This final issue calls for establishment of, and publicity for, some minimum standards of time commitments to services for gifted students. For example, can anyone accept less than three hours per week of direct contact with a specialist as a minimum for a viable program for gifted students? Anyone making such an argument should be asked, at least, to provide some tangible evidence of the attainments of gifted students under such questionable circumstances. The minimum standard might include no less than five hours per week with a support person in general education classrooms (this time would include consultation with the classroom teacher, direct work with cluster groups within the classroom, resource room activities, and individual work with extremely gifted students).

Such standards would avoid the predictable assignment of specialists in gifted education to multiple school buildings and a schedule that results in minimal contact with students or teachers in any one place. Such an exercise in negative educational economics can result in another set of "ghost programs," the "nontherapeutic dose" where parents are told something constructive is happening for their child that cannot possibly happen, given the limited time and availability of educators of gifted students.

STATUS QUO AS OPTION?

Whatever the personal reaction of the readers to these "unthinkable thoughts" and the accompanying suggestions for action, there should be little hesitation in agreeing that the *status quo* is not a viable option. We need to organize ourselves for significant changes in how we deal with the painful issues described above and perhaps many more. In the 21st century, we should be able to say proudly that we saw our limitations and took action against them. Much of this action must be done collectively since we, as individuals, are hardly able to make major institutional changes. It is unlikely that higher education, awash with many other issues, will take the lead here. It is clearly the responsibility of our professional associations to take the leadership on these issues. *The truly unthinkable thought is that we would continue to go on the way we have been without some recognition of the need for change.*

REFERENCES

Baldwin, V. (1994). The seven plus story: Developing hidden talent among students in socioeconomically disadvantaged environments. *Gifted Child Quarterly, 38,* 80–84.

Borland, J. (1997). Evaluating gifted programs. In N. Colangelo & G. Davis (Eds.), *Handbook of gifted education* (2nd ed., pp. 253–266). Boston: Allyn & Bacon.

Bouchard, T., Jr., Lykken, D., McGue, M., Segal, N., & Tellegen, A. (1990). Sources of human psychological differences: The Minnesota study of twins reared apart. *Science, 250,* 223–228.

Bouchard, T., Jr., & McGue, M. (1981). Familial studies of intelligence: A review. *Science, 212,* 1055–1059.

Callahan, C. (1996). A critical self study of gifted education: Healthy practice, necessary evil, or sedition? *Journal for the Education of the Gifted, 19,* 148–163.

Coleman, M., Gallagher, J., & Foster, A. (1994). *Updated report on state policies related to identification of gifted students.* Chapel Hill, NC: Gifted Education Policy Studies Program, The University of North Carolina at Chapel Hill.

Council for Exceptional Children (1995). *What every special educator must know: The international standards for the preparation and certification in special education teachers.* Reston, VA: Author.

Feldhusen, J. (1997). Educating teachers for work with talented youth. In N. Colangelo & G. Davis (Eds.), *Handbook of gifted education* (2nd ed., pp. 547–552). Boston: Allyn & Bacon.

Frasier, M. (1991). Disadvantaged and culturally diverse gifted students. *Journal for the Education of the Gifted, 14,* 234–245.

Frasier, M. (1997). Gifted minority students: Reframing approaches to their identification and education. In N. Colangelo & G. Davis (Eds.), *Handbook of gifted education* (2nd ed., pp. 498–515). Boston: Allyn & Bacon.

Gallagher, J. (1984). Unthinkable thought. *The Exceptional Parent, 14* (5), 13–17.

Gallagher, J. (1998, June). Accountability for gifted students. *Phi Delta Kappan,* 739–742.

Gallagher, J., & Gallagher, S. (1994). *Teaching the Gifted Child* (4th ed.). Newton, MA: Allyn & Bacon.

Gallagher, J., Harradine, C., & Coleman, M. (1997). Challenge or boredom: Gifted students' view on their schooling. *Roeper Review, 19,* 132–136.

Gallagher, S., & Stepien, W. (in press). *Curricula for problem-based learning.* Charlotte, NC: University of North Carolina.

Harrison, A., Coleman, M., & Howard, J. (1994). *Personnel preparation: Academically gifted.* Raleigh, NC: North Carolina Department of Public Instruction.

Klausner, R. (1996). *National science education standards.* Washington, DC: National Academy Press.

Kulik, J., & Kulik, C. (1997). Ability grouping. In N. Colangelo & G. Davis (Eds.), *Handbook of gifted education* (pp. 230–242). Boston: Allyn & Bacon.

Margolin, L. (1996). A pedagogy of privilege. *Journal for the Education of the Gifted, 19,* 164–180.

Morelock, M., & Feldman, D. (1997). High-IQ children, extreme precocity, and savant syndrome. In N. Colangelo & G. Davis (Eds.), *Handbook of gifted education* (2nd ed., pp. 439–459). Boston: Allyn & Bacon.

Oakes, J. (1985). *Keeping track: How schools structure inequality.* New Haven, CT: Yale University Press.

Oakes, J., & Lipton, M. (1992). Detracking schools: Early lessons from the field. *Phi Delta Kappan, 73,* 448–454.

Parker, J. (1987). *Standards for graduate programs in gifted education.* Washington DC: National Association for Gifted Children.

Parker, J. (1996). NAGC standards for personnel preparation in gifted education: A brief history. *Gifted Child Quarterly, 40,* 158–164.

Patton, J. (1992). Assessment and identification of African-American learners with gifts and talents. *Exceptional Children, 59,* 150–159.

Pendarvis, E., & Howley A. (1996). Playing fair: The possibilities of gifted education. *Journal for the Education of the Gifted, 19,* 215–233.

Plomin, R. (1997). Genetics and intelligence. In N. Colangelo & G. Davis (Eds.), *Handbook of gifted education* (2nd ed., pp. 67–74). Boston: Allyn & Bacon.

Ramos-Ford, V., & Gardner, H. (1997). Giftedness from a multiple intelligences perspective. In N. Colangelo & G. Davis (Eds.), *Handbook of gifted education* (2nd ed., pp. 54–66). Boston: Allyn & Bacon.

Reis, S., & Renzulli, J. (1992). Using curriculum compacting to challenge the above-average. *Educational Leadership, 50*(2), 51–57.

Renzulli, J., & Reis, S. (1997). The schoolwide enrichment model: New directions for developing high-end learning. In N. Colangelo & G. Davis (Eds.), *Handbook of gifted education* (2nd ed., pp. 136–154). Boston: Allyn & Bacon.

Sapon-Shevin, M. (1996). Beyond gifted education: Building a shared agenda for school reform. *Journal for the Education of the Gifted, 19,* 194–214.

Sawyer, R. (1988). In defense of academic rigor. *Journal for the Education of the Gifted, 11,* 5–19.

Shore, B., & Delcourt, M. (1996). Effective curricular and program practices in gifted education and the interface with general education. *Journal for the Education of the Gifted, 20,* 138–154.

Shore, B., Cornell, D., Robinson, A., & Ward, V. (1991). *Recommended practices in gifted education.* New York: Teachers College, Columbia University.

Stepien, W., & Gallagher, S. (1993). Problem-based learning: As authentic as it gets! *Educational Leadership, 50*(7), 25–38.

Treffinger, D., & Feldhusen, J. (1996). Talent recognition and development: Successor to gifted education. *Journal for the Education of the Gifted, 19,* 181–193.

VanTassel-Baska, J. (1997). What matters in curriculum for gifted learners: Reflections on theory, research, and practice. In N. Colangelo & G. Davis (Eds.), *Handbook of gifted education* (2nd ed., pp. 126–135). Boston: Allyn & Bacon.

3

Perennial Debates and Tacit Assumptions in the Education of Gifted Children

Laurence J. Coleman

University of Tennessee

Michael D. Sanders

Indiana Department of Education

Tracy L. Cross

Ball State University

For many years, educators of the gifted have debated topics central to the field such as definition, identification, and curriculum (Getzels & Dillon, 1973). This paper explores the possible relationships between gifted educators' periodic debates and the philosophical war among advocates of differing perspectives of social science research. The authors discuss how

Editor's Note: From Coleman, L. J., Sanders, M. D., & Cross, T. L. (1997). Perennial debates and tacit assumptions in the education of gifted children. *Gifted Child Quarterly,* *41*(3), 105-111. © 1997 National Association for Gifted Children. Reprinted with permission.

the acceptance of a particular mode of inquiry embeds tacit ideas into the debate that make resolution difficult. The tacit assumptions of three modes of disciplined inquiry (empirical-analytic, interpretive, and transformative) are presented in conjunction with the accompanying reformulation and reconceptualization of issues (definition, identification, and curriculum) that occur with each mode of inquiry.

INTRODUCTION

Professionals in the field of gifted education have debated such basic topics as definition, identification, and curriculum for many years (Getzels & Dillon, 1973). Popular texts review such topics (Gallagher & Gallagher, 1994). While some consensus on best practices has emerged (Shore, Cornell, Robinson, & Ward, 1991), the perennial debates continue. We have heard comments from colleagues and students about this situation and have wondered why the debate over these topics periodically resurfaces and why our field cannot reach a resolution. Is there something beneath the obvious, something tacit, that might account for our apparent inability to reach a consensus?

Concurrent with these debates in our applied discipline, gifted-child education, the social science community is in turmoil as differing conceptions of disciplined inquiry or research contest with each other. The debate in the larger social science community interacts with our own educationally oriented debates. Could it be that there is some connection between the contested notions of inquiry, sometimes called paradigm wars (Guba, 1990), and the debates in our field?

This paper began as an exploration of the possible relationship between periodic debates in gifted education and the philosophical war among advocates of differing perspectives on social science research. As our understanding of the different philosophical positions grew, we began to formulate ideas about the relationship and presented them to peers, starting in 1990, in papers at meetings of the National Association for Gifted Children (e.g., Coleman, Cross, & Sanders 1992; Coleman, Sanders, & Cross, 1991). In the same time frame, Borland (1990) published a paper entitled "Post Positivist Inquiry" that helped stimulate our thinking. This paper is the result of dialogue among ourselves and with colleagues over the past six years.

Our research has led us to believe that there is explanatory power in the notion that ways of thinking about inquiry or research and the aforementioned debates are linked. Our purpose is to provide readers with an idea of how proponents of different notions of inquiry in the field of gifted education might think about major topics in the field. We believe that people in our field are attracted to different modes of inquiry. By accepting one mode of inquiry as one's own (one may not be aware of that acceptance), a lens is created through which the person judges various practices and issues, in effect, acceptance of a particular mode embeds tacit ideas into the debate that make resolution difficult. Our intent is to expose those tacit assumptions. We name and discuss three modes of disciplined inquiry: empirical-analytic, interpretive, and transformative. Our thinking is influenced by Popkewitz (1984), Guba (1990), and Skrtic (1991). We will show how each mode of inquiry creates a set of lenses pointing toward a reformulation and reconceptualization of notions of definition, identification, and curriculum development in our field. Examples will be supplied of how these lenses refract thinking around each issue so readers will see the outlines of the debates that rage in our field. We describe how they might manifest themselves in our debates. Although we do not believe that uniformity of viewpoint is possible, we will also present an example of mixed thinking and conclude with a reflection on the possibility of reconciling the three positions.

Putting the Research to Use

Recognizing that unspoken and hidden ideas fuel the perennial debates in our field can help us understand the legitimacy of positions that we oppose. The deeper understanding of other's positions can help persons better negotiate conflicts when they appear in practice as well as in research. Furthermore, understanding to which mode of inquiry one has allegiance can lead to educational programs and research agendas that are based solely on a single way of looking at giftedness.

In this paper we do not make a case that one mode of inquiry is superior to another but we do suspect that the perennial debate about major topics is fueled by the irreconcilable differences among the positions. Our assumption is that there is not just one way to look at the field of education for the gifted and talented; rather, all ways are useful for inquiry. By exploring various perspectives, we believe the field can develop a clearer understanding of the phenomenon of giftedness.

Basic Terms

In order to understand our arguments, it is necessary that we clarify the terms "mode of inquiry," "paradigm," and "theory." We see these terms as having increasing levels of specificity. "Mode of inquiry" is at the broadest level. The phrase conveys the idea that scholars start their research armed with a set of philosophical assumptions about the world, about how to conduct research and about the goal of research. The three examples we use in this paper are at this level. Various scholars have attempted to order the social science literature by proposing classification schemes (e.g., Guba, Popkewitz, Skrtic).

"Paradigm" is a very popular term today, as is its partner term "paradigm shift," in both the scientific and the popular media (Hoyningen-Huene, 1993). The term—paradigm—can be traced to Kuhn (1962), who wrote *The Structure of Scientific Revolutions.* We infrequently use "paradigm" in our paper because of the misunderstanding that exists about the term. At the same time there are three ideas that emanate from Kuhn's (1962) work that have relevance to this paper. Although most of Kuhn's writing dealt with the natural sciences, he did make reference to the social sciences. Many scholars in the social science community have used his ideas about paradigms (e.g., Popkewitz, Guba, Skrtic). The first notion is that in the natural sciences fields of disciplined inquiry, such as physics and biology, operate on the basis of a coherent system of thought that defines the important problems, concepts, and research methodology of that field. The second point is that people in a field rarely talk directly about their assumptions guiding their inquiry because they accept them as being obvious and true. This is the part of the notion we find most relevant to our argument. It is the tacit influence of our beliefs that interferes with the debate. The third idea is "incommensurability." The term indicates that one paradigm is not comparable to another. Hoyningen-Huene's (1993) analysis shows how Kuhn's ideas on incommensurability have changed over two decades, but in this paper we use the term to mean "irreconcilability" or "untranslatability."

"Theory" is a term we use to denote a specific coherent body of assumptions, propositions and hypotheses about a phenomenon. Theory is a narrower term than "mode of inquiry" or "paradigm." A theory may or may not presuppose acceptance of a mode of inquiry.

Three Modes of Inquiry

We present three modes of inquiry used in the social sciences or, more specifically in our case, education. Our analysis suggests that the field of gifted education has used one lens, predominantly an empirical-analytic one, to view the phenomena of talent development. We maintain that two other paradigms may also be used as lenses in this way. We assert that perspectives on topical issues change when the lens changes. Each paradigm will be summarized so as to reveal its essence. Guba's (1990) scheme for distinguishing among the paradigms will be used here. Three categories are used: the role of the knower (epistemology); the nature of knowledge (ontology) and how to study a phenomenon (methodology). For purposes of comparison, the characterizations of the paradigms are exaggerated to illuminate their differences.

Empirical-Analytic Mode (EM). People who believe in the empirical-analytic mode of inquiry, a term coined by Popkewitz (1984), see the universe as comprised of universal natural laws that scientists discover. The laws enable scientists to determine the falsity of ideas, uncover causal relationships, and make predictions about events. By using objective methods, researchers strive to control possible sources of error and be neutral observers. The model is a modification of positivism, which has been the predominant paradigm in western science in this century since the absolutist stance of earlier thinkers was abandoned.

The field of gifted education has tended to use the empirical-analytic mode typically associated with natural science while ignoring the possibilities inherent in other research forms. In general, EM researchers view giftedness and talent as quantifiable psychosocial phenomena. This view tends to evaluate instructors, students, and educational programs as definable and measurable. Generally, researchers representing this mode view giftedness as a natural phenomenon that exists relatively free of cultural forces. Talents and abilities are defined by standardized tests and rating scales. Proper identification of giftedness and talent rests on objective measures that can, theoretically, result in a system with the chance of error reduced to an acceptable level. Programs are based on an optimal set of experiences that would be consistent across educational settings and cultures. Mastery is evidenced by objective assessments.

Interpretivist Mode (IM). Researchers representing the interpretivist mode see knowledge of the world as being mediated by the signs and symbols people use to interpret their world. Knowledge is viewed as subjective and what can be learned is how others understand the world. Interpretivist researchers work to uncover the patterns or rules in social relationships as seen by groups and individuals. They do not expect to find a single, most appropriate explanation for all (see Guba, 1990; Popkewitz, 1984). Giftedness is defined and identified by individuals and localized groups as they try to make sense of the idea that some people are more able than others in certain areas at certain times in their lives. The interpretivist researcher views program options as the development of different paths for different people, from talent to talent, and from time to time. Specifics of program outcomes come about as the result of dialogue among the participants, and those outcomes change as participants and circumstances change. Formal measurements might be useful but unlikely to provide all the important information. IM leads to more of a consensus model of program development rather than an authoritative model.

Transformative Mode (TM). Researchers representing the transformative mode see knowledge of the world as being embedded in a cultural matrix of values. All inquiry and human behavior is locked into a web of power relationships grounded in struggles around gender, race, social class, and other culturally and economically determined parameters. Researchers strive to make apparent those relationships so that people can understand their place in the world and be able to transform it. Proponents of this view believe that values are inescapable and values define the ideal relationships among persons.

TM, instead of critical theory (Guba, 1990) or critical science (Popkewitz, 1984), is used as our designation for this mode of inquiry to clarify the distinction between the purpose of inquiry and the methodology of inquiry. In EM and IM the links between purpose for inquiry and methodology are more direct and constant. In TM the uniformity of purpose and method is less steadfast. For example, some critical theorists (e.g., Bourdieu, 1994) take the empirical-analytical modes data analytical tools; and other critical scientists (e.g., Popkewitz) subscribe to more interpretive mode analytical tools (e.g. phenomenological/ constructivist methods).

The transformative mode of inquiry sees giftedness as being defined according to the qualities valued by the powerful and influential in a society to the potential detriment of those whose gifts and talents lie outside those parameters. The measurements for identification and assessment would result in disproportionately low numbers of less powerful (e.g., lower class, cultural minorities, women) being identified and selected for programs. Test bias is a result of the reproduction of power relations within the society. Teachers are seen as transformative intellectuals who can produce and criticize forms of knowledge while legitimating, valuating, and locating student experiences within particular economical based social structures. Programs and curricula encourage student participation in understanding and transforming social forms and in knowledge creation.

Multiple Lenses Made Apparent

In our field, the education of children who are gifted and talented, a mode of inquiry predominates that is apparently accepted by a majority of us. Because of the characteristics of the inquiry modes just described, it is difficult to see the domination of our research endeavors by one mode of inquiry. In order to uncover this mode of inquiry, and its accompanying lens, we begin with a statement about gifted education that most persons in the field would accept on its face value. We then analyze the statement in order to show how adherents of the three modes of inquiry are influenced by each lens, and we reconceptualize that statement. This section is followed by a more complete comparison of the modes of inquiry.

Consider this: *The purpose of the field of gifted education is to identify gifted children in order to place them into programs with appropriate curriculum and with teachers who possess the necessary characteristics and skills for maximizing each student's potentials.* This consensual statement, although others could be written, summarizes major ideas in our field and contains many unspoken assumptions such as:

There is a definable group (the gifted).

They can be identified universally (in any setting). A program with specifiable curriculum is written or can be created.

Teachers have special skills and characteristics.

Putting gifted persons in a program will maximize their potentials.

We will consider each of the assertions contained in the statement and discuss them in terms of the competing mode of inquiry.

The first statement, *There is a definable group,* is a foundation of the EM (empirical-analytic mode). The gifted have a definite universal set of characteristics that enables one to distinguish them from other nongifted groups. This group can be defined independent of social or ethnic-group considerations. To the IM (interpretivist mode) proponents, gifted persons can be defined by all groups according to their own set of attributes as interpreted by persons in that group. There is no universal group. African-American and Hispanic-American and European-Americans would have different definitions. To the TM (transformative mode) followers, gifted persons are defined by attributes that reproduce the dominant values of race, class and gender. There is no universal group. Instead there are issues of value relative to each culture that would be present in the definitions.

The second statement, *They can be identified universally,* is essentially a measurement question that follows from the first statement. The EM proponents see identification as requiring the development of standardized measures and procedures that will locate persons with gifted attributes, independent of environmental, economic, and political considerations and research bias. The same proportion of persons who are gifted should be identified in every society. The IM and the TM groups do not buy the idea of universal identification. To them, the cultural context influences the identification process. Successful measurement occurs when a school district selects children in a manner that satisfies local criteria.

The third statement, *A program with appropriate curriculum can be created,* is viewed differently by adherents of the three modes of inquiries. EM followers believe it is possible to develop curriculum that is best for most gifted students. IM proponents believe that no single best curriculum can be written. Rather, they expect to see the presence of multiple curricula that are appropriate for people in different times and places. The desirable curriculum is one that encourages children to develop their own views in relation to their culture. TM proponents believe that curriculum should help transform persons so that they can better meet their needs. That curriculum should enable them to see the delimiting contradictions in the existent world and provide means for changing that social world.

The fourth statement, *Teachers have special skills and characteristics,* maintains that there are skills that teachers of the gifted should have because those skills work best with gifted students. EM researchers believe that "best" teachers can be identified and that their skills and characteristics can be developed in other teachers. By spreading this set of skills, the educational process will be improved. IM proponents believe that the skills of best teachers could be described in a general way, but each teacher creates his or her own set of skills that fit their students and circumstances. The TM adherent asserts that best teachers need skills and characteristics that will enable them to help children develop their own views so that the students can be freed from their powerless positions and transform themselves.

The fifth statement, *Putting gifted persons in a program will maximize their potentials,* indicates that a program is possible that can maximize potential. The latter term, potential, is presumed to be known and its realization to be knowable too. EM believes it is possible to define and measure potential. We may have difficulty doing it now, but only insufficient technology is the obstacle. IM asserts that potential is a term that has too many meanings to be useful. One must ascertain what those meanings are and in what ways potential is manifested from the perspective of different stakeholders. TM researchers see potential as being defined on the basis of what is deemed valuable by the powerful in a society. Maximizing potential means one's skills and knowledge increase people's awareness of the forces that influence their lives and enable them to free themselves from those circumstances.

It is apparent that even in a general, seemingly innocuous statement like the one describing the purpose of the field of gifted education that began this section, different interpretations of meaning are possible. Taken together, these statements show the general outlines of the modes of inquiry as they relate to the education of children who are gifted and talented. Unfortunately, the abstract nature of the modes of inquiry makes it difficult to see how the lens delimits or impels people to look at issues in different ways. In the next section we present a comparison of modes of inquiry by specific issues in the field so that our point becomes more concrete.

Multiple Issues as Interpreted by Mode of Inquiry

In this section we use major topics to show more specifically how an advocate of a mode of inquiry might view that situation. We do this by presenting Figure 1 to illustrate the variation around three issues. The statements representing the issues are idealized for the purpose of clarifying the tacit and virtual meaning of the mode of inquiries within our field. Although many issues could have been selected for examination, three are presented because they represent recurrent topics of debate. These are:

1. definition of giftedness and talent,

2. identification of individuals, and

3. curriculum.

It is important to keep in mind the distinctions among the modes of inquiry as one reads Figure 1. The essence of each mode of inquiry is presented in regard to each issue.

It is apparent that there are some significant differences about the illustrative topics. Gifted educators who have read the content of Figure 1 at meetings of the National Association for Gifted Children and the Council for Exceptional Children-The Association for the Gifted have remarked on the fact that they engender feelings of familiarity and discomfort. The familiarity of these statements is that some echo arguments heard in the field. The discomfort is that the major gaps among the viewpoints are difficult to reconcile that and parts of each seem reasonable.

Figure I

	Definition: What Is Giftedness	Identification	Curriculum: The Content of Curriculum
EMANCIPATORY	One sees giftedness as a definable category or collection of attributes which exist in nature and are relatively independent of culture.	One believes that objective measures can be devised and used to implement a relatively errorless selection system. The problem in identification is to devise an objective system. Very often the problem is thought to be the tests, rather than people in the process. Articles describing "more sensitive" measurement or process tend to be based on this position.	One might contend that there is an optimum or best set of experiences for fostering giftedness. These experiences override time and type of program and these should be part of every quality program. The objectives of the program are statements of appropriate experiences. The content problem is to build that kind of curriculum. Two variants of this position are present among EAs. One argues that the only proper curriculum is regular subject matter, e.g., math, Shakespeare. The second position argues that the actual material to be studied is not as important as the opportunity to develop a skill. The promotion of higher order thinking or creative thinking using subject-free materials is an example of this kind of curriculum. In both instances mastery is evident from tests.
TRANSFORMATIVE	One sees giftedness as defined by the qualities valued by the powerful and influential in a society. Examples of acceptable talents are those in the federal definition. Examples of unacceptable talents, i.e. those valued by minority groups, may be such things as nonclassical music.	One believes that the measures and the system are designed to favor the power structure; hence, disproportionately low numbers of minorities, women and poor people are selected for gifted programs. The problem in the identification process is that (1) tests are biased (an example of the TM theorist buying part of the EA premise) and (2) those selected mirror or reproduce the power relationships in the society.	Curriculum would be conceived to encourage students to question the fundamental assumptions upon which knowledge is based. Students would be encouraged to use knowledge as a tool for understanding relationships of power within a culture as well as in the construction of "knowledge" itself. One sees the "fun and games" approach to curriculum as a way to prohibit minority youth and women from mastering useful knowledge and skills that will enable them to have an opportunity to have a place in the structure. Further, this "fun and games stuff" is accorded qualities that will promote access, but in reality does not. Instead, that kind of curriculum produces persons who have isolated skills and score well on tests which have no

(Continued)

Figure I (Continued)

	Definition: What Is Giftedness	Identification	Curriculum: The Content of Curriculum
I N T E R P R E T I V E	One sees giftedness as defined by individuals and groups as they try to make sense of the notion that some persons are more able than others in some areas of life. The recurrent articles on what should be included in the definition and the arguments over the *definition of terms* such as "talent," "highly," "superior," etc., illustrate the attempts of persons and groups to fashion a definition which fits their notion of appropriate abilities.	One believes that there are a variety of ways to identify gifted persons; the ones selected will reflect the values of the participants. This is inescapable. The problem of representation in selection cannot be solved unless all those who care about the outcome are involved in the process.	relationship to real life endeavors. Some TM theorists argue for a traditional subject-oriented curriculum. One believes that many curricular options exist for the development of talent and that the paths will differ from person to person, from talent to talent and from time to time. Interpretivists contend that curriculum developers must carefully consider the experiences which will enable students to find a way to master complex bodies of knowledge and skill. The curriculum needs to be flexible to meet the diverse needs, yet organized to deal with real world considerations.

Familiar Echoes and Irreconcilability

Analyses of the research base have revealed that the empirical-analytic mode of inquiry has dominated gifted education (Coleman, Cross, & Sanders, 1992; Rogers, 1989). Major figures in our field such as Terman, Hollingsworth, and Torrance root their life's work in this mode of inquiry, although one should not assume that they were aware of it. Much of the continual debate in the field over the years and criticisms leveled at their scholarship are based on attempts to attain the qualities implicit in EM. In other words, those critics hold up the EM lens to the field and set standards for judging definitions or identification procedures, etc. Acceptable solutions are based on meeting mode of inquiry-specific qualities. Therefore, we become accustomed to thinking about the world in a manner consistent with the tenets of the EM inquiry, and are unable to see possibilities viewable through other lenses.

Thoughtful critics of scholarship and professional practice use a different mode of inquiry-specific criteria to argue against these pioneers (Margolin, 1993; Sapon-Shevin, 1994; see *Journal for the Education of the Gifted, 19(2)*). What is discomforting is not solely the particular arguments, but rather that rebuttals never end the argument.

We maintain that this perplexing situation persists because modes of inquiry are not reconcilable. Proponents of one system of thought cannot readily accept the reasoning and evidence of another mode of inquiry. The reason for this is that each mode views the world in a different way. Their foundational beliefs make it impossible to meld them. Our conventional use of neutral professional language masks divisions and makes it seem possible to bring opposing modes of thought together. On the surface we seem to be talking the same language, but at a deeper level there is not a match in the ideas. The irreconcilability of the situation is further masked by the fact that a person can link criticisms bonded to one mode of inquiry to solutions that fit another mode of inquiry. The result is that the situation remains confused and unsettled.

An Example

An example of embracing contradictory positions from our point of view can be found in an article that appeared in *Exceptional Children* (Patton, 1992). The article is a thoughtful piece on the persistent problem in our field of disproportionately low numbers of African-American children who are identified as gifted. Theoretically, the paper straddles several modes of inquiry. We interpret the article to be an example of mixing elements from various modes of inquiry. Although the paper makes many points, we have selected a few to illustrate our contention. We recognize our selectivity and want to make sure that readers understand that we are not taking issue with the writer's viewpoint. Rather, our only purpose is to put forward the idea that his points and our agreement with them are undermined by the mixing of modes of inquiry. Consider these points:

1. Universal definitions are possible; and culturally relevant definitions are the most valid.

2. Objective measurement is possible, useful, and, desirable; and culturally relevant objective forms of measurement are the most valid.

3. The development of proper assessment devices and procedures will relieve, and maybe eliminate, the problem of identifying minority children who are gifted and talented.

How are the modes of inquiry mixed in these points? Each statement is considered in order to show the unspoken contradiction in it. The empirical-analytic mode of inquiry accepts the first half of points 1 and 2, but the second half moves one into the interpretivist and critical modes of inquiry in that they assert that culturally relevant definitions make universal definitions of giftedness and universal forms of measurement impossible. These points seem to use the empirical-analytic and interpretivist modes of inquiry but shy away from the transformative modes notion that the powerful groups in a culture use definition and measurement to reproduce themselves. IM and TM proponents would argue that one cannot have it both ways as the points do. That is, one cannot argue for the relativity of definitions and also go for the idea that the only way to know things is through measurement that reveals objective reality (an EM idea). One does not follow from the other. Point three about the development of good assessment devices might solve the problem but gets into the same difficulty as the earlier points. Proponents of the empirical-analytic mode of inquiry would subscribe to the point since measurement can reveal the truly gifted. Interpretivists and transformative mode adherents would say that the development of a good assessment device is unlikely. IM proponents assert that a consensus is necessary among the many stakeholders in order to develop proper measurement. Given the variety of multicultural groups (stakeholders), what is the probability of arriving at a consensus? TM would argue that should a consensus emerge, it would reflect the interests of the advantaged in society to the disadvantage of others.

In sum, we have tried to demonstrate how what seem like perfectly plausible statements actually contain parts that are not reconcilable. Thus, what appears to be a solution cannot really satisfy any of the proponents of any of the competing modes of inquiry.

Implications for Gifted Education

This is good news and bad news. The bad news is that one cannot answer criticism launched by proponents of one mode of inquiry by using the terminology and underpinnings of the other. This means we will have to learn to live with discrepant views present in the same field. The good news is that this unsettled state may lead to the emergence of greater understanding of what gifted-child education is and can be.

Our field needs to recognize that the practice of gifted and talented education is complex and is made more complex by the presence of unvoiced modes of inquiry. These modes of inquiry provide us with new ways of looking at what we do and present us with impediments to developing a comprehensive notion of what constitutes giftedness, how it should be, and how the programs should be organized. These modes of inquiry show us that a unified conception of giftedness is impossible.

Acknowledging that differences exist in the field does not dissipate our difficulties. We have tried to demonstrate how some problems cannot be resolved within a mode of inquiry because they lead to circularity and our point that there are issues within modes of inquiry that cannot be resolved within that system. One thing we could do is admit to our differing paradigmatic orientations and use that orientation as a basis for conducting research. As evidence accumulates for each viewpoint, we might create the conditions necessary for the emergence of a more complete conception of giftedness.

REFERENCES

Borland, J. H. (1990). Post positivistic inquiry: Implications of the "New Philosophy of Science" for the field of the education of the gifted. *Gifted Child Quarterly, 34*, 61–67.

Bourdieu, P. (1994). Structures, habitus, power: Basis for a theory of symbolic power. In Dirks, N., Eley, G., & Ortner, S. (Eds.), *Culture/Power/History: A reader in contemporary, social theory.* (pp. 155–199). Princeton, NJ: Princeton University Press.

Coleman, L. J., Cross, T. L., & Sanders, M. (1992, November). *Alternative inquiry in education: Hey can you paradigm?* Paper presented at the National Association for Gifted Children Conference. Los Angeles, CA.

Coleman, L. J., Sanders, M., & Cross, T. L. (1991, November). *Theory development and inquiry: How are they connected?* Paper presented at the National Association for Gifted Children Conference, Kansas City, MO.

Gallagher, J. J., & Gallagher, S. A. (1994). *Teaching the gifted child* (4th ed.). New York: Allyn and Bacon.

Getzels, J., & Dillon, J. T. (1973). The nature of giftedness and the education of the gifted. In R. M. W. Travers (Ed.), *Second handbook of research on teaching* (pp. 689–731). Chicago: Rand McNally.

Guba, E. (Ed.). (1990). *The paradigm dialogue.* Newbury Park, CA: Sage.

Hoyningen-Huene, P. (1993). *Reconstructing scientific revolutions: Thomas S. Kuhn's philosophy of science.* Chicago: University of Chicago Press.

Kuhn, T. S. (1962). *The structure of scientific revolutions.* Chicago: University of Chicago, 2nd ed. 1970.

Margolin, L. (1993). Goodness personified: The emergence of gifted children. *Social Problems, 40*, 510–532.

Patton, J. M. (1992). Assessment and identification of African-American learners with gifts and talents. *Exceptional Children, 59*, 150–159.

Popkewitz, T. (1984). *Paradigm and ideology in educational research: The social functions of the intellectual.* London: Falmer:

Rogers, R. (1989). A content analysis of the literature of giftedness. *Journal for the Education of the Gifted, 13*, 78–88.

Sapon-Shevin, M. (1994). *Playing favorites: Gifted education and the disruption of community.* Albany: State University of New York Press.

Shore, B., Cornell, D., Robinson, A., & Ward, V. (1991). *Recommended practices in gifted education.* New York: Teachers College Press.

Skrtic, T. (1991). The special education paradox: Equity as the way to excellence. *Harvard Educational Review, 61,* 1991.

4

Perceptions of Educational Reform by Educators Representing Middle Schools, Cooperative Learning, and Gifted Education

James J. Gallagher

Mary Ruth Coleman

Susanne Nelson

University of North Carolina at Chapel Hill

The present article describes the results of two surveys comparing the perceptions of educators of gifted students with the perceptions of mainstream educational personnel in middle schools and those specializing in cooperative learning. The results indicated a major gulf between the perceptions of mainstream educators and those of educators of the gifted. In the case of middle schools, the disagreement focused on the value of ability grouping and the social consequences of being labeled gifted. In the case of cooperative learning, there were major differences across the board on practically all items.

The authors conclude that it is in the interest of all concerned to have more extensive dialogue between educators of the gifted and members of the educational reform movement.

The educational restructuring and reform movement of the past few years appears to represent a major change in American education (Fullan, 1993). With broad public acceptance (based upon a general desire for major change in the school systems among public decision makers and the public at large), this movement now envelops the American educational enterprise (*America 2000*, 1992; *Goals 2000*, 1994). There is widespread belief that American education has failed and that many students, at all levels, are receiving a mediocre education.

One striking characteristic of these reform efforts is that educators of gifted students have had little input into these reform initiatives. Whether the topic is middle schools, cooperative learning, authentic assessment, outcome-based education, setting national standards, or site-based management, few educators of gifted students have had an opportunity to participate in the major decision making that characterizes this potential reshaping of American education. At the same time, there has been a clear warning that our most gifted and talented students are one group that has been negatively affected by the educational status quo, with its lack of challenge and low expectations. U.S. Secretary of Education Riley has referred to this situation as "The Quiet Crisis" (quoted in Ross, 1993).

This lack of participation of educators of gifted students in the reform movement raises a number of questions. One important question is, "How similar are the perceptions of the educators of the gifted to those in mainstream education about these reform movements?" The purpose of this paper is to compare the perceptions of educators representing the middle school movement, cooperative learning, and the education of gifted students on reform movement issues as they impact the education of gifted students.

We know that perceptions drive actions (cf. Kelly, 1970), and if there are major differences in the perceptions of the groups on this issue, then it will be difficult to bring these groups of teachers into harmony with one another. For example, if we see a shadow on the wall and think it is a burglar, we will react to that perceived danger. If we perceive some of our colleagues as enemies to our interests, our reactions may well not be pleasant or appropriate.

Mutually held perceptions, on the other hand, can become an entry point for collaborative efforts.

Background

The two reform areas that formed the basis for the comparisons in this study were the middle schools movement and cooperative learning. The middle schools were selected as a major movement in this country that predates the current reform movement but has now been incorporated into it. Cooperative learning was chosen because it is a set of definable educational strategies that has been put into operation in many school systems.

Although the middle schools movement represents a structural change across an entire school and cooperative learning stresses internal classroom strategies, they both emphasize similar changes. They are both currently featuring heterogeneous grouping, and they both have an emphasis on "equity goals" which often emphasize social behavior rather than academic and cognitive excellence. Both of these approaches have come into real or potential conflict with educators of gifted, who have stressed the educational goal of excellence.

Putting the Research to Use

The present article raises questions regarding the relationships of educators of the gifted with members of the educational reform movement. There were substantial differences between how educators of the gifted saw the educational world and the vision of the groups who were concerned with middle schools and cooperative learning. These latter two groups felt that their reform efforts were sufficient to address the needs of gifted students without the special programs provided by educators of the gifted. Even if they are wrong, and the authors believe that they are, there is a danger of limited support for gifted programs where these contrary views are held. It is important for educators of the gifted to seek more dialogue with educational reformers to stress the special needs of gifted students and to examine how to accept the positive aspects of the reform movements without abandoning the educational needs of gifted students.

Middle schools. The middle schools movement represents an attempt to restructure the program for students usually in Grades 6–8. Its aim has been to replace the traditional junior high school with a program and educational environment stressing affective education, interdisciplinary curriculum, team teaching and planning, and the development of personal identity (George, 1988; Lounsbury & Vars, 1978; Scales, 1992). The middle school movement has become a source of concern for educators of gifted students due to the recent emphasis by some leaders in the middle schools movement on the benefits of heterogeneous grouping. This emphasis has led to a policy of opposing programs—such as those in gifted education—that separate gifted students (or any exceptional children) for differentiated instruction (Epstein & MacIver, 1990; George, 1988; Oakes, 1985; Sicola, 1990; Tomlinson, 1992).

Cooperative learning. Cooperative learning has become a popular educational strategy within the educational reform movement. Although there are many variations, cooperative learning generally stresses student cooperation and active student learning and participation (Johnson & Johnson, 1990; Kagan, 1990; Slavin, 1988). Teachers using cooperative learning establish small groups of students who work together to address a common task. Cooperative learning emphasizes group cooperation and the mastery of various skills needed to work cooperatively. As with the middle schools movement, there has been a strong emphasis by many leaders of cooperative learning on the usefulness of heterogeneous grouping of students within these small groups. There is the implicit assumption that the key curriculum needs of *all* students can be met through such heterogeneous grouping strategies (Allan, 1991; Oakes, 1992; Slavin, 1990). One by-product of that assumption has been a reduction of honors programs or other special programs for gifted students (Joyce, 1991; Slavin, 1990; Robinson, 1990).

Problem

The question posed in the present research was, "How are the perceptions of educators committed to gifted students similar to, or different from, those of middle school and cooperative learning practitioners regarding the impact of these reforms on gifted students?"

METHOD

Procedure

Middle schools. The primary tools for comparing these groups were two surveys that were developed in a similar manner. For the middle school survey, an open-ended questionnaire was sent to 25 key people selected from both the middle school movement and gifted education. The questionnaire asked each respondent to identify five areas of concern that needed to be addressed when blending the goals of middle schools and programs for gifted students. Six major issues emerged from the responses and became the basis for developing individual stem items on the survey: (a) grouping strategies for gifted middle grades learners; (b) identification strategies for gifted middle grades students; (c) curriculum modifications for gifted middle grades students; (d) teacher preparation needs; (e) program evaluation types; and (f) social and emotional needs of gifted middle grades students.

The draft survey based upon these issues was then sent to the original respondents for further comments. The resulting survey included 23 stem items reflecting the six themes. A Likert scale response asked participants to rate their opinions on each item from 1 (*strongly disagree*) to 4 (*strongly agree*). We also provided the option of N (*no opinion*). In addition to the 23 scale items, a second section of the survey asked participants to rank the six areas of concern by selecting the three most essential issues and placing these in priority order. The third section consisted of an open-ended request for comments.

Examples of the survey items on the middle school survey are:

The label "gifted" may cause feelings of social elitism. Gifted students who are heterogeneously grouped for academic subjects may not be able to advance at their own learning rate.

Current programs designed for middle school gifted students could benefit all students, in addition to gifted students.

Cooperative learning. The survey developed for the cooperative learning respondents followed a procedure similar to that of the middle schools survey. An open-ended questionnaire was sent to 20 well-known experts in cooperative learning and gifted education and, again, six major issues emerged from their responses: (a) the need for teacher preparation; (b) which form of cooperative learning works best with gifted students; (c) how best to combine cooperative learning with gifted education; (d) meeting school and emotional needs of gifted students through cooperative learning; (e) how to evaluate cooperative learning with gifted students; and (f) the use of ability grouping during cooperative learning.

These issues formed the basis for a draft survey of 27 items that was returned to the experts for further comment. The survey also included the opportunity for extended comments on the part of the respondents. After a further revision, the survey was ready for use.

Examples of the items from the cooperative learning survey are:

Many gifted students are able to develop leadership abilities through participation in CL groups.

Gifted students in CL groups often become the "junior teacher" and feel responsible for instructing other students.

CL is a strategy that enables teachers to educate all students effectively within a heterogeneous classroom.

Sample

The membership lists of key professional organizations in each of these areas were obtained. One hundred names were randomly selected from each of the lists. In the case of the middle schools, the National Middle Schools Association and the Association for Supervision and Curriculum Development Middle Schools Network were utilized; in the case of cooperative learning, the International Association for the Study of Cooperative Learning (IASCL) and the Cooperative Learning Network of the Association for Supervision and Curriculum Development were used.

In each comparison, the membership lists of TAG (The Association for the Gifted, a Division of CEC) and the National Association for Gifted Children (NAGC) were used to obtain educators of gifted students. A separate sample was drawn from the gifted associations' membership lists for the middle school and the cooperative learning comparisons. For each study, then, 400 surveys were sent out.

The return rate was remarkable for survey research. Over 84% returned the middle schools survey; 75% returned the cooperative learning survey. Perhaps this reflects the intense interest in these topics. The high return may also have been due to providing self-addressed, stamped envelopes and employing follow-up letters to spur participation. In addition, over half of the respondents took advantage of the invitation to provide personal comments on the issues presented in the surveys.

Data Analysis

The responses to the survey items were checked by item cluster for internal consistency using Cronbach's alpha. Some additional clusters were established as a result of this analysis, and the results will be reported as such. A multivariate analysis of variance (MANOVA) was at first considered as a way to compare and analyze the responses of the groups. This method, however, was rejected in favor of the effect size statistic, which more accurately describes differences between large samples (Cohen, 1988). Effect size is determined by dividing the differences in group means by the total group standard deviation. An effect size of .80 is considered large; an effect size of .50 is seen as moderate; an effect size of .20 implies minimal influence.

RESULTS

Middle School/Gifted Comparisons

The results calculated from the survey responses of the 175 gifted educators and the 147 middle school educators can be seen arranged in order of the effect size in Figure 1. The number of high effect sizes confirmed that there were major differences in the attitudes and perceptions of these two groups. In most instances, the differences between the groups were ones of intensity of feeling rather than flat-out disagreements. For example, on the cluster that reflects the statement that "the regular curriculum challenges gifted students," there was a major effect size difference, even though both groups, on the average, rejected that idea. The educators of gifted students just rejected it more enthusiastically than did the middle school educators.

However, there are two domains in which there existed, on average, clear disagreement between the two groups. These are represented by the cluster stating that "gifted students benefit from being grouped together." As seen in Figure 1, the average ratings of the middle school group disagreed with the proposition that gifted students benefit from being grouped together, whereas the gifted educators agreed with the statement by a large margin. There was also substantial disagreement between the two groups on the item "identifying students as 'gifted' causes social difficulties." The gifted educators did not believe that students being identified as "gifted" caused social difficulties, whereas the middle school personnel believed that it did. A discussion of each cluster group in Figure 1 will help shed light on the survey analysis.

Cluster Item Responses

1. *Gifted students benefit from being grouped together.* This cluster dealt with whether gifted students should be educated within a heterogeneous or a homogeneous grouping. This issue showed the widest discrepancy between the two groups of educators. Educators from the middle school group felt that gifted students may not benefit from ability grouping, whereas educators from the gifted group felt that grouping was important to meet the needs of gifted learners. The effect size of 1.76 indicated that this issue clearly separated these two groups of educators.

2. *Identifying students as gifted causes social difficulty.* Educators from the middle school generally agreed with this statement. Their feelings seemed to be that the "gifted" label and accompanying special programs often create social adjustment problems for gifted students. The educators of gifted students generally disagreed with this statement, feeling that "giftedness" does *not* necessarily interfere with social development and that the label and services provided might assist gifted students with their social adjustment. An effect size of 1.39 indicated a major difference in the attitudes of the two groups.

3. *The regular middle school curriculum is challenging for gifted students.* These items addressed whether or not the regular middle school curriculum could meet the needs of gifted students. Both groups felt that the standard curriculum was *not* challenging enough for gifted students; however, the strength of this perception varied by group. Although the middle school educators disagreed with this statement, the educators of gifted students strongly disagreed. With an effect size of 1.07, this difference in intensity seemed important.

Figure 1   Comparisons of Means for Gifted and Middle School Respondents on
Survey Clusters

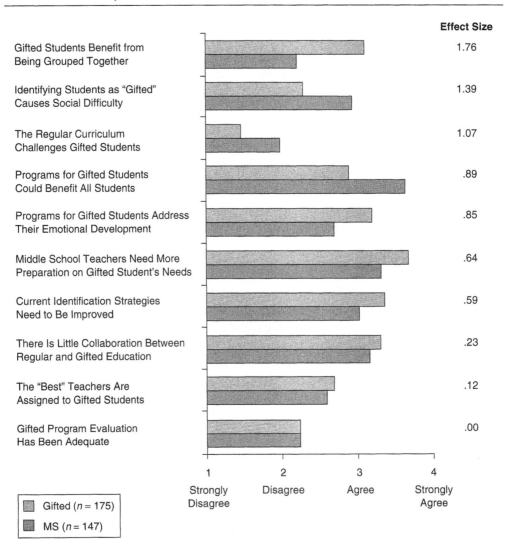

4. *The program designed for gifted students could benefit all students.* The middle
   school educators voiced strong agreement with this sentiment, whereas
   the educators of gifted students expressed mild agreement. The educators of gifted students felt that, to some extent, components of the program for gifted students would be good for other students, as well. The
   effect size of .89 indicated that these groups differed in their intensity of
   agreement with the statement.

5. *Current programs for gifted adequately address emotional development for
   gifted students.* These items dealt with whether or not sufficient support

and guidance were available to gifted middle grade learners to meet their emotional needs. Both groups agreed with this statement. However, the educators of gifted students strongly agreed that programs for gifted students do address the emotional needs of the students and that sufficient social support and attention to their affective development is included in such special programs. The large effect size of .85 indicated that the intensity of feelings differed for the two groups.

6. *Teachers at the middle grades need additional staff development in the characteristics and needs of gifted students.* This set of items addressed whether or not teachers of middle grade students have enough preparation to meet the needs of gifted students. The sense here was that there is need for more staff development and support to assist teachers in meeting the needs of the gifted students in their classes. Although both groups agreed with this theme, the teachers of gifted students strongly agreed. The effect size of .64 indicated a moderate difference in the intensity of agreement between the two groups of educators. This area seemed to be a point of mutual concern and may be a point of future collaboration, as well.

7. *Current identification practices need to be improved.* This cluster looked at two issues: the failure of current practices to recognize underachieving gifted students, and the need for student identification in order to assure appropriate services. There was overall agreement in this area. However, the focus was slightly different. The middle school educators felt that current practices overlook many students, whereas the educators of gifted students focused on the need for identification to assure services. The moderate effect size of .59 indicated that the groups reported some divergent views on these issues.

8. *Little collaboration takes place between educators in regular and gifted education on curriculum development.* This topic seemed particularly important given the middle schools' philosophical emphasis on interdisciplinary units and the inclusion of thinking strategies within the curriculum. Both of these areas have been extensively used in planning differential education for gifted students. The groups agreed that little collaboration has taken place. The effect size of .23 indicated that their feelings were quite similar on this issue. Additionally, both groups seemed to feel that collaboration would be mutually beneficial.

9. *The "best" teachers are assigned to teach the gifted students.* We included this cluster because it is a complaint sometimes voiced. The group responses, however, indicated neither agreement nor disagreement. The average of both groups fell into the *no opinion* category, indicating the perception that excellent teachers—as well as poor teachers—can be found in all areas of education. The effect size of .12 indicated no real difference between the groups on this cluster.

10. *Evaluation of gifted programs has been adequate.* These items explored the program assessment for special groups of students. Both groups disagreed with this statement, indicating that program evaluation is an area that needs attention. There was no difference (effect size of 0) between the groups on this cluster.

Table 1 provides some samples of the comments volunteered by those responding to the middle school survey. In many respects, the extemporaneous comments paralleled the survey issues. The specific comments indicated a shading of opinion, with some middle school teachers clearly aware of the special needs of gifted students and teachers of the gifted reacting to some of the perceived good qualities of the middle school (see Table 1, pp. 64-67).

The overall findings of the survey with middle school personnel indicated some clear differences in how the two groups viewed the middle school programs for gifted students. The heart of the differences appeared to be ability grouping, an issue that needs resolution between these professional groups. It is particularly important, given these differences, that we have completed five case studies on schools that describe how such schools have successfully blended a middle school philosophy with ability grouping when needed (Coleman, Gallagher, & Howard, 1993).

Cooperative Learning/Gifted Comparisons

In a manner similar to that employed in the middle schools comparison, a Cronbach alpha was calculated for each of the item clusters to guarantee consistency within the cluster. All of the clusters obtained alphas in the range of .51 to .80, with the exception of the cluster on ability grouping. All three of the stem statements in that cluster were, as a consequence, reported as individual items. Figure 2 gives the effect sizes for each item cluster or item.

Cluster Item Responses

The clusters were arranged in Figure 2 according to effect size, except for the single item statements on ability grouping. Each cluster will be discussed separately.

1. *The curriculum used in cooperative learning is not challenging enough for gifted students.* The particular thrust of this cluster was that the tasks chosen for the cooperative learning activities might tend to be too easy for the gifted students involved. The effect size of 1.68 represented an impressive difference between the two groups, with the gifted educators (GT) agreeing with this negative statement and those educators involved with cooperative learning (CL) rejecting the idea that cooperative learning did not challenge gifted students.

Figure 2   Response to Item Clusters from Cooperative Learning and Gifted
Educators

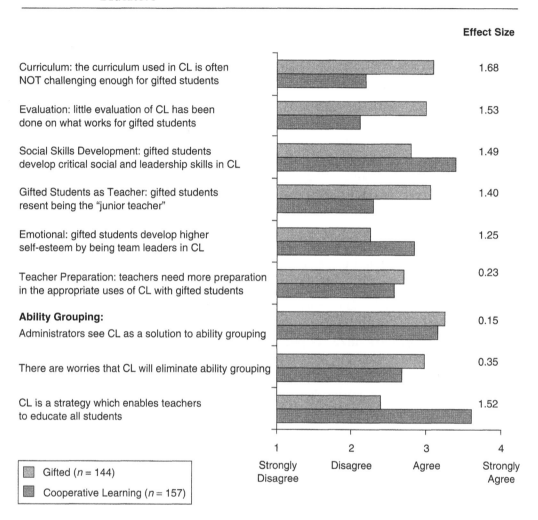

Effect Size

Curriculum: the curriculum used in CL is often
NOT challenging enough for gifted students — 1.68

Evaluation: little evaluation of CL has been
done on what works for gifted students — 1.53

Social Skills Development: gifted students
develop critical social and leadership skills in CL — 1.49

Gifted Students as Teacher: gifted students
resent being the "junior teacher" — 1.40

Emotional: gifted students develop higher
self-esteem by being team leaders in CL — 1.25

Teacher Preparation: teachers need more preparation
in the appropriate uses of CL with gifted students — 0.23

Ability Grouping:
Administrators see CL as a solution to ability grouping — 0.15

There are worries that CL will eliminate ability grouping — 0.35

CL is a strategy which enables teachers
to educate all students — 1.52

1   2   3   4
Strongly   Disagree   Agree   Strongly
Disagree   Agree

Gifted (*n* = 144)
Cooperative Learning (*n* = 157)

2. *Little evaluation of CL has been done on what works for gifted students.* The
GT group agreed that there is little evidence available on what works
for gifted students; that statement was strongly rejected by the cooperative learning group. Once again, there was a major effect size of 1.53.
This represented a strong difference between the two groups. On this
cluster, as well as on some of the others, the responses seemed to reflect
an emotional commitment rather than an expression of facts or data.
Few of the practitioners in either group would likely have had solid
information regarding the research literature available to support their
point of view.

3. *Gifted students develop critical social and leadership skills in cooperative learning.* The cooperative learning group showed a very strong agreement with this cluster theme, but the GT group did not. This accounts for the rather high effect size of 1.49 separating the groups. The fact that the GT group was negatively inclined on this item was particularly important in view of the strong emphasis in many cooperative learning programs on social skills development.

4. *Gifted students resent being the "junior teacher."* A strong agreement by the GT educators to this statement reflected a rather common observation of the role in which gifted students are sometimes placed in small-group sessions in cooperative learning. Yet the statement was generally rejected by the cooperative learning group. On the basis of the response to these items—and the strong effect sizes obtained—there would seem to be a generalized reaction by these groups to the concept of cooperative learning. It seems that the cooperative learning groups were seeing cooperative learning in a positive light under any circumstances. The GT groups seemed to be seeing the negative side of cooperative learning regardless of the setting.

5. *Gifted students develop higher self-esteem by being team leaders in cooperative learning.* Given the above supposition that cooperative learning people see the positive side of cooperative learning and GT people see the negative, there is nothing surprising about the response to this item. The cooperative learning group agreed with this positive outcome for gifted students in cooperative learning situations, but the GT group did not agree. Again, a very high effect size (1.25) can be noted.

6. *Teachers need more preparation in the appropriate uses of CL with gifted students.* Perhaps the most telling difference was obtained on this single item. This item produced the strongest reactions by the cooperative learning group, with a highly positive rating. The GT group, however, did not accept this proposition. This discrepancy is probably at the heart of the difficulty in reaching some accommodation between the two groups. It seems that the cooperative learning educators feel that their strategies will meet the needs of gifted students; the GT people believe that there needs to be something special in the curriculum in addition to cooperative learning.

7. *Other items.* There are several items or clusters in which the effect sizes were .35 or less, representing substantial agreement between the two groups. Both groups accepted the need for more preparation for teachers working with gifted students in cooperative learning. Both agreed that administrators see cooperative learning as a solution to ability grouping (though they may differ in how they feel about that "solution"). They agreed that cooperative learning gets the administrator off a "hot spot" by allowing him/her to say that the needs of gifted students are

being met by this strategy of cooperative learning and allowing a reduction or elimination of special programs. Both groups agreed that cooperative learning could eliminate ability grouping programs—indeed, this would be at the heart of the GT group's concerns.

Open-Ended Comments

One of the limitations of a rating scale is that it gives a statement about a current attitude of the respondent but does not show any rationale for why the attitude exists or what shading the attitude might have. That is why it was particularly important for the authors to review the spontaneous comments of the respondents. These comments revealed some complex thought patterns about these issues.

Some samples of these comments may be seen in Table 2. These responses reveal that educators involved in the educational reform movements were not necessarily insensitive to the needs of gifted students and that educators of gifted students were, in many instances, responsive to the reform agenda (Gallagher, Coleman, & Nelson, 1993; Nelson, Gallagher, & Coleman, 1993) (see Table 2, pp. 68-70).

Comments such as these make it clear that there is a basis for further discussion about these difficult issues. Certainly it seems that many persons at all levels of the educational enterprise wish to find some type of accommodation to these problems.

DISCUSSION

These comparisons indicate that educators who work with gifted students are in substantial disagreement with their educational colleagues who are proponents of cooperative learning and those in the middle schools movement concerning what is needed for gifted students. In the case of the cooperative learning survey, this disagreement appears to be across the board on practically all issues. In contrast, the middle school educators disagreed with educators of the gifted on two major points: ability grouping and the social consequences of being labeled "gifted." Other differences were ones of intensity, not direction.

The basically negative posture taken by the GT groups toward cooperative learning and the middle schools movement is partially modified by the more extended comments made by the GT respondents. These personal comments indicated that they valued the educational reform effort of middle schools and cooperative learning but felt that it was not sufficient to meet the needs of gifted students. Similarly, many of the personal comments of those educators using cooperative learning and those who are in middle school education indicated their sensitivity to, and concern about the needs of, gifted students. Nevertheless, the overall effect of these results was to reveal that a major gulf exists between the perceptions of these key groups of educators. This gulf, if allowed to persist, is sure to create problems at local levels as well as in policy development at the state and federal levels.

It would seem to be in the interests of all concerned to find ways to engage those in gifted education and those in the reform movement in meaningful, useful dialogue. Perhaps actual observation of classroom situations would help to reconcile these quite different viewpoints by showing the observers the good points of the opposing view. Surely there are many positive statements to be made for the effective implementation of some of the educational reform efforts. Certainly the general reception of the middle school movement and of cooperative learning in the broader educational community has been impressive. It would seem wise to seek ways in which the best of gifted education and the educational reform movements can be merged or synthesized.

We have also examined school systems that seem to have been successful in implementing the current educational reform efforts *and* providing effective programs for gifted students (Coleman, Gallagher, & Howard, 1993; Coleman, Gallagher, & Nelson, 1993). Based upon our observations, it is possible to combine successfully effective examples of the current reform programs with effective programs for gifted students. The education field in general would profit from a careful study of how such a blending of interests and practices can be produced.

REFERENCES

Allan, S. (1991). Ability grouping research reviews: What do they really say to the practitioner? *Educational Leadership, 48*(6), 60–65.

America 2000. (1992). Washington, DC: U.S. Department of Education.

Cohen, J. (1988). *Statistical power analysis for the behavioral sciences* (2nd ed.). Hillsdale, NJ: Erlbaum.

Coleman, M., Gallagher, J., & Howard, J. (1993). *Middle school site visit report: Five schools in profile.* Chapel Hill, NC: Gifted Education Policy Studies Program, University of North Carolina at Chapel Hill.

Coleman, M., Gallagher, J., & Nelson, S. (1993). *Cooperative learning and gifted students: Report on five case studies.* Chapel Hill, NC: Gifted Education Policy Studies Program. University of North Carolina at Chapel Hill.

Epstein, J., & MacIver, D. (1990). *Education in the middle grades: National practices and trends.* Columbus, OH: National Middle Schools Association.

Fullan, M. (1993). *Change forces.* Bristol, PA: Falmer.

Gallagher, J., Coleman, M., & Nelson, S. (1993). *Cooperative learning as perceived by educators of gifted students and proponents of cooperative education.* Chapel Hill, NC: Gifted Education Policy Studies Program, University of North Carolina at Chapel Hill.

George, P. (1988). Tracking and ability grouping. *Middle School Journal, 20*(1), 21–28.

Goals 2000. (1994). Washington, DC: U.S. Department of Education.

Johnson, D., & Johnson, R. (1990). *Cooperation and competition: Theory and research.* Edina, MN: Interaction Book Company.

Joyce, B. (1991). Common misconceptions about cooperative learning and gifted students. *Educational Leadership, 48*(5), 72–74.

Kagan, S. (1990). The structural approach to cooperative learning. *Educational Leadership, 47,* 12–15.

Kelly, G. (1970). A brief introduction to personal construct theory. In D. Bannister (Ed.), *Perspectives in personal construct theory.* New York: Academic.

Lounsbury, J. H., & Vars, G. (1978). *A curriculum for the middle school years.* New York: Harper & Row.

Nelson, S., Gallagher, J., & Coleman, M. R. (1993). Cooperative learning from two different perspectives. *Roeper Review, 16,* 117–121.

Oakes, J. (1985). *Keeping track: How schools structure inequality.* New Haven, CT: Yale University Press.

Oakes, J. (1992). Can tracking research inform practice? Technical, normative, and political considerations. *Educational Researcher, 21*(4), 12–21.

Robinson, A. (1990). Cooperation or exploitation? The argument against cooperative learning for talented students. *Journal for the Education of the Gifted, 14,* 9–27.

Ross, P. (1993). *National excellence: A case for developing America's talent.* Washington, DC: U.S. Department of Education.

Scales, P. (1992). *Windows of opportunity: Improving middle grades teacher preparation.* Chapel Hill, NC: Center for Early Adolescence, University of North Carolina at Chapel Hill.

Sicola, P. (1990). Where do gifted students fit? An examination of middle school philosophy as it relates to ability grouping and the gifted learner. *Journal for the Education of the Gifted, 14,* 37–49.

Slavin, R. (1988). *Cooperative learning: Theory, research, and practice.* Englewood Cliffs. NJ: Prentice-Hall.

Slavin, R. (1990). Ability grouping, cooperative learning, and the gifted. *Journal for the Education of the Gifted, 14,* 3–8.

Tomlinson, C. (1992). Gifted education and the middle school movement: Two voices on teaching the academically talented. *Journal for the Education of the Gifted, 15,* 206–238.

Table I   Sample Quotes from Middle School Survey

MS Educators	Issue	Educators of Gifted
We must group students in appropriate classes for English and math. Equally important, we *must* mainstream in other subjects. Call it, if you wish, elaboration. A prevailing need is to help teachers develop classroom approaches applicable to the needs of all children. I feel strongly that middle level students should *not* be ability grouped. A middle school needs to ensure that the social and emotional needs and the potential of all students are best met by hiring and developing a staff that tries its best to do all they can for each student with the capital they have available. Gifted students should be heterogeneously grouped some of the day and homogeneously grouped with gifted peers some of the day. They need both. The basic task is to develop designs and strategies that allow for heterogeneous grouping while providing opportunities for G/T students to reach their potential.	**Ability Grouping**	The problems of heterogeneous grouping, skills levels, boredom, and challenge are all daily events. How does a teacher learn to teach everyone? What strategies are effective with the whole class? The current trend to heterogeneous grouping, right or wrong, makes identification less important than open access to challenging experiences. I am concerned that movement away from ability grouping will hurt the development of gifted students. Educators must accommodate student differences so that gifted students do not lose ground academically. I would love to see gifted students grouped with the top 15% to 20% of the population in most classes. This way, they can be gifted all the time instead of only 3, 5, or more hours per week. I am very concerned about middle schools short-changing gifted students in academic challenges. Further, our district has gone toward site-based management, heterogeneous grouping, cooperative learning, etc., at the expense of students with special needs.
I strongly feel that the strategies used by teachers of the gifted should be used by all teachers.	**All students should have what gifted students have**	If the programs at the middle school level were more differentiated, all students could not benefit from them. Unfortunately, most of the programs I know are merely centered around more enrichment

MS Educators	Issue	Educators of Gifted
"Curriculum modification" that ensures gifted MS kids will reach their potential should also work for all students. I think it's possible, if you take a more strategic, less skills-oriented approach.		activities and science, which all students could handle and benefit from. I believe that much of what we do in gifted education should be done with all students. Then, those students who are highly creative or academic could be focused on.
Stop labeling gifted—train teachers to meet individual needs in a homogeneous class from K-8. Grouping takes place naturally in high school, with the wide range of courses. The teacher is the key. *All* teachers must be trained in successful use of strategies to meet student needs. Gifted students must be recognized for their gifts and encouraged to use them. Sad to say, in our parish there is an elitism associated with G/T students and the additional monies poured into the magnet schools for these students. The teachers themselves develop an elitism attitude, and this has caused much resentment between magnet schools and neighborhood schools, principals, and staff.	**Staff Development**	Current staff has little idea of how to adequately differentiate curriculum—no matter how challenging—for gifted students. Senior administrators are generally uninformed and lack support for programs. I feel it is essential to involve the *classroom teacher* in the education of the gifted middle school student. Educators of gifted children need to find a program "niche" within current reform and restructuring efforts—and within the "middle school" design. I am very concerned that, with the middle school concept being implemented more widely, administrations will recognize this but not give adequate training and support to teachers for successful integration of gifted students into heterogeneous groupings. We have teachers who resent the term "gifted" applied to students. Many teachers have no concept of the term and how it applies to teaching.
I believe in the gifted curriculum for all students, at least the great majority. I feel strongly that	**Challenging Curriculum**	If students are not challenged by curriculum or peers, they are in fact being taught to underachieve.

(Continued)

Table I (Continued)

MS Educators	Issue	Educators of Gifted
attempts should be made to include those adaptations within a heterogeneously grouped classroom at the middle school level.		They will not be prepared to cope with challenging curriculum beyond high school and will feel inadequate compared to students who have had more challenging curriculum. We have been successful in negotiating with proponents of the "middle school philosophy" to provide an effective academic program for academically talented students in math and language arts. Middle school is a key age; abilities/gifts can/should blossom in new kinds and ways. The curriculum needs to be strong, challenging, and experimental for all kids—so all learn to be max of their potential. Rescue middle grades from its "wasteland" reputation and put the best teachers and curricula there.
The education of gifted students has become, in many cases, an item of high *social* importance for parents as well as the more basic issue of appropriate education. My biggest concern with gifted students in homogeneous groups is the development of social skills. I would like to see research on gifted college graduates who fail in and/or frequently change jobs. I wonder if they develop appropriate social skills. Because middle school students are at a transitional and impressionable stage, we need to be careful not to label them—"gifted" or otherwise.	**Social Problems**	I feel it is very important not to isolate "gifted" students from the rest of the school. They must learn to work with people of all learning abilities. Our goal should not be to create an elite group, but instead a well-balanced group of people that can effectively lead others and make new discoveries in life. A special concern for me is the social and emotional needs of gifted girls at the middle school level. Middle school seems to be a tremendous turning point in social development, with girls often experiencing serious decline in self-esteem. I fear this may be even

MS Educators	Issue	Educators of Gifted
		more serious among gifted girls, especially in a society that values women for their physical appearance and little else. At this age, the biggest success has been—these adolescent people have a group, a place with which to identify—a safe place to go and "do their thing."

MS Educators	Issue	Educators of Gifted
Parents in elementary have had self-contained gifted classes, which are dissolved in MS. This is creating a PR problem, because gifted students are homogeneously grouped for only a portion of the day, vs. full day. We must recognize that the needs of the parents should not drive program development or implementation.	**Parents**	Parents who have gifted children assume they are gifted, too. Parents are often concerned that students are missing "traditional classes" when in a gifted/talented program.

Table 2 Sample Quotes from Cooperative Learning

CL Educators	Issue	Educators of Gifted
I have a problem with it ... I don't want to overburden the gifted student with the responsibility of teaching, yet I know there is much to be gained by such CL activities. How to find the appropriate balance? CL is best used when the goal of instruction is the development of conceptual understanding and critical thinking—and all students need that and can achieve that.	**CL in mixed ability groups**	CL must be used with care for the gifted, or we are putting an artificial ceiling on their learning. In heterogeneous classes, the gifted kids are not challenged intellectually by CL but may be hard put socially to keep their image as just one of the guys intact when the others look to them to come up with the answers. A main concern of these students now is that the regular classroom holds them back. This [CL] indicates a further impediment.
While many teachers have received training in CL, they do not receive the coaching and assistance for successful implementation...Principals need to monitor CL's use with the gifted. They, too, should be trained. I personally would like to see more evidence from research of what strategies I should be encouraging all teachers to use to meet both the top and the bottom students. CL is a deceptively simple strategy that requires more training and forethought than many teachers misusing CL have.	**Need for more staff development**	... teachers are not skilled in CL much less dealing with gifted learners. Preparing all teachers in the use of a variety of techniques for students of differing ability levels...preservice level as well as inservice.
CL is one of many tools which should be done correctly with all students. I'm concerned that some teachers use group work and call it CL without building in the appropriate skills. I don't feel that I can use one strategy to teach. My teaching	**CL as a tool and not a model**	Why the emphasis on CL with gifted? It should be but one of many tools...CL needs evaluation now that it has been in practice for a while—lack of individual initiative has developed. Will a group be with you throughout life to help you learn?

CL Educators	Issue	Educators of Gifted
changes as my students' needs change . . . Some days are great, some aren't. We view CL as one instructional strategy available to teachers—not as a panacea for ability grouping, social skills development, etc.		I think CL is another viable setting for learning, but as with most issues in education, we grab the ring for the wrong reasons and ride the merry-go-round without boarding properly. Clarification is needed to distinguish CL as an instructional strategy rather than an administrative program design for children.
I do not believe that CL can or should replace the grouping of gifted students—there is a place for both. Our district has full-time classes for the gifted...CL has been highly successful in these situations. X High is presently experimenting with CL in honors and college level classes...The teacher and I were amazed at the creativity and depth of the work produced by the students.	**Use of CL in same ability groups**	I feel grouping could work well if gifted students are frequently in the same group. Gifted children find working in a group of equal ability peers to be a positive experience when problem solving and participating in higher level thinking skills. Used within a gifted program, I believe CL is a wonderful process.
Gifted students most definitely need CL, but teachers are ill-prepared to facilitate them to teach them the required social skills. Gifted students need socialization skills as they tend to be intolerant, competitive, creative, independent, and individualistic.	**CL's value in self-esteem, social skills, and leadership**	If it is true that the gifted student is most likely to assume leadership activities in CL, then we should arm them with these skills first before engaging them in CL. They [teachers] should be made aware that some people do not necessarily achieve peak performance in a group...before we presume that they make good group leaders, I think, it is time we help them learn to lead and manage themselves. CL techniques have been great for social skills and conflict management among gifted students.

(Continued)

Table 2   (Continued)

CL Educators	Issue	Educators of Gifted
If structured appropriately, CL would not set gifted students up to be junior teachers nor allow them to become responsible for the entire group. As long as some trainers reinforce to teachers to group H-M-L and use a group grade, we will continue to have problems. Parents, administrators, and teachers need to understand the appropriate and inappropriate uses of CL. As a trainer and support person for CL, I see some abuses with gifted students, but usually not intentionally.	**Inappropriate uses of CL**	The idea of CL and the reality are often very different. The appropriate utilization of CL is hampered due to the lack of sufficient CL training, just as gifted education is often not part of regular ed. training. . . . it is very wasteful to think that the best academic and intellectual ideas emerge from groups. They don't, and learning has got to have the major emphasis on personal effort. Gifted students are often assigned responsibilities as TAs to regular classroom teachers. Such practices deny gifted students equitable opportunities for education and harm peer relationships. It appears that the major objective of group practices is to reduce differences rather than to adapt to differences.

5

The Effects of the Elimination of Gifted and Talented Programs on Participating Students and Their Parents

Jeanne H. Purcell

The University of Connecticut

The present burden for the education of the gifted and talented falls upon parents "who weep alone for their children."

—Ruth Martinson (1972)

Editor's Note: From Purcell, J. H. (1993). The effects of the elimination of gifted and talented programs on participating students and their parents. *Gifted Child Quarterly,* 37(4), 177-187. © 1993 National Association for Gifted Children. Reprinted with permission.

Interviews were conducted with 19 parents of students identified and served by a gifted program eliminated in 1990 to determine the effects of the elimination of the program on participants. To triangulate the findings of the interviews, mail surveys were sent to 49 additional parents of students who were also served and identified by the program. Results indicated that parents perceived that their children were experiencing a decline in energy, curiosity, and intrinsic motivation to achieve at high levels and were beginning to disengage from the traditional curriculum. Interviewed parents also reported that the process of program elimination resulted in so much divisiveness that more than half of them had considered alternative educational avenues for their children's remaining years in school.

INTRODUCTION

What happens to students who have been identified as gifted and talented when the gifted and talented program in their school is eliminated? Although little research exists about this phenomenon, several researchers have raised concerns about the current state of education for high-ability students. Renzulli and Reis (1991) reviewed the effects of the reform movement on gifted education and suggested that the accumulating effects of this movement are causing a quiet crisis and a step backward for the field. Specifically, they believe that the dumbing down of the curriculum, the elimination of grouping, and the national focus in recent years on standardizing curriculum in the form of mastery learning models have compromised efforts to provide a meaningful and appropriately differentiated curriculum for high-ability students. Feldhusen (1989) believes that students with high abilities in the public school system are ignored and offered only a limited number of high-quality curricular options. For the most part, he predicted a continuing and serious decline in the educational attainments of all students and the "systematic demotivation" (p. 59) of our students with high abilities.

Starko (1990) considered reasons for the discontinuation of a gifted program and suggested that the perceived negative effects of the program were factors that contributed to the program's demise. She documented negative comments from teachers and students, including problems with parents over identification, increased pressure (from students themselves), feelings of segregation experienced by identified students, perfectionism among students in the program, and "students leveling off and no longer seeming to be superior students once they were in the program" (p. 36). Starko (1990) concluded that programs for the gifted will remain vulnerable until there are solutions to some of the perceived negative effects of these programs.

Journalists have also documented that programs for high-ability students are experiencing difficulties in light of the current zeitgeist, and this trend is especially apparent in the New England area. A recent front page story in *The Boston Globe* stated that "education for the brightest public school students in New England is falling far behind what is offered their peers in other parts of the country" (Radin, 1991). *USA Today* reported that programs for the gifted "have suffered varying fates, suffering mostly where economies are poor" (Kelly, 1991, p. 18). Even though programs for these students throughout New England and elsewhere in the country are being eliminated, no research has been located which examines the effects of the elimination of a program on previously served students.

Putting the Research to Use

Increasing numbers of programs for high-ability students are being threatened, reduced, and eliminated, especially in states without mandates and in poor economic health (Purcell, 1993). To date, little research exists which examines the effects of program reduction or elimination on students previously served by programs. The effects described in the current research, while provocative, cannot be generalized beyond the sample studied. However, this study suggests four areas for further inquiry. First, what are the school behaviors of students who have suffered the loss of a gifted and talented program? Is the negative behavior pattern of high-ability students found in this study occurring in students from other geographical locations where programs have been reduced or eliminated or are other behavioral patterns emerging? Second, what is the extent of underachievement among students who have lost program services during the course of their educational program? Third, what are the effects of the elimination of programs for high ability children on their parents? Does the process of elimination necessarily have the divisive effects on parents and other community members described in the current study? Finally, further inquiry is necessary to determine the reasons for the elimination of gifted programs. Are the reasons related to financial issues or are the reasons related to more deep-seated issues, such as attitudes toward high-potential students? Clearly, the findings of the current research underscore the need for parents, those working with high-ability students, and researchers to elaborate upon the findings presented here in order to develop a better understanding of the numerous effects related to program reduction and elimination.

The purpose of this study was two-fold: (a) to describe parental perceptions of the positive and negative effects of special programming for high-ability students and (b) to describe parental perceptions of what happens to children identified as gifted and talented when a program specifically designed to meet their needs is eliminated. The following research questions were investigated: (a) What are the perceived positive academic and social effects of the program for high ability students? (b) What are the perceived negative academic and social effects of the program? (c) What are the perceived short-term effects, positive and negative, of the elimination of the program for high-ability students? (d) What are the perceived long-term effects, positive and negative, of the elimination of the program? (e) What are the effects of the elimination on parents of children identified as gifted and talented?

METHOD

The research presented here is a qualitative case study in which multiple sources of data were used to triangulate the findings. Sixty eight parents were initially contacted and 19 (hereafter referred to as interviewed parents or interviewees) agreed to interviews in which a phenomenological approach was taken. To verify the findings from interviewed parents, four additional sources of information were used: an anonymous survey (designed to parallel the interview questions) of 27 of the 49 initial respondents who preferred not to be interviewed (hereafter referred to as surveyed parents to distinguish them from the interviewed parents); documents (i.e., nine newspaper articles and 33 letters to the editor); interviews with two teachers of the gifted from the eliminated program; and a videotape of a board of education hearing in which 13 citizens expressed their opinions regarding the proposed elimination of the program for high ability students.

Subjects

A public school district which had eliminated its gifted and talented program in the 1989–1990 school year was selected as the site for the study from a pool of seven other communities in the state that eliminated programs during that academic year. Three of the seven communities were eliminated as possible sites because the average income of the citizens was well above the state mean. Another community was eliminated as a possible site because it was a regional district: that is, three or four diverse localities comprised the educational community. A final site was eliminated because one researcher was known to community members. A parent in each of the two remaining districts was contacted for information concerning the longevity of the program for students with high abilities and the extent to which each believed parents in the respective communities understood the goals of the program and would be willing to participate in the research. Final selection was based upon the longevity of the program for students with high abilities and the degree to which parents were believed to have understood the goals of the program.

The targeted site, a suburban, culturally homogeneous New England community with a population of 15,200, claims marinas, tourism, and distribution centers as its principal industries. The income was about the state mean, and the parents interviewed perceived the town to be made up of professionals, including doctors, lawyers, and scientists for several large research companies and energy production centers in the area. The schools were highly regarded by the citizens of the community and the surrounding area. Comments such as the one that follows were typical: "I chose to settle in this town in 1978 because of its excellent school system, good political management, and because it had vision. . . ." Statistics about funds allocated to education supported this perception. In recent years, the community allocated a large portion of its taxes to education, and in 1987–1988 the town spent $916.50 per capita for education, which was 11.44% more than the state average.

The interviewed parents and surveyed parents were similar populations with respect to the number of children per family involved with the program for the gifted, the total number of years experience with the program, and parents' understanding of the program's goals. Twelve (63%) of the 19 interviewees had one child who participated in the program and these 12 parents had, on average, 2.3 years experience with the program. The remaining 7 interviewed parents had two children who participated in the program and had 7 years experience. Eighteen interviewees believed that they understood the goals of the program. Nineteen (70%) of the 27 surveyed parents had one child who participated in the program with an average of 2 years experience with program services. The remaining 8 surveyed parents had two children involved and 5 years experience with the program. Nineteen (70%) of surveyed parents believed the goals of the program had been made clear to them, 4 (15%) were unclear about the goals, and another 15% believed that they did not understand the goals.

A program for academically able students based on the Enrichment Triad Model (Renzulli, 1977) began in this school district in 1978 in Grades 3–5, and an additional component was added 6 years later to serve students in Oracles 6–8. One teacher coordinated activities in the three elementary schools and another teacher coordinated activities in the middle school. Both teachers reported that they provided services to approximately the top 10% of the students within their respective schools, and students in all grades were identified using multiple criteria (i.e., achievement test scores. IQ scores, teacher recommendations, writing samples, and creativity test scores). Students in the elementary grades participated in a pull-out program that met for a block of time each week, approximately 60–90 minutes; students in the middle school had the program built into their schedules and met for at least 45 minutes a day. Students at both levels were provided more time in the resource room if they elected to work on self-selected independent investigations.

Both teachers of high-ability students related in interviews that they had similar goals for the programs in their schools: to provide cognitively appropriate enrichment and acceleration experiences to lead students to first-hand investigations of self-selected topics. Although there had been some concerns about elitism during the 12 years of the program's existence, neither teacher had believed that the elimination of the program was imminent.

Parents of children who had been identified for the program, Grades 3–8, were selected for this study because it was believed that they would be most aware of changes in their children's attitude and/or behavior with respect to school and academic achievement. Access to a list of parents was difficult because records about the gifted program were believed by parents to have been destroyed after its elimination. Although neither teacher of the gifted believed records had been destroyed, neither possessed program documents and believed documents had been turned over to administrators when the program ended. Thus, a "gatekeeper" (Lincoln & Guba, 1985, p. 234) who had been a key figure in a communication network established by parents to keep each other informed of events surrounding the proposed elimination prepared the initial list of possible participants. He identified subjects in the following ways: by generating a list from his memory, by asking both his children (who had been involved in the program) to recall names of their friends who had been in the program, by soliciting names of parents from each parent liaison in the three elementary schools and one middle school, and serially (one parent often supplied him with names of other parents). Thus, subjects selected other subjects which Bogdan and Biklen (1982) describe as "snowball sampling" (p. 66). The initial list of possible participants consisted of 68 parents of children who had been involved in the gifted and talented program in the 1989–1990 school year, and it is estimated from newspaper accounts and informants that this list represented approximately one half of all parents whose children had been identified for the program.

The 68 parents were sent an initial contact letter that briefly introduced the study, requested a 15 to 20-minute interview, and listed seven questions for the interview. Consent was obtained formally by the respondent's signature on a return post card, and 19 parents, or 28% of the initial respondent pool, agreed to be interviewed. Ten of the 19 represented one of the elementary schools; the remaining respondents were equally divided among the other two elementary schools and the middle school. All 19 parents were interviewed.

A follow-up survey was designed for the purpose of triangulating findings from interviewees. The anonymous survey consisted of Likert-scale items and spaces for surveyed parents to provide additional comments and description. The survey was mailed to the 49 parents who had not returned post cards indicating their willingness to be interviewed. Twenty-seven surveys were returned for a response rate of 59% for the written survey. The research had an overall response rate of 68%.

Instrumentation

A 10-item Likert-scale survey was designed to parallel the questions outlined in the initial contact letter to interviewed parents. Questions 1–3 collected demographic information from surveyed parents and questions 4–5 contained items dealing with positive and negative effects of the gifted program on which surveyed parents were asked to respond on a 4-point interval scale: 1 = *not at all*, 2 = *a little*, 3 = *some*, 4 = *a great deal*. Additionally, these parents were encouraged to add and rate their own positive and negative effects on blank items and scales. A 5-point scale (1 = *very negative effect*, 2 = *slight negative effect*, 3 = *none*, 4 = *slight positive effect*, 5 = *very positive effect*) was used to categorize answers to questions 6–7, which concerned parental perceptions of the short-term and long-term effects of the elimination of the program for high-ability students. Questions 8–10 asked surveyed parents their perceptions about the appropriateness of the curriculum prior to and after elimination of the gifted program, as well as their plans regarding their children's educational future (i.e., remain with public schools, thinking about private school, have already decided on private school, other).

The survey was based upon initial interviews with interviewed parents; that is, the survey was designed after three interviews with parents had been conducted. Support for the instrument's content validity was also established in a field trial with parents of gifted and talented children and teachers of the gifted.

Procedure

Interviewed parents. Each of the 19 interviewed parents was engaged in dialogues ranging from a minimum of 15 minutes to a maximum of 80 minutes. The interviewee was encouraged to elaborate upon whatever he or she thought was relevant about the seven questions and to diverge and structure his or her own account; answers and questions came from these parents. Interviews were audiotaped and transcribed literally.

Interviews were conducted by phone for two reasons. First, since most interviewed parents worked full-time, phone interviews were believed to have the least impact upon their schedules. Second, phone interviews were used because the content in the interviews was sensitive; initial contact with the gatekeeper indicated that the elimination process had caused a strained relationship between many parents and the school community. The gatekeeper reported that he, along with other interviewed parents, had received harassing phone calls and that parents were fearful the information they provided might be used "against their child" if people within the school learned of their participation. (Subsequent interviews with interviewees revealed that only 2 of the 19 had received such phone calls.) Phone interviews were perceived as least invasive, and, therefore, it was believed that participants would be more willing to share their perceptions regarding the effects of the elimination of the program for high-ability students.

Surveyed parents. The follow-up survey of nonrespondents to the requests for interviews was mailed and collected concurrently with the interviews.

Documents. Documents, nine newspaper articles and 33 letters to the editor, related to the elimination process were collected from interviewed parents and from three local newspapers. One interviewee had kept a scrapbook of newspaper articles which chronicled events leading to the elimination of the program, and he provided a copy of all the articles to the researcher.

Video. Another interviewee provided a videotape of a board of education hearing in which citizens from the community were provided time to express their views concerning the need for a program to provide services to high-ability students. The videotape recorded all 13 citizens who registered to address the board of education.

Teacher interviews. Interviews were conducted with both teachers of the gifted to determine their perceptions regarding the goals of the program, the positive and negative effects of the program, and short-term and long-term effects of the elimination of the program. Teacher interviews were audiotaped and transcribed literally.

Data Analysis

Interviewed parents. Data analysis was completed in two parts. Transcribed interviews were initially analyzed in an ongoing process similar to the "constant comparative method" (Glaser & Strauss, 1967, p. 105) to determine the categories and properties of positive and negative effects of the gifted program and the short-term and long-term effects of the elimination. When data collection was completed, intensive analysis was conducted to identify themes based on repeating regularities in the descriptive data.

Surveyed parents. The surveys were analyzed in two ways: by computing means and standard deviations on the scaled items and using "across category clustering" (Miles & Huberman, 1984, p. 155) on open-ended items.

Documents. The content of all documents was examined by highlighting positive effects in one color and negative effects in another color. Two lists were compiled: perceived positive effects of the program and perceived negative effects of the program. Across category clustering was used to assemble lists of the most frequently mentioned positive and negative effects.

Video. The videotape was analyzed for themes using across category clustering in a manner similar to the technique utilized for document analysis described above. The content of each speaker's comments was analyzed; the positive effects were highlighted (no negative effects were mentioned by the speakers) and then assembled according to the frequency with which they were mentioned.

Teacher interviews. Teacher interviews were analyzed in two stages which were identical to the stages outlined for interviewed parents described above.

RESULTS

The findings are organized by research question. Additionally, findings related to each research question are categorized by source (i.e., interviewed parents, surveyed parents, documents, videotape, and teacher).

Research Question #1: What Were the Perceived Positive Academic and Social Effects of the Program for Students with High Abilities?

Interviewed parents. Research question #1 concerning the perceived positive effects of the gifted and talented program yielded three categories of positive effects from the 20 individual effects reported by interviewed parents: a differentiated curriculum, support for interpersonal issues, and support for intrapersonal issues (see Figure 1).

Two of these 20 effects, "sparked or facilitated an interest" and "generated energy and/or excitement," surfaced prominently and can be considered primary findings. "Sparked or facilitated an interest" was identified by 13 of the 19 interviewed parents (68%), and "generated energy or excitement" was mentioned by 10 interviewees (53%). Another set of positive effects which emerged from the interview data included "increased opportunity to interact with intellectual peers" and "being able to go beyond the curriculum." These effects were cited by 9 (47%) and 8 (42%) interviewed parents, respectively.

Surveyed parents. The positive effects rated highly by surveyed parents were similar to the ones most frequently mentioned by interviewed parents. Parents who were surveyed rated a total of eight positive effects on a 4-point scale (1 = *not at all*, 2 = *a little*, 3 = *some*, 4 = *a great deal*) and rated "increased opportunity to interact with intellectual peers" ($X = 3.79$; $SD = 0.49$) and "exposed to lessons not normally covered in the classroom" ($X = 3.62$; $SD = 0.54$) the highest. Both of these effects were findings that emerged from the interview data.

Documents. Forty-two newspaper articles, including 33 letters to the editor, collected from three local newspapers were used to verify the findings from interviewed parents to research question #1. Two thirds of the letters to the editor supported retention of the gifted program because it provided students with a more challenging curriculum, a positive effect mentioned frequently by interviewed parents.

Videotape. The videotape also provided support for the data collected from interviewed parents with respect to research question #1. Thirteen citizens

Figure 1   Categories and Frequency of Positive Effects Reported by Interviewers

Category	Frequency	
	No. of responses	% of all responses*
Provided appropriately differentiated curriculum		
1. Sparked/facilitated interests	13**	16
2. Provided opportunities to go beyond the traditional curriculum	8	10
3. Developed critical-thinking skills	4	5
4. Provided opportunities for students to work at an appropriate intellectual level	3	4
5. Broadened students' horizons with enrichment	3	4
6. Stimulated thoughts	2	2
7. Exposed students to careers	2	2
8. Provided freedom and choice	2	2
9. Provided students opportunities to learn process skills	2	2
10. Eliminated boredom	2	2
11. Encouraged creativity	2	2
12. Provided students with the opportunity to go in-depth	1	1
13. Provided students with the opportunity to see the "whole process"	1	1
14. Kept students connected to school	1	1
Total responses in category	46	(55)
Supported intrapersonal issues		
15. Energized/excited students	10	12
16. Increased self-esteem	7	8
17. Increased self-confidence	6	7
18. Encouraged risk taking	3	4
Total responses in category	26	(31)
Supported interpersonal issues		
19. Increased the opportunity to work with intellectual peers	9	11
20. Increased opportunities for students to work with more accepting peers	2	2
Total response in category	11	(13)

*Percentages do not total 100 because they have been rounded
**Responses do not total 19 (the number of interviewees) because interviewees provided multiple responses

spoke at the board hearing recorded on this tape and all spoke in favor of retaining the program. Positive effects were organized into three categories: the differentiated curriculum, support for interpersonal issues, and support for intrapersonal issues. With respect to the first category, 6 speakers believed the program provided a more challenging curriculum, 2 speakers believed the program encouraged creativity, and 2 other speakers believed the program provided advanced-level training in thinking skills. Two speakers believed the most positive aspect of the program was the time it provided students to interact with their intellectual peers. Three speakers (2 of whom had also spoken concerning the importance of a differentiated curriculum) also spoke about intrapersonal issues, stating that positive aspects of the program included the promotion of risk taking and the encouragement of students toward high goals and standards.

Teacher interviews. The data from the teachers of the gifted concerned all three categories of positive effects. They believed the program's curricula went beyond what was provided in the classroom and was "interactive, experiential, and investigatory." Additionally, they believed the program helped students realize that there were other students who were "'as adept intellectually and academically" as they were and encouraged risk taking.

To summarize, categories of positive effects utilized by the four sources for triangulation (i.e., survey data, documents, videotape, teacher interviews) confirmed the categories of positive effects (i.e., differentiated curriculum, support for interpersonal issues, and support for intrapersonal issues) reported by interviewed parents. Furthermore, many of the specific effects (i.e., the challenge of the differentiated curriculum, the time with intellectual peers) were mentioned by all sources as important positive effects.

Research Question #2: What Were the Perceived Negative Academic and Social Effects of the Program for Students with High Abilities?

Interviewed parents. Although the majority of interviewees felt there were no negative effects, 43% of these parents reported eight negative effects which were organized into five categories: teasing by nonidentified peers, make-up work, elitism, labeling and/or singling out students, and lack of communication among teachers regarding the educational plans for and needs of students identified as gifted (see Figure 2). Of the five categories of negative effects cited by interviewees, "teased by nonidentified peers" was most frequently mentioned (three citations), followed by a concern for make-up work (two citations).

Surveyed parents. Three of the five negative effects mentioned by interviewed parents were supported by surveyed parents. Parents who were surveyed indicated negative effects and the extent of negative effects in two ways: by responding to Likert-type questions (i.e., had to complete class work missed while participating in the gifted program, felt singled out and different from other students, and was teased by nonidentified peers) and in open-ended questions in which they were asked to report and rate negative effects not mentioned in the scaled items. High scores on the scaled questions ($1 = not\ at\ all$, $2 = a\ little$, $3 = some$, $4 = a\ great\ deal$) indicated effects that were most troublesome for surveyed parents' children. These parents believed that completing make-up work was the most troublesome aspect of the gifted program for their children ($X = 2.30$; $SD = 1.23$), and it is important to note that the most highly rated negative effect was rated only 2.3, indicating that negative effects did not feature prominently in the surveyed parents' data.

Figure 2   Categories and Frequency of Negative Effects Reported by Interviewees

	Frequency	
Category	No. of responses	% of all responses*
Teasing by nonidentified peers	3	38
Make-up work	2	25
Elitism	1	13
Labeling/singling out of students	1	13
Lack of communication among teachers regarding identified students' activities in the program	1	13
Total responses	8	

*Percentages do not total 100 because they have been rounded

Documents. Eighteen documents, 14 letters to the editor and 4 articles, mentioned elitism (specialized treatment of a select group) as a negative effect of the program or referred to it as a problem perceived by others. Although this negative effect was not prominent in either the interviewed parents' or surveyed parents' data, it did feature prominently in the data of many of those not directly involved with the program. The discrepancy between the perceptions of the two populations (i.e., interviewees/surveyed parents and letter writers) is one possible reason for the degree of controversy that emerged within this community during the elimination process.

Video. None of the speakers at the board of education hearing spoke against the program or mentioned negative effects related to the program.

Teacher interviews. The elementary teacher of the gifted and talented reported no negative effects related to the program for students with high abilities. The middle school teacher of the gifted and talented indicated that there were two negative effects. One concerned the necessity of selection criteria and the fact that these criteria "upset parents and students who weren't in it." The other concerned the nature of the activities pursued by students selected for the program. These learning activities were perceived as "wonderful" by nonselected parents and students and resulted in a desire for these services by nonselected students and their parents.

In summary, interviewed parents' perceptions regarding the negative effects of the gifted program in this community were corroborated by the data from surveyed parents. Less than half of the interviewees believed there were negative effects, and the negative effects rated by surveyed parents were perceived to have little or no effect on their children. The data from the documents and teachers present a different picture of the negative effects of the program. Almost half (43%) of the documents referred to elitism either as a problem with the program or as a problem perceived by others about the program. The middle school teacher believed the program's selection criteria and activities caused a negative reaction among students and parents of students who were not involved with the program.

Research Question #3: What Are Perceived Short-Term Effects, Positive and Negative, of the Elimination of the Program?

Interviewed parents. Over three fourths of those interviewed (84%) perceived outcome behaviors which they attributed to the elimination of the gifted and talented program. Their children missed the challenge that the gifted program had provided, were going "too slow," and were bored.

> I think he misses it. Particularly during math because that's another area where he's really good. And they do go slow and that drives him a little bit crazy.

One interviewee perceived great frustration in her child:

> I remember him coming home and telling me he was upset, frustrated, and angry because they were doing a chapter on telling time. Now this is fourth grade. He said, "I know all this stuff." And I tried to explain to him that other students needed time to learn about time. And he was very angry and said to me, "Well what about me?" And you know, I didn't know what to tell him. He felt very bored and frustrated, and that he was just not getting enough.

Interviewed parents indicated a spectrum of behaviors occurring as a result of the boredom, including daydreaming, disruptive behavior, and academic demotivation.

> He finds himself to be very bored in class. He tells us that he turns it off. He says, "I can't do the science work in class because I'm busy trying to solve pollution problems." And we say to him, "do the work for class." But in his head he's thinking about the greenhouse effect and the ozone layer and he's trying to figure out how he could solve them, rather than do the work that was mundane.
>
> Now he's in this fifth-grade basal reader, even though he reads at the eighth-grade level. He's in the fifth-grade math class, even though he tests well above fifth-grade . . . It's boring. It's very boring. And he's becoming a little disruptive at times.

> A: School is a chore, there's no motivation, and both my children hate school. They take no initiative in their work. One of my sons is doing terribly.
> Q: Can you tell me what you mean by "terribly"?

A: He's failing, he's one of the brightest kids in the school, and he's failing.

Q: Across the board?

A: Three Fs and two Ds.

Q: How did he do last year?

A: He made the honor roll. His attitude in school now is, he knows what they're teaching, he doesn't see any point in homework or in repeating or in giving back any of his work that he knows. He'll get 100 on a quiz, but a zero on homework. That means 50 or failing. . . . With the gifted program he was able to think and consistently got As. And he was excited about learning. There's none of that this year.

The majority of interviewed parents perceived that their children were bored in school to varying degrees. Many believed that an appropriate curriculum option for their children no longer existed within the school environment and perceived their children as overtly seeking avenues, some socially unacceptable and some more self-destructive than others, to find a place for their intellectual energy. The school-based behaviors associated with boredom in classes and identified by parents in this sample are reflected in a spectrum of outcome behaviors in Figure 3.

Additionally, interviewees' comments indicated that the abilities of their children have not been valued, have even been sabotaged, and included, for example, "[my child] feels discriminated against," "was given dirty looks by other students [when she went to the talented and gifted resource room]," and "my daughter was the only girl in her grade in the program. The teacher wouldn't tell her the missed assignments. Her classmates told her the wrong assignments on purpose." After the elimination of the program, one parent indicated that her child had been told by her teacher to "stop doing her in-depth work." Another parent commented that her child said her teachers "resent" her when she goes beyond the regular curriculum. One parent, speaking about the elimination process and the attitude of community members, stated: "One thing that came out . . . was an attitude. It was that kids who are gifted shouldn't be singled out, that they reflect badly on everyone else."

Surveyed parents. Surveyed parents were asked to respond to one scaled item related to this research question and provided spaces on which to explain their response. The item asked the question: Has the elimination of the gifted and talented program had any effect, positive or negative, on your child in the past year?

Surveyed parents' data supported the beliefs of interviewees; overall, surveyed parents believed that their children were experiencing short-term difficulties associated with the elimination of the program for the gifted and talented. This was indicated by the mean score (1.9) of surveyed parents' responses to the aforementioned survey question ($SD = 0.76$, [1 = *very negative*, 5 = *very positive*]), and the nature of the explanations they provided, which ranged from "missing the program" to lack of academic motivation, described by one correspondent as follows:

Figure 3   Perceived Behavioral Outcomes of the Elimination of the Gifted and Talented Program

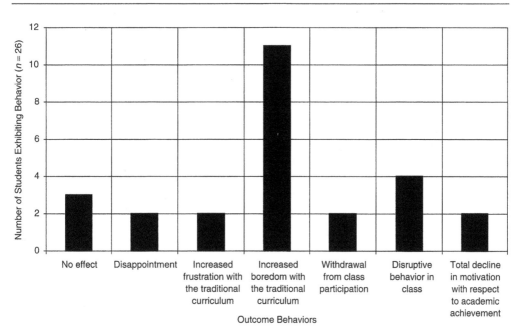

My child no longer has the motivation to do anything but the minimum required for assignments. He is bored and coasting. We are watching his work, effort, and productivity set back 2–3 years.

Teachers. Both teachers reported short-term negative effects related to the elimination of the program. Although the elementary teacher indicated she no longer had contact with the majority of students from the program, she still saw two students. She believed one was "shooting along just fine," but the other had "really kind of disappeared as far as not wanting to be noticed as being very bright." The middle school teacher, who left the district after the program was eliminated, indicated that she could not report on specific students but believed there was an "amazingly negative impact" on the students who had participated: no longer would they have exposure "to unusual ways of thinking and the fact that learning could take place in diverse environments."

Research Question #4: What Are the Perceived Long-Term Effects, Positive and Negative, of the Elimination of the Program for Students with High Abilities?

Interviewed parents. Eighty-four percent of interviewees believed the elimination of the gifted program would have long-term effects on their children.

Responses emerged in two categories: long-term effects on students and long-term effects on education in general and world competitiveness. Interviewees did not believe their children's potential would be realized.

> I think it's a waste. . . . Each child should be allowed to develop to his/her potential and be challenged. . . . We felt before that the system could deal with children like my daughter, and now we feel that public schools are only interested in children of middle and below-average learning abilities.
>
> If there are no programs to excite them about learning, I don't even want to think about it. Maybe later on in life something will be reawakened in them . . . My hope is that someday they'll say, "Oh yes, I will do this for myself," and will go on to develop some initiative and joy in learning. I'm very depressed about my sons' futures.

Many perceived that their children were disengaging from school. One parent commented: "Undoubtedly, there are going to be more [students with above-average ability] who are going to turn off . . . and that's very, very scary." Other informants saw long-term effects on education and the future work force: "I do think . . . schools are not performing up to the kind of educational standards that we need, and that the quality of the work force will not be competitive with the rest of the world."

Fourteen percent of parents surveyed did not believe there would be any long-term impact of the elimination of the gifted and talented program. Because the gifted program never existed beyond the eighth grade in this community and because the children of some of those interviewed had advanced into high school, these parents believed that the elimination had no effect upon their children.

Surveyed parents. Parents who were surveyed were asked to respond to one scaled item related to this research question and provided spaces on which to explain their response. The item asked the question: In your opinion, what overall effect will the elimination of the gifted program have on your child during his/her remaining years in the school system? Survey data supported the beliefs expressed in interviews, as indicated by the mean score (1.9) of surveyed parents' responses to the aforementioned question ($SD = 0.77$ [1 = *very negative*, 5 = *very positive*]), and the nature of the explanations they provided. Open-ended responses centered around several themes, including:

> It has a very negative impact on our son's future. If we didn't take up the slack at home, I feel the elimination would have a very negative effect. Even with our attempts, it will have a negative effect because we can't duplicate the atmosphere of peers.
>
> Without stimulation and the right challenges, I fear further regression, frustration, anger, and acting out.

Teachers. Both teachers reported that the potential of many of their former students would not be realized. The middle school teacher concluded, "As a society, we have got to come to terms with these kids."

Research Question #5: What Are the Effects of the Elimination on the Parents of Students with High Abilities?

Interviewed parents. Another long-term effect emerging from the interview data was the impact that the elimination process had on parents of children identified as gifted and talented and upon the children themselves. The divisiveness became so intense that some parents who had traditionally believed in the need for special services for their more able child began to question their beliefs.

> I thought I always believed that it was absolutely necessary for those children to have something extra to keep them interested in school . . . but I don't know. I know so many parents, believe it or not, who are anti, who are friends of mine. One woman in the neighborhood did not think it was fair that my son went to that program. . . . She didn't think he should be singled out. She didn't think that any child should be singled out and given that opportunity. . . . And I wondered if she might be right.

Finally, children were drawn into the dispute.

> **A:** It was a big to-do with the whole town. They had kids fighting with kids, parents with parents, the school board . . . It turned into a public debate and it carried over into the school and the children who had been identified . . . there was some bitterness.
>
> **Q:** Can you give me an example of that?
>
> **A:** One day my daughter came home in tears because they had debated it in class, and children can be quite cruel.

The data suggest that the process of elimination was not only divisive but also caused a spectrum of effects among three fourths of those interviewed. Twelve percent of interviewees indicated disappointment, 43% indicated discouragement and disenchantment, and 24% indicated skepticism or open distrust of the educational system and/or its leaders. Twenty-one percent of these parents did not feel that the elimination process affected them. Those who were affected expressed their frustration, discouragement, and distrust in comments such as the following:

> **A:** I'll tell you the truth, I've banged my head against the wall. I've spent hours with our superintendent. I've spent hours with our principal. Their pat answer is, the company line is, that this [outcomes-based behaviors program] is a new program and we need time to get

> it on board. My answer to them is that "Well, if it needs time to get on board . . . what's the interim program you have in mind while we're going from A to Z?" They had planned nothing!

Q: What did they say?

A: They said, "Oh no, Mrs. Jones. Your child is being challenged. You just don't see it because you're not in your son's class." And I clearly say, "Obviously I'm not in the class, but I do know that he comes home and says. 'God, it was boring today. Why can't I do more? Why can't I do something else? Why do I have to do this if I already know it? Why do I have to sit through the review of a test that I got 100% on?'"

The dissatisfaction among some of those interviewed caused adversarial relationships between parents and the school system which varied in intensity and is echoed in the following responses:

> Our feelings about the school system have changed drastically. We came here because of the school system. I turn that around right now, and I would never tell anybody to move here for the educational system. I'm very, very disturbed by it, and I don't see it getting any better.
>
> Through this whole process last year . . . the frustration with the school was just incredible. And just for the sake of saving a few dollars. I feel my kids' education has been sabotaged . . . I still try to support the school, but it's become much more of an adversarial relationship.

Interviewed parents and surveyed parents. The dissatisfaction with the public school system engendered by the process of elimination caused many who were interviewed to consider alternative educational routes for their child's remaining years of school. The consideration of alternative schooling options is reflected not only by interviewees, but also by those who were surveyed. Thirty-nine percent of those surveyed indicated they have considered and/or already selected alternative arrangements for the education of their children; 53% of interviewees have already considered and/or selected alternative educational avenues for their children. It is believed that these numbers actually, underrepresented the number of parents who would like to send their children to different schools because many surveyed parents and interviewed parents said that although they wished they could send their children elsewhere to school, they were not in a financial position to do so. Clearly, the process of elimination affected not only high-ability children but also their parents.

Documents. The documents supported the controversial nature of the elimination process in three ways. First, the large number of citizens who wrote letters to the editor indicated the extent of concern related to the issue of education for students with high abilities. Second, the titles of the articles and letters attested to the strength of beliefs, even anger, of many in the community, for example:

"Save a Buck and Short-Change a Mind," "Town-Hurts Tomorrow's Leaders for a Measly $7,000," "The Gifted Don't Need the Extras," "Cutback of the Gifted Program Causes a Furor," and "All School Children Are Not Equal." Third, reports about harassing phone calls, vandalism, and threatening mail were documented in newspaper articles and letters and verified earlier reports by interviewees.

DISCUSSION

This study raises provocative issues, but caution in generalization is needed because external reliability (Goetz & LeCompte, 1984) is difficult to attain in qualitative studies. Although descriptions of context, the interviewees, the surveyed parents, the relationship between the researcher and participants, constructs, and the methods of data collection and analysis are outlined, and several sources of data are used to triangulate the data from the group investigated, the findings presented here pertain to the effects of program elimination in this one community.

It is clear from interviews and surveys in this study that the elimination of a gifted program did have a spectrum of effects on many of the parents and students once served by the gifted program in this community. Four major findings will be highlighted: the decline of student motivation to achieve at higher levels, student underachievement with respect to the traditional curriculum, the effect of the process of program elimination on students and parents, and the effect of deep-seated attitudes about high-ability students on their academic performance.

Decline of Student Motivation at Higher Levels of Functioning

Energy or excitement, one of the most frequently mentioned positive effects of gifted programming by interviewees, is recognized as a characteristic of the gifted by researchers (MacKinnon, 1960; Oden, 1983; Piechowski, Silverman, Cunningham, & Falk, 1982), and early research suggested that high-ability students may come to programs with higher levels of energy. Parental observations from this investigation suggested a heightened sense of excitement and/or energy as *a result* of their child's interaction with the program's challenging activities and with intellectual peers. Accordingly, parents indicated that the heightened challenge of program activities and peer interaction were two program elements that their children missed the most after the program was eliminated. Several parents commented that even their children noticed differences about themselves. "My son told us he knows he would be learning so much more about what he's interested in if he still had the program." The data supplied by many parents in this sample suggest that there has been a decline in the intrinsic motivation of their children: their children no longer have the same level of intellectual curiosity and energy. Without the opportunity to undertake more difficult curricular challenges and to be recognized for their special abilities, many parents believed their children were becoming less motivated and consequently settling for lower standards.

Student Underachievement with Respect to the Traditional Curriculum

Concomitantly, some of these students were beginning to disengage from and underachieve with respect to the traditional curriculum because its low level and slow pace made them "frustrated," "bored," and "disruptive," according to their parents. It seems reasonable to conclude from the data that while the gifted and talented program was operating in this community, it motivated students and may have helped to keep many of them connected to the traditional school experience. When it was eliminated, parents reported that their children began to "tune out" of the regular curriculum in a variety of outcome behaviors and expressed concern that their children's future achievement would be negatively affected. Parents of children who were currently in the middle school grades were especially concerned about their children's disengagement from the traditional curriculum. They believed their children were developmentally ready to separate themselves from adult figures and the school, and that teachers and the curriculum no longer nurtured a group of academically motivated students.

Accordingly, this research has important implications for those who are responsible for establishing and implementing educational policy, as well as those involved with educational research. Increasing numbers of gifted programs are being eliminated (Purcell, 1992, 1993). Once gifted programs are eliminated, research suggests that little remains in traditional classrooms to stimulate the child with above-average ability. Reis and Purcell (1993) suggest that as much as 24%–50% of the curriculum in math, language arts, science, and social studies can be eliminated without affecting the achievement levels of high-ability students. Westberg, Archambault, Dobyns, and Salvin (1993) examined the instructional and curricular practices used with high-ability students in regular elementary classrooms across the country, and their data suggest that across all five subject areas, high-ability students received no differentiation in 84% of the activities in which they were involved.

A small percentage of the students with high abilities in this study may continue to function well without program services in traditional classes. A much larger percentage of students in this study, however, may already be disengaging from school and beginning to underachieve with respect to the traditional curriculum. Policy makers need to become aware of the declining number and scope of some appropriately differentiated educational alternatives for high-ability students and of the experience at this one community. Those in educational research need to conduct additional studies to examine the extent of the outcome behaviors suggested by this research.

The Effect of the Process of Program
Elimination on Students and Their Parents

The data in this study suggest that the process of elimination affected both students and parents. The process caused some of the parents in this community to question the value that society places on the abilities of their children. The process of elimination also caused several parents who had always believed that their children needed differentiated instruction to question the necessity of those services. Furthermore, the process of program elimination alienated parents of gifted and talented children to such an extent that many, perhaps as many as half, have given serious thought to private school.

Attitudes Toward High-Ability Students
and the Academic Performance of These Students

Finally, the findings in this study suggest that deep-seated attitudes toward students with high abilities may exist within this school and community and can affect the academic performance of these learners. Brown (1990) studied high school students and reported two phenomena related to peer expectations and achievement among adolescent cohorts. First, he found that although academic pressures to finish high school were quite strong, there was little pressure to excel academically. Second, Brown explained that peers may bring sanctions to bear upon the more academically able student because the more capable students "set standards of performance that increase the efforts that their peers have to put into school work" (p. 16). Rather than regard their peers with esteem, the less able peers try to "get even" with the "curve wreckers" (Brown, 1990, p. 28); esteem for their more able counterparts is transformed by their own frustrations into enmity and ridicule.

The data from the present study indicate that normative pressures and sanctions have been brought to bear upon some of the high-ability students in the current study and at a much earlier age than the high school students Brown studied. Interviewed parents from this study indicated, for example, that as early as third grade nonidentified students told identified peers who had been out of the room to participate in gifted program activities the wrong assignment to make up *on purpose*. Furthermore, interviewees from this study indicate that *parents of nonidentified students and some teachers* brought sanctions to bear upon identified students during and after the elimination process. Brown does not offer any explanation for why some parents or teachers might deride the accomplishments of the more able students, although he does suggest that the seeming dislike for intellectuals apparent in adolescents may be a "reflection of a prejudicial view of intellectuals common to the larger culture" (1990, p. 15).

CONCLUSION

A paucity of research exists about the effects of the elimination of gifted programs on students the program once served and their parents. The research presented here suggests that the majority of parents in one community perceive that the elimination of the gifted and talented program has affected their children. Further, the elimination process was divisive and caused such dissatisfaction among parents of high-ability children that over half have considered sending their children to other schools. It is hoped that the present study will encourage further research to elaborate upon the present findings and to understand the longitudinal effects of the elimination of gifted and talented programs upon students, schools, and communities.

REFERENCES

Bogdan, R. C., & Biklen, S. K. (1982). *Qualitative research for education.* Boston: Allyn and Bacon.

Brown, B. B. (1990, November). *School, culture, social politics, and the academic motivation of U.S. students.* Paper presented at a conference on student motivation sponsored by the Office of Educational Improvement. Arlington, VA.

Feldhusen, J. F. (1989). Why the public schools will continue to neglect the gifted. *Gifted Child Today, 12*(61), 55–59.

Glaser, B. G., & Strauss, A. I., (1967). *The discovery of grounded theory: Strategies for qualitative research.* New York: Aldine.

Goetz, J. P., & LeCompte, M. D. (1984). *Ethnography and qualitative design in educational research.* New York: Academic Press.

Kelly, D. (1991, October 23). Programs for the gifted: Equitable or elitist? *USA Today,* p. 18.

Lincoln, Y. S., & Guba, E. G. (1985). *Naturalistic inquiry.* Newbury Park. CA: Sage.

MacKinnon, D. W. (1960). The highly effective individual. *Teachers College Record, 61,* 376–378.

Martinson, R. A. (1972). An analysis of problems and priorities: Advocate survey and statistical sources. In S. P. Marland. *Education of the gifted and talented: Background papers,* (Vol. 2. pp. 121–136). Washington, DC: U.S. Governmental Printing Office.

Miles, M. B., & Huberman, A. M. (1984). *Qualitative data analysis.* Newbury Park, CA: Sage.

Oden, M. (1983). A 40-year follow-up of giftedness: Fulfillment and unfulfillment. In R. S. Albert (Ed.), *Genius and eminence* (pp. 203–212). Oxford, UK: Pergamon.

Piechowski, M. M., Silverman, I. K. Cunningham, K., & Falk, F. (1982). March). *A comparison of intellectually gifted and artists on five dimensions of mental functioning.* Paper presented at the American Educational Research Association Annual Meeting, New York, NY.

Purcell, J. H. (1992). Programs in states without a mandate. *An "endangered species"? Roeper Review, 15*(2), 93–95.

Purcell, J. H. (1993). *A study of the status of programs for high-ability students in twenty states and the factors that contribute to their retention and elimination.* Unpublished doctoral dissertation. The University of Connecticut. Storrs, CT.

Radin, C. A. (1991, September). Gifted students face test of indifference. *The Boston Globe*, pp. 1, 14.

Reis, S. M., & Purcell, J. H. (1993). An analysis of content elimination and strategies used by elementary classroom teachers in the curriculum compacting process. *Journal for the Education of the Gifted, 16*(2), 147–170.

Renzulli, J. S. (1977). *The enrichment triad model: A guide for developing defensible programs for the gifted.* Mansfield Center, CT: Creative Learning Press.

Renzulli, J. S., & Reis, S. M. (1991). The reform movement and the quiet crisis in gifted education. *Gifted Child Quarterly, 35,* 26–35.

Starko, A. J. (1990). Life and death of a gifted program: Lessons not yet learned. *Roeper Review, 13*(1), 33–38.

Westberg, K. L., Archambault, F. X., Dobyns, S. M., & Salvin, T. (1993). The classroom practices observations study. *Journal for the Education of the Gifted, 16*(2), 120–146.

6

Precocious Reading Ability: What Does It Mean?

Nancy Ewald Jackson

University of Washington

The results of studies of precocious reading ability are reviewed, and the implications of these results for parents, teachers, and educational policy makers are discussed. Precocious reading ability is a complex skill, and levels of specific subskills vary widely among individuals. Although precocious reading ability is moderately associated with general intelligence, some highly intelligent children do not read early and some precocious readers are of average or subnormal intelligence. Although parents should not expect to be able to teach their infants to read, they may encourage the early development of reading through natural and mutually enjoyable activities.

Editor's Note: From Jackson, N. E. (1988). Precocious reading ability: What does it mean? *Gifted Child Quarterly, 32*(1), 200-204. © 1988 National Association for Gifted Children. Reprinted with permission.

Imagine yourself having dinner at a restaurant. There is a family at the next table with a boy who looks about three years old. When the waitress brings their menus, the boy asks for one of his own and reads it aloud. Most of us would find such a scene unsettling, but the exact nature of our reactions is likely to reflect what we know or assume about the causes and implications of such extreme precocity. Some observers might assume that the child is extraordinarily intelligent. Those who believe that conscientious parents can and should encourage the early development of academic skills are likely to admire this couple's apparent success. Other observers might worry that the child has been pushed into activities that are inappropriate for his age and that might interfere with other aspects of his development (Zigler & Lang, 1985). Whether approving, jealous, or worried, all onlookers are likely to assume that a child's extremely precocious attainment of the ability to read is a sign of something important about the parents' childrearing practices or about the child's current intellectual abilities and academic future. Some of these assumptions may be inconsistent with the results of empirical studies of precocious readers.

The purpose of this article is to summarize the evidence about what precocious reading is and what it implies. This information may help parents, teachers, and policy makers develop informed positions on such questions as what other exceptional intellectual achievements should be expected of a child who has learned to read at an unusually early age, how reading instruction in the primary grades should be adapted for children who have begun reading before starting school, and whether and how parents should foster precocious reading ability.

ARE PRECOCIOUS READERS LIKELY TO BE HIGHLY INTELLIGENT?

One way of addressing the question of what else one might expect of precocious readers and the related question of what attributes indicate that a child is likely to become a precocious reader is to consider the relationship between precocious reading and general intelligence. The relationship between general intellectual ability, as measured by scores on standard tests, and precocious reading ability has been investigated repeatedly and always has been found to be modest. As a group, precocious readers tend to be somewhat above average in IQ, but individual precocious readers have had test scores ranging from below average to above the scale limits (Durkin, 1966; Jackson, Cleland & Donaldson, in press; Roedell, Jackson, & Robinson, 1980). Within a group of bright preschoolers, those with the highest IQ's are not particularly likely to be the best readers (Jackson & Myers, 1982). As readers progress to more and more difficult texts, the upper limits of their comprehension will be related to their general language and reasoning abilities and their knowledge of the subject. (Curtis, 1980; Resnick, 1984). However, the texts that beginning readers read rarely challenge those limits. The major difficulty faced by beginning readers is breaking the code of the written text, and excellent decoding ability sometimes occurs in children who are not especially intelligent or even verbally adept. The most extreme cases of discrepancy between decoding ability and other intellectual abilities occur among autistic, mentally retarded children who exhibit a pattern of behavior that has been called "hyperlexia." Hyperlexic children begin reading, often compulsively, before reaching normal school age. They may attain very advanced levels of ability to decode, or sound out, written texts. Such children's ability to understand what they are reading is likely to be very limited, but they can use letter-sound correspondence rules very well, even in pronouncing realistically patterned pseudowords that they cannot have seen before (Healy, 1982). Even though the typical precocious reader is a normal child of above-average intelligence, the existence of hyperlexia is a dramatic reminder that early reading ability is not in itself a sure sign of any particular level of general ability.

Neither does a high level of general intelligence guarantee that a child will be a precocious reader. Among the high-IQ children in Terman's longitudinal study sample, about half were described by their parents as having begun reading by the age of five years, about 20 percent by age four. Early reading was most often reported for the subgroup with the highest Stanford-Binet IQs. Nonetheless, some of the brightest children were not early readers (Terman & Oden, 1947). Similar results have been found in more recent studies of gifted children (Cassidy & Vukelich, 1980; Price, 1976; Roedell, Jackson, & Robinson, 1980).

Attempts to link the emergence of precocious reading ability to a particular constellation of specific intellectual abilities have not yet had conclusive results (Torrey, 1979), but there is some evidence that precocious reading achievement is moderately associated with the ability to name letters rapidly and, perhaps, with auditory short-term memory span (Jackson & Myers, 1982; Jackson et al., in press). In one study of gifted preschoolers who had been exposed to a varied curriculum of activities designed to encourage pre-reading and reading development, some children learned letter names but made little progress in word recognition. Those who advanced the most were those who could identify letters rapidly as well as accurately (Jackson & Myers, 1982). The results of studies of more typical groups of older beginning readers suggest that rapid letter naming is evidence of a more general efficiency in retrieving information from long-term memory that may be one aspect of reading readiness (Blachman, 1983; Ehri & Wince, 1983).

DO PRECOCIOUS READERS CONTINUE TO PERFORM EXCEPTIONALLY WELL IN LATER LIFE?

Biographical and anecdotal evidence reveals that many eminent adults were precocious readers (Albert, 1971; Cox, 1926). However, these results must be balanced against reports that some adults who have attained eminence for remarkable intellectual and professional achievements were abnormally slow to begin reading (Schulman, 1986). Also, these retrospective reports tell us nothing about the prospective odds that children identified as precocious readers will attain eminence in adulthood.

What about the intermediate implications of precocious reading achievement? The little evidence that is available indicates that precocious readers are likely to continue to do well in school. Durkin (1966) identified a large group of first graders who were at least moderately advanced readers. Later in the children's elementary school years, she compared their achievement with that of IQ-matched children who had not read early. Both groups were doing well, and the precocious readers' academic achievement still surpassed that of the comparison group. However, Durkin's comparison does not provide strong evidence that precocious reading is a cause rather than just a statistical predictor of continued high performance. There is no way to achieve a perfect match between existing groups, and it is possible that the continued superiority of the precocious readers was due to unmeasured factors, such as parental emphasis on achievement, specific intellectual abilities, or chance fluctuation in test scores, on which the precocious readers had an unrecognized advantage over the comparison group.

Skepticism about a specific causal relation between precocious reading and a continued advantage in reading achievement is consistent with the results of a controlled experimental study of this relation. Durkin (1974–75) assigned 4-year-olds at random to two years of pre-first grade reading instruction or to a control condition in which the children received some reading instruction during their kindergarten year. The initial advantages of the experimental group were no longer statistically significant by the time the children were in the third grade.

While giving unselected groups of preschoolers early instruction in reading may not have long-term benefits, the results of a more recent Durkin study further support the conclusion that "naturally occurring" precocious readers are likely to continue to be good readers. Durkin (1982) surveyed inner-city public elementary schools in a study that she hoped would identify aspects of the school environment related to high performance in reading by black children from low-income families. When she reviewed the school histories of these superior readers, she found nothing that seemed like a key to their success. However, interviews with their parents revealed that almost all of these children had started learning to read at home before beginning first grade. As in Durkin's earlier (1966) correlational study, one cannot tell whether the early reading achievement itself or associated factors were the real determinant of success. Nonetheless, there is no evidence that precocious reading achievement does children any harm, and it may be an advantage in some circumstances.

Even though precocious readers are likely to continue to perform well academically, they may not be the best candidates for placement in special programs for the gifted. When achievement test scores are used as a criterion for admission of primary-grade children to special programs for the gifted, early readers have a substantial advantage, and nonreaders who are very able in other intellectual realms are penalized. Basing admission to a first- or second-grade program on a test that emphasizes reading ability makes sense if the program stresses advanced reading or requires the children to read independently in order to complete assignments. One would not want nonreaders to miss needed instruction in beginning reading or precocious readers to endure many hours of lessons in skills they already have mastered. However, selection into or exclusion from an elementary school gifted program often determines a child's placement for many years. The modest association between precocious reading achievement and general intelligence means that some precocious readers will not be especially adept at the kinds of learning and reasoning required for success in many gifted programs during the later elementary school years. School personnel find it difficult to remove children from a desirable and prestigious special program once they have been admitted, and additional places for academic late bloomers may be scarce. Under such circumstances, it may be prudent to devise a selection system in which the presence or absence of precocious reading achievement is not a critical factor.

WHAT SPECIFIC SKILLS
DO PRECOCIOUS READERS HAVE?

Educational planning for a precocious reader would be easier if one knew exactly what skills such children have mastered. For example, evidence that precocious readers rely on a memorized sight vocabulary but cannot decode unfamiliar words would suggest that, despite their advanced achievement in some aspects of reading, these children need basic instruction in phonics. However, the results of the few studies that have addressed this question suggest that precocious readers are a very heterogeneous group (Backman, 1983; Jackson, et al., in press).

There is some evidence that, on the average, precocious readers are more advanced in their ability to use context to aid fluent word identification and comprehension than they are in their ability to identify individual words (Jackson & Biemiller, 1985). Nonetheless, the pattern of their oral reading errors indicates that precocious readers typically are well able to attend both to graphic information within individual words and to the meaning of what they are reading (Malicky & Norman, 1985). Precocious readers' ability to use letter-sound correspondence rules to decode unfamiliar words may, on the average, be less well developed than their ability to recognize a variety of familiar words (Jackson et al., in press). However, the evidence for the relative strength and weakness of the typical precocious reader's specific skills is inconsistent (Backman, 1983; Jackson et al., in press). Perhaps the most remarkable aspect of precocious readers' achievement eventually will be found to be each individual's ability to capitalize on whatever specific strengths he or she might have to overcome weaknesses in other areas. In this respect, precocious readers may be like children who show other forms of intellectual giftedness (Jackson & Butterfield, 1986).

In a comprehensive study of precocious reading, Jackson et al. (in press) found that this ability consists of both a general set of skills and some specialized differences in reading style. The performance of 87 normal, kindergarten-age precocious readers on 11 measures of various reading subskills was factor analyzed. Individual differences in the group's performance on these measures were best characterized by a hierarchical model consisting of a superordinate general factor and three specific factors. All of the measures—tests of decoding and word identification skills, text reading speed and accuracy, and ability to make inferences from context—contributed to the general factor. In other words, there was some tendency for children to perform comparably well, relative to others in the group, across all the measures. As one might expect, performance on this general reading skill factor was related to reading comprehension and to verbal intelligence. However, many of the measures also contributed to the three specific factors. Independently of their overall reading ability, the children varied in the speed and precision of their oral reading and in their ability to use decoding rules. Readers with high scores on the specific reading speed factor were likely to be imprecise and to be poor decoding rule users. These factor-analytic results are consistent with the study of hyperlexic children cited above (Healy, 1982) in indicating that some aspects of the ability to master decoding rules may be unrelated to reading comprehension and verbal intelligence. In hyperlexic readers, one sees variance in decoding ability without the variance in general skills and comprehension that characterizes normal precocious readers.

The variation in normal precocious readers' styles is dramatic. Some precocious readers are able to decode virtually any word, even those whose pronunciation is governed by unusual or complex rules. Others rely heavily on context, combining minimal graphic information from the word itself with a well-developed sense of what a word in that position should be. Some precocious readers also write and spell at an early age; others don't develop these skills until their reading comprehension is quite advanced (Backman, 1983; Salzer, 1984).

Some aspects of the diversity among precocious readers were evident among those whose early development was followed as part of a longitudinal study of gifted children (Roedell et al., 1980). A child called Susan was one of the first precocious readers encountered in that study sample. From the age of 2 years, Susan's Stanford-Binet IQ was above the scale limits for the test, and she performed particularly well on vocabulary and verbal reasoning items. Her scores on repeated administrations of the Wechsler block design and mazes subtests ranged from average to moderately superior levels (scaled score range 10–17). At age 3 years, she read fluently but imprecisely, seeming to rely on an extensive sight vocabulary. She disliked reading aloud, and when she did so, she skipped quickly over unfamiliar words without pausing to decode them. She showed little interest in printing or spelling, and her skills in those areas were far behind her reading comprehension level. At age 5 she announced to her teachers that she knew how to read very well and would like to learn how to write. Despite Susan's initially limited mastery of phonics, she was able by age 4 to read independently such challenging books as *Charlotte's Web* and the *Little House* series. Throughout her preschool years, Susan delighted in the creation of imaginative poems, stories, and plays. By age 5 she was able to write these herself rather than dictate them to her parents and teachers. When Susan was 6 years old, reading and writing were her favorite activities.

Bruce was another extremely precocious reader from the same longitudinal study sample, but his development was strikingly different from Susan's. His scores on the Wechsler block design and mazes subtests were consistently very high, sometimes above the scale limits for his age. Although Bruce's Stanford-Binet IQ rose gradually from 132 at age 3 to 163 at age 6, his scores on the vocabulary subtest of that instrument were never very high. By his third birthday, Bruce was an enthusiastic and skilled printer as well as a competent reader. His mastery of phonics was excellent, and he read aloud in a slow, precise manner. During his preschool years, Bruce's favorite reading materials were picture books of cars and trucks, alphabet books, and dictionaries. At age 6 he still did not read the advanced stories that Susan had enjoyed for years. In the children's kindergarten year, while Susan was creating fanciful stories and poems, Bruce concentrated on projects such as the preparation of a beautifully illustrated, factually correct, and logically organized essay, "All about Apples." He was the mathematics star of the kindergarten program, mastering multiplication virtually the moment the system was explained to him. At age 6 his passion was mathematics. Outside of school he read for information but not for pleasure.

As these and other (e.g., Torrey, 1969) case histories illustrate, the diversity among precocious readers is so great that it would be foolish to prescribe a single curriculum for all. Appropriate reading instruction must be based on consideration of each child's mastery of the many different skills that contribute to reading comprehension and to literacy in general. For example, giving an advanced comprehender a list of unfamiliar or nonsense words to read aloud may reveal an inability to decode these words without support from a passage context. Even a child who has been compensating effectively for inability to use basic decoding rules might profit from brief instruction in these rules (J. Bradley, personal communication, March 1983). Other precocious readers may need help moving from heavy reliance on decoding rules to a more fluent reading style. Many may need basic instruction in spelling or the mechanics of writing. Consultation with a reading specialist is just as appropriate in planning instruction for an unusually precocious reader as it is in planning for a reader who is progressing slowly.

HOW CAN PARENTS FOSTER PRECOCIOUS READING ABILITY?

In this era of pressure to produce "superbabies," manuals are available that purport to tell parents how they can teach their infants to read. However, there is no evidence supporting the claims of these programs (Zigler & Lang, 1985). Formal preschool instruction in reading tends to have limited success (Durkin, 1970, 1974–75; Feitelson, Tehori, & Levinberg-Green, 1982; Fowler, 1971; Jackson & Myers, 1982). With such instruction, many young children learn letter names and sounds and acquire a modest vocabulary of words they can recognize at sight. For example, after two years of instruction beginning at age 4, Durkin's (1970; 1974–75) experimental group could identify an average of 125 words (compared with 18 for the control group) and knew 15.5 of the 22 letter sounds taught. Precocious advancement beyond this point into fluent reading with a high level of comprehension may depend on fortuitous juxtaposition of individual aptitudes and interests with well-timed facilitating experiences.

During 10 years of work with hundreds of precocious readers and their parents (Jackson et al., in press; Jackson, Krinsky, & Robinson, 1977; Jackson & Myers, 1982; Roedell et al., 1980), I have developed an impression of these families that is consistent with the descriptions given in earlier studies (Durkin, 1966; Plessas & Oakes, 1964; Price, 1978). Parents of precocious readers are highly involved in fostering their children's intellectual development and provide many experiences of the sort that would be expected to increase early awareness of words and interest in reading (Jackson et al., in press). They read to their children, point out individual letters and words, help with printing, and so on. However, these parents rarely give the impression of having pushed their children toward goals that the children did not share. Some even report having been surprised at the first signs that their child could read independently. One foreign-born couple avoided reading to their son in English because they did not want him to acquire their accent, but he somehow managed to combine things he had learned at home, from a babysitter, and from television into extraordinarily precocious reading achievement. Even unfortunate circumstances may contribute to an early interest in reading. For example, one mother thought that her daughter's reading ability had developed because this was one activity that the young girl could enjoy while confined to bed for long periods by rheumatoid arthritis.

Parents of precocious readers frequently credit the television programs "Sesame Street" and "The Electric Company" with helping their child learn to read (Jackson et al., in press; Salzer, 1984). Instruction at preschool does not seem to be an important factor, at least among precocious readers selected from kindergarten classes in suburban public schools (Jackson et al., in press). Help received at home is not necessarily amateur help. About 20 percent of the precocious readers in one recent study had at least one parent with training in elementary education, but the skills of this subgroup did not differ significantly from those of the group whose parents did not have such a background (Jackson et al., in press).

Some developmental psychologists have reacted against the current pressure for precocious achievements in young children by suggesting that parents should not give their preschoolers formal instruction in reading. For these developmentalists, "formal" instruction has fixed objectives not dependent upon the child's readiness or expressed desire to learn, and it places the parent in the role of a teacher who makes approval contingent upon successful intellectual performance. Parents are advised to avoid giving such instruction and instead to devote the limited time they have with their children to activities generally considered appropriate for the child's age and developmental stage (Elkind, 1981; Zigler & Lang, 1985). There is merit in such a view to the extent that it counters an argument that parents should expect to be able to teach their young children to read and should commit considerable time and energy to that project (Doman, 1983). However, research suggests that precocious reading is a natural and appropriate attainment for some children—an accomplishment that sometimes, somewhat unpredictably, grows out of the kinds of experiences that most young children and parents enjoy. Thus it seems as foolish to discourage parents from helping their children learn to read as it does to prescribe that they should do so. Perhaps the most sensible advice professionals can give is for parents to trust their own perceptions of their child's developing interests and to encourage those interests in any ways that are enjoyable for both parent and child.

CONCLUSION: WHAT DOES PRECOCIOUS READING ABILITY MEAN?

Understanding the nature and implications of precocious reading requires careful interpretation of patterns and associations. Any simple statement about precocious readers is likely to be distorted or incomplete in important ways. Precocious reading ability is associated with general intelligence, but not all precocious readers have high IQs and not all children with high IQs learn to read early. Some precocious readers are better at comprehending text and learning words from context than they are at using decoding rules; others are excellent decoders. Most parents of precocious readers have helped their children learn, but they are not likely to have pushed a child into inappropriately advanced activities.

Such complexities can be frustrating. Advising parents and planning the education of precocious readers would be much simpler if one could draw a broad set of conclusions simply from knowing that a child has learned to read early. However, early readers are so diverse and prospective evidence regarding their development in later childhood and adulthood so sparse, that each child's abilities and needs are best evaluated on an individual basis.

Caution is also warranted in responding to the question, "Are precocious readers gifted?" One appropriate reply is, "It depends on what you mean by 'gifted' and what you mean by 'reading.'" Exceptionally early attainment of the ability to read is in itself a demonstration of gifted performance as I would define it (Jackson & Butterfield, 1986). On the average, precocious readers will continue to do well in school. However, the extent to which precocious reading is a sign that a child some day will demonstrate other kinds of remarkably advanced or creative accomplishments is not yet known. Furthermore, the predictive significance of precocious reading eventually may be found to depend on the circumstances in which a child has learned to read and the particular pattern of reading skills attained.

REFERENCES

Albert, R. S. (1971). Cognitive development and parental loss among the gifted, the exceptionally gifted, and the creative. *Psychological Reports, 29*, 19–26.

Backman, J. (1983). Psycholinguistic skills and reading acquisition: A look at early readers. *Reading Research Quarterly, 18*, 466–479.

Blachman, B. A. (1984). Relationship of rapid naming ability and language analysis skills to kindergarten and first grade reading achievement. *Journal of Educational Psychology, 76*, 610–622.

Cassidy, J. & Vukelich, C. (1980). Do the gifted read early? *The Reading Teacher*, 578–582.

Cox, C. M. (1926). *Genetic studies of genius (Vol. 2). The early mental traits of three hundred geniuses.* Stanford, CA: Stanford University Press.

Curtis, M. E. (1980). Development of components of reading skill. *Journal of Educational Psychology, 72*, 656–669.

Doman, G. (1983). *How to teach your baby to read.* Garden City, NY: Doubleday.

Durkin, D. (1966). *Children who read early.* New York: Teachers College Press.

Durkin, D. (1970). A language-arts program for pre-first grade children: Two-year achievement report. *Reading Research Quarterly, 5*, 534–565.

Durkin, D. (1974–75). A six-year study of children who learned to read in school at the age of four. *Reading Research Quarterly, 10*, 9–61.

Durkin, D. (1982, April). *A study of poor black children who are successful readers.* Reading Education Report No. 33, Center for the Study of Reading, University of Illinois at Urbana-Champaign.

Ehri, L. C. & Wilce, L. S. (1983). Development of word identification speed in skilled and less skilled beginning readers. *Journal of Educational Psychology, 75*, 3–18.

Elkind, D. (1981. *The hurried child.* Reading, MA: Addison-Wesley.

Feitelson, D., Tehori, B. Z., & Levinberg-Green, D. (1982). How effective is early instruction in reading? Experimental evidence. *Merrill-Palmer Quarterly, 28*, 485–494.

Healy, J. M. (1982). The enigma of hyperlexia. *Reading Research Quarterly, 17*, 319–338.

Jackson, N. E. & Biemiller, A. J. (1985). Letter, word, and text reading times of precocious and average readers. *Child Development, 56*, 196–206.

Jackson, N. E. & Butterfield, E. C. (1986). A conception of giftedness designed to promote research. In R. J. Sternberg & J. E. Davidson (Eds.), *Conceptions of giftedness* (pp. 151–181). New York: Cambridge University Press.

Jackson, N. E., Donaldson, L. N. & Cleland (in press). *The structure of precocious reading ability. Journal od Educational Psychology.*

Jackson, N. E., Krinsky, S., & Robinson, H. B. (1977, March). *Problems of intellectually advanced children in the public schools: Clinical confirmation of parents' perceptions.* Paper presented at the biennial meeting of the Society for Research in Child Development, New Orleans, LA. ERIC Doc. Reproduction Service No. ED 143 453.

Jackson, N. E., & Myers, M. G. (1982). Letter naming time, digit span, and precocious reading achievement. *Intelligence, 6*, 311–329.

Malicky, G. & Norman, C. (1985). Reading processes of 'natural' readers. *Reading-Canada-Lecture, 3*, 8–20.

Mason, J. M. (1980). When do children begin to read? An exploration of four-year-olds' letter and word reading competencies. *Reading Research Quarterly, 15*, 203–277.

Plessas, G. P. & Oakes, C. R. (1964). Prereading experiences of selected early readers. *The Reading Teacher, 17*, 241–245.

Price, E. H. (1976). How thirty-seven gifted children learned to read. *The Reading Teacher,* 44–48.

Resnick, L. B. (1984). Comprehending and learning: Implications for a cognitive theory of instruction. In H. Mandl, N.L. Stein, & T. Trabasso (Eds.), *Learning and comprehension of text* (pp. 431–444). Hillsdale, NJ: Erlbaum.

Roedell, W. C., Jackson, N. E., & Robinson, H. B. (1980). *Gifted young children.* New York: Teachers College Press.

Salzer, R. T. (1984). Early reading and giftedness—Some observations and questions. *Gifted Child Quarterly, 28*, 95–96.

Schulman, S. (1986). Facing the invisible handicap. *Psychology Today, 20*, (2), 58–64.

Terman, L. M. & Oden, M. H. (1947). *The gifted child grows up. Genetic studies of genius* (Vol. 4). Palo Alto, CA: Stanford University Press.

Torrey, J.W. (1969). Learning to read without a teacher: A case study. *Elementary English, 46*, 550–556.

Torrey, J. W. (1979). Reading that comes naturally: The early reader. In T. G. Waller & G. E. MacKinnon (Eds.), *Reading research: Advances in theory and practice* (Vol. 1) (pp. 117–144). New York: Academic Press.

Zigler, E. & Lang, M. E. (1985). The emergence of "superbaby": A good thing? *Pediatric Nursing, 11*, 337–341.

7

Contributions of Gifted Education to General Education in a Time of Change

Carol Ann Tomlinson and Carolyn M. Callahan

The University of Virginia

Educators in the field of gifted education should be involved in the educational dialogue known as the School Reform Movement both because of the need of gifted learners for positive changes in education and because of the potential of the field to contribute to improved education for a wide range of students.

Gifted youngsters, like others, suffer from inadequately trained teachers, test-driven instruction, low-level texts, and curricula which engage neither

Editor's Note: From Tomlinson, C. A., & Callahan, C. M. (1992). In the public interest: Contributions of gifted education to general education in a time of change. *Gifted Child Quarterly, 36*(4), 183-189. © 1992 National Association for Gifted Children. Reprinted with permission.

thought nor interest. They are further at risk in settings which mandate student homogeneity and in which teachers are prone to "teach to the middle."

Further, the field of gifted education, by virtue of its principles and practices, has the opportunity to provide educational leadership in expanding views of intelligence, attention to underserved populations, a broadened view of democracy in education, differentiation and individualization of instruction, and varied instructional models and strategies.

We have a colleague who tells us he finds the field of gifted education "uninteresting" because it does not focus on *the real problems* which exist in education today. We, of course, find it necessary to argue with the notion that the education of our most able youngsters is free of the problems which beset all of contemporary American education and the idea that the gifted should be ignored in the attempts to address the "real problems" in our educational system. Once that argument is made, however, it occurs to us that much of what is now under the rubric of gifted education may well be—or certainly could be—a focal point for finding many of *the real solutions* to contemporary education dilemmas for all youngsters in American public education.

SCHOOLING FOR THE GIFTED: ALSO IN NEED OF REFORM

Gifted youngsters, like all youngsters, are, for significant portions of their youth, students in schools. Whatever enriches and enlivens education benefits them—as it benefits other students. Whatever impedes learning works to their detriment—as it works to the detriment of other students. When Toch (1991) decries assignment of teachers to subjects they are ill-equipped to teach, test-driven emasculation of instruction, monosyllabic texts, instructional management systems which he calls the pedagogical equivalent of painting-by-numbers, and teaching strategies which render classrooms lifeless, he is calling attention to maladies which infect the learning process of all students, including the gifted.

When Goodlad (1984) notes that most teachers simply do not possess the understanding and skills necessary to teach higher levels of thinking, he is delineating a condition which stunts the growth of highly able students as well as students for whom learning is not as swift. When Sizer (1984) laments the failure of schools to foster intrinsic motivation in students, or Welsh (1986) points toward the tendency of teachers to "teach to the middle," or Brady (1989) decries curricula which are incoherent and disjointed, or Nehring (1989) depicts the sense of futility experienced by a teacher at the near impossibility of individualizing instruction for 140 pupils a day, their concerns are translated into reality for all students who negotiate their way through the corridors and classrooms of late 20th-century public schools in America.

Oakes (1985), Goodlad (1984), and a chorus of other writers in both scholarly and popular publications lament the practice of tracking, which they believe preserves quality education for high-ability students while sacrificing quality education for students perceived to be less able academically. Although few would attempt to counter the argument that schools are vastly missing the mark with at-risk students, there is evidence that high-ability students are also losing rather than gaining educational ground (i.e., International Association for the Evaluation of Educational Achievement, 1988; Educational Testing Service, 1989; Anderson et al., 1990: Applebee, Langer, & Mullis, 1989; Callahan, 1992; Dossey, Mullis, Linguist, & Chambers, 1988; Fetterman, 1988; Hammack et al., 1990). In a study of the achievement of 251 gifted students, Zettel and Ballard (1978) found that well over half were working at levels below those of which they were intellectually capable. A majority were working at least *four* grade levels below their potential. Boyer (1983) notes that gifted students represent a special challenge to schools if those students are to reach their potential, and he recommends special arrangements such as accelerated programs, independent study, and special academies. Thus, even if one believes that current administrative arrangements favor the able, those administrative arrangements clearly are not adequate to ensure growth commensurate with ability in those students either.

As Brandwein (1981) suggests, however, it is unwise to engage in a prolonged argument about which group's problems take precedence over another's. A child alienated by schooling is likely lost. Talent atrophied is likely irretrievable. Those are truths regardless of the ability of the child. Those are unacceptable patterns in American education when they occur systematically for any learner. Brandwein advises, "The aim is clear: Each child, each of the young, should be able to advance to full capacity in accordance with general and special ability and aptitude" (p. 266).

It seems wiser, then, rather than arguing about who is hurt more by the problems of schools, to set about looking for solutions to some of those problems which impede the learning of virtually all students. The field of gifted education seems well-equipped to take a leading role in the problem-solving process. Indeed, it is our belief that general education could be enriched in philosophy, instruction, pedagogy, and practice through dialogue with educators of the gifted. Of course, we are not so arrogant as to believe that the dialogue would yield benefits in only one direction. The field of gifted education would certainly be enriched and informed by careful examination of the concerns and practices of general education as well.

PHILOSOPHICAL CONTRIBUTIONS
OF GIFTED EDUCATION

Expanded Views of Intelligence

Because gifted education has drawn heavily upon cognitive psychology as a field of study, many in gifted education have commended an expanded view of intelligence. Drawing upon the insights of writers and researchers such as Gardner (1983), Guilford (1967), Ramos-Ford & Gardner (1991), Sternberg (1985, 1991), and Sternberg & Detterman (1979), educators of the gifted such as Cox, Daniel, and Boston (1985), Khatena (1986), Passow (1985), Piechowski (1991), Renzulli (1977), Richert (1991), and Tannenbaum (1983) have encouraged looking beyond a test-score-definition of intelligence to seek manifestations of talent in the arts, leadership, creativity, "emotional giftedness" (which is similar to Gardner's [1983] notion of "intrapersonal giftedness"), and other forms of individual ability or talent. These educators of the gifted have encouraged use of multiple criteria or sources in searching for talent, including observation of students in complex settings, samples of student work produced from student interest in a topic, input from parents and community members, and student portfolios. Thus gifted education espouses not only the notion that intelligence itself is multifaceted, but also that manifestations of intelligence are likewise complex and must be sought through nontraditional as well as more conventional expressions.

Finally, educators of the gifted have advocated translating into classroom practice the development of both higher level cognitive processes (such as analyzing, comparing and contrasting, defending positions, seriating or ordering, detecting bias, etc.) and metacognitive processes (such as planning, articulating problem-solving strategies, rehearsing ideas for retention, etc.), both of which are necessary for effective intellectual functioning. They have stressed the need for development of both convergent and divergent thinking abilities and have encouraged teachers to allow students to develop specific interests and talents rather than mandating well-roundedness or specialization in all areas. Materials and strategies for encouraging these behaviors already exist in the literature of gifted education and in the repertoires of teaching skills of teachers in the field. Thus educators of the gifted are in a position to make powerful contributions to general education through the application of broadened principles of talent recognition and talent development in the regular classroom.

Attention to the Underserved

Although it is often perceived as a field concerned only with the advantaged, gifted education has also had a long and expanding interest in seeking out and developing ability in "underserved" populations of students. Baldwin (1985, 1991); Callahan (1986, 1991); Feldhusen, VanTassel-Baska, and Seeley (1989); Fox, Brody, and Tobin (1983); Frasier (1989); Gay (1978); Karnes (1979,

1983); Kerr (1985); Maker and Schiever (1989); Ortiz and Volkoff (1987); Reis (1989); Reis and Callahan (1989); Torrance (1977); VanTassel-Baska, Patton, and Prillaman (1989); Whitmore (1980), and many others, have offered specific advice for identifying and developing talent in Black, Hispanic, Asian, and other minorities, as well as in underachievers, handicapped learners, and females. Currently, the National Research Center on Gifted/Talented Education, a 5-year, $7.5 million project funded by the federal government through the Javits grants and located at the University of Connecticut, the University of Virginia, the University of Georgia, and Yale University, is studying nationwide practices in working with such youngsters. In addition, approximately 37 other Javits-funded projects are also actively addressing the needs of nontraditional gifted learners. Insights such as those gained through these and related efforts are important for discovering and fostering potential in school populations which are decreasingly white and middle-class.

Broadened View of Democracy

In regard to educational philosophy, gifted education can benefit general education by providing the basis of a strengthened view of democracy as it relates to education. Former Secretary of Health, Education, and Welfare, John Gardner (1961), and others point to our national schizophrenia regarding highly able youngsters. On the one hand, we understand as a nation that much of our strength is deeply rooted in the creative and productive potential of able individuals who have been born into a society which refuses to put a lid on the heights to which ingenuity may rise. On the other hand, perhaps the hallmark of our democracy is the single phrase, "all men are created equal." Thus we are torn as a nation between the powerful poles of individual excellence and group equality.

At times in our history, our nation has embraced the highly able as a vehicle for acquisition of strength or stature. We have opted for excellence over equity. More often, however, we have tended to be angry with those who have great academic ability, as though the anger would somehow atone for the difficulty of those whose academic ability is not as evident, and we have opted to stress equity over excellence. Typically, then, "excellence" has meant a focus on the highly able. "Equity" has meant a focus on the "disabled" (whether the disability was physical, social, or economic).

Because gifted learners are a minority which, as is often the case with minorities, is frequently misunderstood, devalued, and underserved, educators of the gifted have, of necessity, examined the conflict between excellence and equity and may offer insight in at least two important regards. First, they have defined democracy in education not as equality of capacity but as equality of opportunity to develop one's capacity, whatever its level. Second, the field of gifted education commends a multiple-talent approach to ability development. The definition of democracy rightly understood, and combined with multi-faceted definitions of intelligence, would give general education a mandate for recognizing diversity and fashioning schools to fit children rather than children to fit prefabricated agendas of schools. It would be a voice in commending the goal of providing of both equity and excellence to all students.

We are told that in matters of policy, equality and excellence are competing values which, in reality, are seldom served simultaneously (Mitchell & Encarnation, 1984). In the history of our nation's schools to date, we have lived by that belief, alternately neglecting one group to the benefit of the other. Educators of the gifted are one voice, in what should be a chorus of voices, seeking to help citizens and policy makers alike understand that a school system which does not pursue excellence for all students (even those from whom we have traditionally expected little) as well as equity for all students (even those whom we have seen as "ahead of the game") is doomed to fail all students and the society which supports it. Both equity and excellence should be identified with all students, and educators of the gifted come from a tradition which makes them uniquely able to play a role in helping to develop the national will to ensure that they do.

Instructional Contributions of Gifted Education

Gifted education is an especially strong resource to general education instructionally because of its understanding and application of cognitive psychology. For nearly half a century, writers and practitioners in the field of instruction for the gifted have studied, described, applied, and evaluated the kind of cognitively based instruction which is now being commended broadly for all students. For example, Goodlad (1984) calls for curricula organized around a limited number of themes, application of concepts rather than memorization of facts, and student engagement in solving problems which engage their interest. Toch (1991) looks toward learning which is student-centered, generating energy and enthusiasm. Brandwein (1981) speaks out for self-activated learning, discovery learning, healthy growth of self-concept and self-esteem as goals of learning, and abandonment of tests as a basis for judging growth. Sizer (1984) speaks out for students' responsibility for their own learning, and Adler (1982) for both active learning and rigor in learning.

Gifted education has been a laboratory for creating classrooms which are based on these very recommendations. It has developed models for classrooms which are student-centered (Maker, 1982) and in which teaching by themes (Kaplan, 1986) enables students and teachers to traverse the traditional boundaries of disciplines. It has been a pioneer in teaching for thinking (Gallagher, 1985; VanTassel-Baska, 1988) and in ensuring that development of individual creativity is prized (Callahan, 1978; Gowan, Khatena, and Torrance, 1981; Torrance, 1979; Treffinger, 1980). It has broad experience in helping students apply information learned to "real problems" rather than only "school-house" ones (Renzulli, 1982). At the same time, however, the field of gifted education has insisted on maintaining a high level of academic rigor in schools (Passow, 1982; VanTassel-Baska, 1988; Ward, 1980). Further, gifted education utilizes an approach to instruction which stresses affective development and guidance which spring from both cognitive and social/emotional profiles (Clark, 1983; Coleman, 1985; Davis & Rimm, 1989). Gifted education has long argued for evaluation of student growth by means broader and richer than tests (Callahan & Caldwell, 1984; Feldhusen & Baska. 1989) and has experience with use of portfolios, student self-evaluation, evaluation via presentation to meaningful audiences, and establishing criteria for assessment of growth which are more qualitative than quantitative in nature. In fact, it is likely that gifted education is the oldest, best laboratory and model for cognitive-based education which exists in American public education today.

PEDAGOGICAL CONTRIBUTIONS OF GIFTED EDUCATION

Differentiation

Gifted education as a field is a fertile resource for general education in the area of pedagogy from at least three standpoints: differentiation of instruction, individualization of instruction, and use of multiple modes of instruction. First, the field of gifted education has come to grips with the futility of trying to teach students all of the information in the text or on the standard syllabus, an accommodation necessary before the profile of education can change. Educators of the gifted understand the preferability of teaching students pivotal concepts upon which understanding of a subject is based and then showing students *how* to be learners and inquirers. Instruction which is appropriately differentiated, they believe, will be based upon concepts or themes which cut across and bind disciplines, provoke high-quality thought, require student independence and interdependence, and seek solutions to significant problems. Theme-based learning (Kaplan, 1986), problem solving (Feldhusen & Treffinger, 1985), self-directed learning (Treffinger, 1986), research (Kaplan, 1986), and productivity (Renzulli, 1977) are at the core of the pedagogy of gifted education from kindergarten through high school.

By way of illustration, a gifted elementary student learning about American life during the early 1800s recently explored the concept of economics as a determiner of quality of life. She then raised questions about the economy in her own geographical area during the early 1800s, learned how to find primary and secondary print sources related to her questions, found out how to use courthouse records to learn about the past, and became proficient at interviewing so that she could talk effectively with both experts in the history of her county as well as elderly citizens with family stories to tell. She planned and executed a research project to make an educated hypothesis about the death of a 10-year-old girl whose grave bore 1807 as her date of death. This young student came to understand quite richly life in her county in the early 1800s, how the economy affected health and standards of living, and how the political climate of the time molded the economy. In the end, she was conversant regarding key concepts in economics, politics, health, and medicine. She had no doubt accumulated far more information than would have been possible from a fact-driven curriculum. She had learned skills of planning, problem solving, decision making, research, and self-evaluation, and in addition created products which expanded her skill as a writer of fiction and nonfiction, photographer, and researcher.

Gifted education is a source of instructional models and a very broad array of teaching strategies which are concept driven rather than fact driven and which teach the skills of discovery, research, independence, group cooperation, inquiry, creativity, and application of these skills to all disciplines.

Individualization

Goodlad (1984) calls for schooling with a highly individualized character. A second way in which gifted education can serve as a pedagogical resource to general education arises from the persistent advocacy of the field of gifted education for determining and teaching according to individual student needs within a regular classroom. Generally, the assumption has been that the "standard" curriculum and teaching level has been designed for "typical" students of a given grade level. Thus, atypical students (among whom will fall gifted learners) require curricular adjustments suited to their learning profiles in order to be appropriately challenged. When differentiation of instruction for gifted learners has not been provided, the result has often been apathy, disenchantment with school, underachievement, misbehavior, and lowered expectation and performance. Thus a pivotal injunction of the field of gifted education has been that teachers understand and employ practices of instructional individualization which allow students to learn at varied rates and degrees of depth. With the current trend in general education to group students heterogeneously, there appear to be two choices. One is to pretend that all students are enough alike cognitively so that they will all benefit from one academic diet (although we would never presume they all needed the same size clothing or portions of food). The second is to understand that with an increasingly divergent classroom population, the skills of individualization are an imperative for all teachers.

Again by way of example, a group of eighth graders within an English class proved to be quite able with reading and far more knowledgeable about Greek and Roman mythology than their classmates. Rather than assuming that all students in the class needed to study the same mythology unit at the same pace, the teacher arranged for the advanced students to study myths of oriental, American Indian, Slavic, and African cultures to compare and contrast the forms and contents of the myths and to develop a model for explaining the structure and purpose of myths to younger children in a neighboring school.

Gifted education provides a philosophical and practical impetus for recognizing and teaching according to differing needs of individuals within a group.

Multiple Modes of Instruction

If the philosophies of differentiation and individualization are pursued, then a third pedagogical contribution of gifted education becomes important—its role in developing multiple modes of instruction to translate those philosophies into classroom practice. Gifted education as a field has never embraced the lecture-read-worksheet mode of instruction as especially effective in promoting rich learning experiences. Rather, practices such as learning styles assessment, compacting, independent study, inquiry learning, acceleration, product differentiation, and related strategies have been tested in the field of gifted education and should be invaluable to a broader group of educators attempting to develop facility with modes of instruction which recognize and accommodate individual differences. In decades of use with gifted learners, these mechanisms for differentiation of instruction have been developed, practiced, and refined, and would likely enrich education for most American students in most schools when properly employed. As Sizer (1984) notes, "That students differ may be inconvenient, but it is inescapable. Adapting to that diversity is the inevitable price of productivity, high standards, and fairness to the students" (p. 194). Gifted education has developed procedures and practices relating to differentiation and individualization which enable educators to deal positively and effectively with learner differences.

CONTRIBUTIONS TO THE GENERAL PRACTICE OF EDUCATION FROM GIFTED EDUCATION

Teaching Models

In addition to philosophical, instructional and pedagogical contributions which the field of gifted education can share with general education, there are at least two contributions which may be termed "practical" in that they address practical or pragmatic issues in the current practice of education. First, gifted education is a ready source of teaching models which encourage a more student-centered, process-oriented, content-rigorous approach to curriculum than is typically practiced in today's schools. The Schoolwide Enrichment Model (Renzulli & Reis, 1985), the Multiple Menu Model (Renzulli, 1988), the Purdue Model (Feldhusen, 1980), the Grid Model (Kaplan, 1986), the Enrichment Matrix Model (Tannenbaum, 1983), and others provide guidance to teachers seeking to assist students in becoming thinkers who deal with significant problems relevant to professionals in a variety of fields, who are creative problem solvers, and who earn a sense of self-efficacy as independent, self-actualized learners. The task of helping massive numbers of teachers develop such approaches to instruction which typically were neither taught to them in teacher preparation courses nor modeled for them in their own education is formidable. The presence of a cadre of well-trained teachers of the gifted across the nation is an invaluable resource for sharing and modeling useful techniques with colleagues. In addition, gifted education has much that is positive and advantageous to share about magnet schools and alternative programs suggested by writers such as Toch (1991) and Brandwein (1981) as one possible source of solutions to current educational problems.

Standard Setting

A second practical contribution which can be appropriately made by the field of gifted education is to hold a standard of excellence before educators. No company prospers or grows without acknowledging and seeking to enlarge a cadre of superior performers—be they inventors, idea people, sales staff, or leaders. No successful athletic program fails to acknowledge and reward its superstars. Art exhibits the work of those believed to be most creative or most challenging in prime gallery space. Music recognizes first chair. Theater places a star on certain doors and gives top billing on the marquee. Likewise, education must unashamedly acknowledge the presence of children who challenge the definitions of quality, whose thinking surpasses that of their teachers, whose capacity to learn appears without limit, whose products are of professional quality. Gifted education should lead in that acknowledgment as well as in the insistence that the potential of gifted children be freed and appropriately guided to develop. Currently, for example, it is essential that educational leaders and practitioners understand the danger which exists in lowering a performance ceiling for highly able learners in an attempt (albeit well-intentioned) to raise the performance ceiling for other learners. For example, when schools and school divisions mandate heterogeneity without teacher enthusiasm for the practice and with little or no preparation for managing student diversity, maintaining extraordinary expectations for extraordinary students, mechanisms for helping learners whom we call "at risk" bridge, the chasm of inexperience, or even modes of assisting students to adapt to the changes inherent for all of them in the new environment, it is unlikely that desirable results will be forthcoming.

In being an advocate for genuine (as opposed to political or rhetorical) excellence, by researching practices which enable or impede growth in highly able learners, and by insisting upon utilization of best practice (even in the face of a climate of rejection), gifted education can play a critical role in the positive growth of gifted students and education as a whole.

A Plea for Joining Forces Toward Positive Change

This article is not an argument that gifted learners should be served in public education to the exclusion or to the detriment of other students. On the contrary, it argues that educational change is needed for all kinds of learners, including the highly able. It argues that schools cannot succeed until all kinds of students are highly likely to maximize their possibilities there.

This article is not an attempt to suggest that the field of gifted education has all the answers to enriching and enlivening education in America. Clearly it does not.

It is not an attempt to say that we in gifted education have done everything right. Most assuredly we have not.

It is, however, a plea that at a time when we need rich and varied answers to complex educational dilemmas, all educators work together for solutions.

Educators of the gifted have an obligation (and an opportunity) to move into the mainstream of educational reform, with confidence that we have essential ideas to share, and with the understanding that we have important lessons to learn. Educators in other facets of practice have an obligation (and an opportunity) to expand the dialogue about educational reform to ensure that as changes come, the changes are carefully designed to embrace *all* students—even the highly able.

To this end, it would be beneficial for educators of the gifted to seek out opportunities for presentations at general education conferences in a wide variety of fields, including specific subject area conferences, general curriculum and instruction conferences, and conferences related to various age groups and to administrative concerns. Editors of publications in the field of gifted education, both scholarly ones and those oriented toward specific classroom practice, should invite general educators to contribute to their journals on topics of mutual concern and interest and should consider re-publication of general education articles likely to expand dialogue and understanding between gifted education and general education. Educators of the gifted at university, school division, and local school levels should seek opportunities to share beliefs and practices which have been a part of their repertoires and which might benefit students broadly. Reciprocally, general educators would profit from including presentations by educators of the gifted at their conferences, re-publishing articles from gifted education print sources in general education journals, inviting educators of the gifted to submit articles on topics of shared interest, and seeking out educators of the gifted at all levels of education to share insights and practices which could enrich teaching across grades, subjects, and ability levels. Further, it would be an important step in an exchange to plan meetings, seminars, and conferences at national, state, and local levels with the specific agenda of developing strategies and timelines for dialogue between general education and gifted education.

In a time when there are calls for integration of disciplines previously viewed as discrete, it would be more than mere symbolism for educators to seek out opportunities to integrate the theory and practice of educational specialties which have lamentably been dealt with as distinct from one another.

The need for educational specialties will endure. Differences in student readiness and aptitude will remain. Nonetheless, sharing strategies which can assist a wide range of educators in dealing effectively with those differences and with developing aptitude in all students seems a reasonable step in this time of educational change.

REFERENCES

Adler, M. (1982). *The Paideia proposal*. New York: Collier Books.

Anderson, L., Jenkins, L., Leming, J., MacDonald, W., Mullis, I., Turner, M., & Wooster, J. (1990). *The civics report card*. Princeton, NJ: Educational Testing Service.

Applebee, A., Langer, J., & Mullis, I. (1989). *Crossroads in American education: A summary of findings*. Princeton, NJ: Educational Testing Service.

Baldwin, A. (1985). Programs for the gifted and talented: Issues concerning minority populations. In F. Horowitz & M. O'Brien (Eds.), *The gifted and talented: Developmental perspectives* (pp. 223–250). Washington, DC: American Psychological Association.

Baldwin, A. (1991). Ethnic and cultural issues. In N. Colangelo & G. Davis (Eds.), *Handbook of gifted education* (pp. 416–427). Boston: Allyn & Bacon.

Boyer, E. (1983). *High school: A report on secondary education in America*. New York: Harper & Row.

Brady, M. (1989). *What's worth teaching: Selecting, organizing, and integrating knowledge*. Albany, NY: State University of New York.

Brandwein, P. (1981). *Memorandum: On renewing schooling and education*. New York: Harcourt, Brace, Javanovich.

Callahan, C. (1978). *Developing creativity in the gifted and talented*. Reston, VA: The Council for Exceptional Children.

Callahan, C. (1986). The special needs of gifted girls. *Journal of Children in Contemporary Society, 18*, 105–117.

Callahan, C. (1991). An update on gifted females. *Journal for the Education of the Gifted, 14*(3), 284–311.

Callahan, C. (1992, April). *Performance of high ability students in the United States on national and international tests*. Paper presented at the meeting of the American Education Research Association, San Francisco, CA.

Callahan, C., & Caldwell, M. (1984). Using evaluation results to improve programs for the gifted and talented. *Journal for the Education of the Gifted, 7*(1), 60–74.

Clark, B. (1983). *Growing up gifted*. Columbus, OH: Charles E. Merrill.

Coleman, L. (1985). *Schooling the gifted*. Menlo Park. CA: Addison-Wesley.

Cox, J., Daniel, N., & Boston, B. (1985). *Educating able learners: Programs and promising practices*. Austin. TX: University of Texas Press.

Davis, G., & Rimm, S. (1989). *Education of the gifted and talented*. Englewood Cliffs, NJ: Prentice Hall.

Dossey, J., Mullis, I., Linquist, M., & Chambers, D. (1988). *The mathematics report card: Are we measuring up?* Princeton, NJ: Educational Testing Service.

Educational Testing Service. (1989). *What Americans Study*. Princeton, NJ: Author.

Feldhusen, J. (1980). *The three-stage model of course design*. Englewood Cliffs, NJ: Educational Technology Publications.

Feldhusen, J., & Baska, L. (1989). Identification and assessment of the gifted. In J. Feldhusen, J. Vantassel-Baska, & K. Seeley (Eds.) *Excellence in educating the gifted* (pp. 85–101). Denver, CO: Love

Feldhusen, J., & Treffinger, D. (1985). *Creativity in thinking and problem solving far gifted education*. Dubuque, IA: Kendall-Hunt.

Feldhusen, J., VanTassel-Baska, J., & Seeley, K. (1989). *Excellence in educating the gifted*. Denver, CO: Love.

Fetterman, D. (1988). *Excellence and equality: A qualitative different perspective on gifted and talented education*. Albany, NY: State University Press of New York.

Fox, L., Brody, L., & Tobin, D. (1983). *Learning-disabled gifted children: Identification and programming* Austin, TX: Pro-Ed.

Frasier, M. (1989). The identification of gifted Black students: Developing new perspective. In J. Maker (Ed.), *Critical issues in gifted education: Defensible programs for cultural and ethnic minorities* (pp. 213–225). Austin, TX: Pro-Ed.

Gallagher, J. (1985). *Teaching the gifted child.* Boston: Allyn & Bacon.

Gardner, H. (1983). *Frames of mind: The theory of multiple intelligences.* New York: Basic Books.

Gardner, J. (1961). *Excellence: Can we be equal and excellent too?* New York: Harper & Row.

Gay, J. (1978). A proposed plan for identifying Black gifted children. *Gifted Child Quarterly, 22,* 353–360.

Goodlad, J. (1984). *A place called school: Prospects for the future.* New York: McGraw-Hill.

Gowan, J., Khatena, J., & Torrance, P. (1981). *Creativity: Its educational implications.* Dubuque, IA: Kendall-Hunt.

Guilford, J. (1967). *The nature of human intelligence.* New York: McGraw-Hill

Hammack, D., Hartoonian, M., Howe, J., Jenkins, L., Levstik, L., MacDonald, W., Mullis, I., & Owen, E. (1990). *The U.S. history report card.* Princeton, NJ: Educational Testing Service.

International Association for the Evaluation of Educational Achievement. (1988). *Science achievement in seventeen countries: A preliminary report.* Oxford, UK: Pergamon Press.

Kaplan, S. (1986). The grid: A model to construct differentiated curricula for the gifted. In J. Renzulli (Ed.), *Systems and models for developing programs for the gifted and talented* (pp. 180–193). Mansfield Center, CT: Creative Learning Press.

Karnes, M. (1979). Young handicapped children can be gifted and talented. *Journal for the Education of the Gifted, 6,* 157–172.

Karnes, M. (1983). The long-term effects of early programming for the gifted/talented handicapped. *Journal for the Education of the Gifted, 6,* 266–278.

Kerr, B. (1985). *Smart girls, gifted women.* Columbus, OH: Ohio Psychology Publishing Company.

Khatena, J. (1986). *Educational psychology of the gifted.* New York: Macmillan.

Maker, J. (1982). *Curriculum development for the gifted.* Austin, TX: Pro-Ed.

Maker, J., & Schiever, S. (1989). *Critical issues in gifted education: Defensible programs for cultural and ethnic minorities.* Austin: TX: Pro-Ed.

Mitchell, D., & Encarnation, D. (1984). Alternative state policy mechanisms for influencing school performance. *Educational Researcher, 13*(5), 4–11.

Nehring, J. (1989). *"Why do we gotta do this stuff, Mr. Nehring?": Notes from a teacher's day in school.* New York: Fawcett Columbine.

Oakes, J. (1985). *Keeping track: How schools structure inequality.* New Haven, CT: Yale University Press.

Ortiz, V., & Volkoff, W. (1987). Identification of gifted and accelerated Hispanic students. *Journal for the Education of the Gifted, 11,* 45–55.

Passow, H. (1982). The relationship between the regular curriculum and differentiated curricula for the gifted/talented. In *Selected Proceedings of the First National Conference on Curricula for the Gifted/Talented.* Ventura, CA: Ventura Superintendent of Schools Office.

Passow, H. (1985). Intellectual development of the gifted. In F. Link (Ed.), *Essays on the intellect* (pp. 23–43). Alexandria, VA: Association for Supervision and Curriculum Development.

Piechowski, M. (1991). Emotional development and emotional giftedness. In N. Colangelo & G. Davis (Eds.), *Handbook of gifted education* (pp. 285–306). Boston: Allyn & Bacon.

Ramos-Ford, V., & Gardner, H. (1991). Giftedness from a multiple intelligences perspective. In N. Colangelo & G. Davis (Eds.), *Handbook of gifted education* (pp. 55–64). Boston: Allyn & Bacon.

Reis, S. (1989). We can't change what we don't recognize: Understanding the needs of gifted females. *Gifted Child Quarterly, 31,* 83–88.

Reis, S., & Callahan, C. (1989). Gifted females: They've come a long way—or have they? *Journal for the Education of the Gifted, 12,* 99–117.

Renzulli, J. (1977). *The enrichment triad model,* Mansfield Center, CT: Creative Learning Press.

Renzulli, J. (1982). What makes a problem real: Stalking the illusive meaning of qualitative differences in gifted education. *Gifted Child Quarterly, 4,* 147–156.

Renzulli, J. (1988). The multiple menu model for developing differentiated curriculum for the gifted. *Gifted Child Quarterly, 32,* 298–309.

Renzulli, J., & Reis, S. (1985). *The schoolwide enrichment model: A comprehensive plan for educational excellence.* Mansfield Center, CT: Creative Learning Press.

Richert, S. (1991). Rampant problems and promising practices in identification. In N. Colangelo & G. Davis (Eds.), *Handbook of gifted education* (pp. 81–96). Boston: Allyn & Bacon.

Sizer, T. (1984). *Horace's compromise: The dilemma of the American high school.* Boston: Houghton Mifflin.

Sternberg, R. (1985). *Beyond IQ: A triarchic theory of human intelligence.* New York: Cambridge University Press.

Sternberg, R. (1991) Giftedness according to the triarchic theory of human intelligence In N. Colangelo & G. Davis (Eds.), *Handbook of gifted education* (pp. 45–54). Boston: Allyn & Bacon.

Sternberg, R., & Detterman, D. (1979). *Human intelligence: Perspectives on its theory and measurement.* Norwood, NJ: Ablex.

Tannenbaum, A. (1983). *Gifted children: Psychological and educational perspectives.* New York: Macmillan.

Toch, T. (1991). *In the name of excellence.* New York: Oxford University Press.

Torrance, P. (1977). *Discovery and nurturance of giftedness in the culturally different.* Reston, VA: Council for Exceptional Children.

Torrance, P. (1979). *The search for satori and creativity.* Buffalo, NY: Creative Education Foundation.

Treffinger, D. (1980). *Encouraging creative learning for the gifted and talented: A handbook of methods and techniques.* Ventura, CA: Ventura County Superintendent of Schools Office.

Treffinger, D. (1986). Fostering effective independent learning through individualized programming. In J. Renzulli, (Ed.), *Systems and models for developing programs for the gifted and talented* (pp. 429–460). Mansfield Center, CT: Creative Learning Press.

VanTassel-Baska, J. (1988). *Comprehensive curriculum for gifted learners.* Boston: Allyn & Bacon.

VanTassel-Baska, J., Patton, J., & Prillaman, D. (1989). Disadvantaged gifted learners at risk for educational attention. *Focus on Exceptional Children, 3*(22), 1–15.

Ward, V. (1980). *Differential education for the gifted.* Venture. CA: Ventura Superintendent of Schools Office.

Welsh, P. (1986). *Tales out of school.* New York: Viking.

Whitmore, J. (1980). *Giftedness, conflict, and underachievement.* Boston: Allyn & Bacon.

Zettel, J., & Ballard, J. (1978). A need for increased federal effort for the gifted and talented. *Exceptional Children, 44,* 261–267.

8

Are Teachers of the Gifted Specialists? A Landmark Decision on Employment Practices in Special Education for the Gifted

Joseph S. Renzulli

The University of Connecticut

The relative newness of many gifted education programs and the lack of certification regulations sometimes means that teachers of the gifted must face employment insecurities that result from their lack of seniority in new instructional situations. Threatened with the termination of her teaching contract during a period of declining enrollment, a five-year gifted specialist became embroiled in a grievance procedure to determine her fitness

Editor's Note: From Renzulli, J. S. (1985). Are teachers of the gifted specialists? A landmark decision on employment practices in special education for the gifted. *Gifted Child Quarterly, 29*(1), 24-28. © 1985 National Association for Gifted Children. Reprinted with permission.

for employment in preference to a tenured senior classroom teacher who did not have special training.

Adjudication hearings involved both teachers, the Board of Education, and the American Arbitration Association. At issue were many factors that could have far reaching impact for teachers of the gifted and the field at large.

One of the most important issues facing gifted education today is the need for policies that will help the teachers in our profession gain recognition as specialists. This issue is important for several reasons, the foremost of which is the decline in enrollments and subsequent reductions in staff that are taking place in many schools throughout the nation. Because gifted programs are a relatively new addition to the schools' overall effort to provide comprehensive services to all students, teachers of the gifted frequently fall into the "last-person-hired" category. Low status on the seniority list has already resulted in the elimination of positions for persons who have made special efforts to pursue advanced training in the area of gifted and talented. More importantly, some trained professionals who have made a career commitment to education of the gifted are being replaced by teachers who are not only untrained in this area but, in some cases, do not want to work with gifted and talented students. This situation could have far reaching implications for the quality of gifted programs and the cadre of dedicated professionals we have been attempting to build over the years. Although most persons in the profession would agree that teaching gifted and talented students unquestionably requires special competencies, training, and commitment, only 16 of the 50 states have thus far seen fit to develop special teacher certification regulations governing this area of special education.

The absence of special certification in 34 states has already resulted in numerous "casualties" among teachers of the gifted. However, a recent decision by the American Arbitration Association may serve as a precedent-setting case that can be used to support the positions of other teachers of the gifted and talented who are in danger of losing their jobs due to reductions in force.

OVERVIEW OF THE CASE IN QUESTION

The American Arbitration Association Case Number 1139-1912-83 involved a grievance filed by the Dedham Education Association (hereafter referred to as the Association) against the Dedham, Massachusetts Board of Education[1] when the Board retained a teacher of the gifted (hereafter referred to as the Junior Teacher) during a reduction in force effective during the 1983–84 school year. The grievance was denied by the Board, whereupon the case was submitted for adjudication by the American Arbitration Association (AAA). The contract between the Board and the Association stipulates that the AAA shall serve as an arbitrator in cases of unresolved grievances and that the decisions of the arbitrator shall be final and binding on all parties. Arbitration is a judicial procedure whereby grievances are submitted to an impartial person or persons for determination on the basis of evidence and arguments presented by both parties. By contractual agreement, the parties in this case agreed in advance to accept the decision of the arbitrator as final and binding.

This case concerned a situation in which the Board laid off a teacher with seniority and retained a junior teacher because, in the Board's judgment, the Junior Teacher possessed special qualifications and training for the teaching of gifted and talented students at the elementary level. Since Massachusetts does not have certification guidelines for teachers of the gifted and talented, both teachers in this case possessed standard elementary certificates. In spite of the absence of special certification, the Associate Commissioner of Education for the Commonwealth of Massachusetts has stated that " . . . local school boards have the authority, absent any state law or regulation, to set up qualifications beyond certification for the teachers they employ" (Case, 1984). The rights of school boards to set standards for teachers' qualifications that are *above* and *beyond* state certification regulations was an especially crucial factor in the final determination of this case.

The essence of this case is embodied in the following statements in the contract between the Board and the Association governing reductions in staff:

> . . . should reductions in force [beyond non-tenured teachers or teachers who have performed in an unsatisfactory manner] be necessitated, it shall be effectuated in the inverse order of seniority within a discipline with the exception of those instances where a junior teacher holds a position within a discipline which no other teachers within the discipline are qualified to fill; in which case, the next most junior teacher holding a position for which another teacher within the discipline is qualified shall be laid off first. (Dedham Educ. Assoc., Article XXXI,C)

In the absence of special certification for teachers of the gifted in the Commonwealth of Massachusetts, both teachers in this case were classified under the "discipline," Elementary: K-6. The essence of the case, therefore, was whether or not the Junior Teacher had special qualifications for teaching the gifted and talented that would allow her to be retained in favor of a senior teacher who did not possess such qualifications.

POSITION OF THE PARTIES

Position of the Association

The Association contended that the Senior Teacher had taught students of every level of ability, including students who were gifted and talented [although this teaching experience took place in a regular classroom and was not part of a formally organized program for gifted and talented students]. The Association further argued that qualities cited by authorities as being desirable for teaching the gifted and talented had been attributed to the Senior Teacher by her supervisors. The Association also claimed that the Senior Teacher had shown a desire to work with the gifted and talented within the classroom setting throughout her career and that for such students, the Senior Teacher had provided experiences aimed at creative, literary, and academic enrichment. The Association further contended that Article XXXI,C of the contract does not speak of being the best or most qualified, but only of being qualified, maintaining that the School Board offered no proof that the Senior Teacher could not perform the job as teacher of the gifted and talented.

Position of the School Board

The position of the Board was presented by Mr. John V. Woodard, Attorney with the firm of Powers and Hall. The strategy he employed will be described in detail and offered as a "prototype" for other cases involving teachers of the gifted who are not protected by state certification regulations in cases of reduction in staff.

Mr. Woodard contended that certification as an elementary teacher does not establish a teacher as being qualified to teach the gifted and talented, per se. The law permits local boards to establish additional qualifications beyond those necessary for elementary certification. Mr. Woodard pointed out that the Board did, in fact, establish such qualifications in this case. He also emphasized that the Massachusetts Department of Education has consigned matters related to gifted and talented education to local control. Mr. Woodard's argument centered around three major factors which will subsequently be described.

Job Announcement

In 1979, the Board established the position of Teacher of the Gifted/Talented (elementary) and also set forth the qualifications necessary for holding such a position. In addition to a statement about previous classroom teaching experience at the appropriate grade levels, the job announcement stated that:

> . . . at least one course in Gifted/Talented Education will be required. . . . The candidate must plan to attend the Summer Conference/ Institute on the gifted/talented sponsored by the Connecticut State Department of Education and the University of Connecticut. . . .

Since the program for the gifted and talented in Dedham is based on the Enrichment Triad Model, it was deemed necessary for the teacher to have appropriate training in this particular approach to gifted education. This training was provided at the aforementioned institute.

It is important to point out that at the time the original job announcement was made, the Senior Teacher did *not* apply for the position. The Junior Teacher, on the other hand, did apply and subsequently attended two summer institutes at the University of Connecticut. Although attendance at such institutes does not, in and of itself, guarantee proficiency in teaching the gifted and talented, it is a de facto expression of interest. The fact that the Junior Teacher completed the institutes with high evaluations also helped to make a strong case that this teacher does possess those special competencies required to successfully implement a Triad program for the gifted and talented.

Specification of Competencies

A major thrust in Mr. Woodard's argument for the Board was based on information about specific skills involved in teaching the gifted and talented. Through contact with me and other professionals in the field, he was able to compile a description of teaching activities and skills which helped to highlight those specialized competencies which define the role of teachers of the gifted. Three documents played an especially important role in preparing this argument.

The first document is entitled, A Taxonomy of Type II Enrichment Processes, and consists of a categorical listing of more than 200 cognitive and affective process skills that constitute the central focus of most programs for the gifted and talented. Although this taxonomy included many skills and abilities that are desirable objectives for general education, it nevertheless highlighted the broad array of skills that should be a primary focus in programs for gifted and talented students.

Two other documents focused more specifically on the types of teaching skills that are involved in guiding gifted students through individual and small group investigative and creative experiences (Reis & Cellerino, 1983; Renzulli, 1983). Among other things, these materials focus upon the following list of specific skills.

1. Analysis of individual interests, abilities, and learning styles.

2. Organization and implementation of specific activities designed to stimulate a wide variety of new interests among students.

3. Guidance in the processes of problem finding and problem focusing.

4. Systematic strategies for making appropriate modifications in the regular curriculum, which include elimination of skills already mastered, the ability to work at one's own pace, and appropriate subject matter acceleration.

5. Assistance in the identification of methodological (research skills) resource materials.

6. Assistance in the identification and appropriate use of advanced level and diverse reference materials and resource persons.

7. Procedures for providing students with appropriate feedback and guidance in the revision of creative products and the general escalation of early drafts of scientific, literary, or artistic endeavors.

8. Assistance in the exploration of various formats and modes of communication for the production of student endeavors.

9. Assistance in the identification of appropriate outlets and audiences for student work.

10. Specific examples of these teaching behaviors were described in the two documents cited. These descriptions helped to lay the groundwork for the third dimension of Mr. Woodard's argument.

The Issue of Special Qualifications for Teachers of the Gifted and Talented

An important issue in this case is the interpretation of the word "qualified" in Article XXXI, C.2.B of the Agreement between the Board and the Association. Since this word is used, but not defined, in the Agreement, it is open to differing interpretations. In addition to material drawn from the documents described above, Mr. Woodard based his argument on a logical analysis of the use of this term in the agreement. The fact that teachers of the gifted and talented are included in the Agreement under the heading of "the elementary discipline," provides no basis for the inference that theirs is like every other elementary position or not unique *within* that discipline. The fact that both parties (i.e., the Board and the Association) inserted such language in the Agreement clearly implies that within every discipline there are positions which require unique qualifications. The Board did not dispute the fact that the position of gifted and talented teacher requires an elementary teacher certificate. However, that does not preclude the Board from prescribing additional qualifications and/or training. The requirement of a certificate is simply a *minimal* requirement. In this regard, Mr. Woodard cited the following section from the Massachusetts General Law (Section 71, 38G):

No teacher shall be eligible for employment by a school board as a teacher . . . unless he (sic) has been granted by the Board a certificate with respect to the type of position for which he (sic) seeks employment; *provided, however, that nothing herein shall be construed to prevent school committees from prescribing additional qualifications* . . . [Emphasis added]

The absence of a separate certificate in Massachusetts is no basis for the inference that the position of gifted and talented teacher is not unique, or that additional qualifications are unwarranted. It was pointed out that the reason Massachusetts has not established certification for teachers of the gifted is in large part due to the fact that gifted and talented education has been left to local control.

Two documents developed by the Massachusetts State Department of Education were especially useful in supporting this section of the Board's argument. A 1979 publication entitled, *A Resource Guide for the Education of Gifted and Talented,* states:

> The [State] Board of Education acknowledges the role of schools in addressing the educational needs of gifted and talented students and supports the development of programs for these students in local school systems.

The State Board's acknowledgment of the uniqueness of gifted and talented education is also reflected in their approval of a 1978 position paper on the gifted and talented and the creation of an Office of Gifted and Talented within the State Department of Education's Division of Curriculum and Instruction. Mr. Woodard further helped establish the uniqueness of the position of teachers of the gifted and talented by citing statements from the aforementioned document (Case, 1984) written by the Associate Commissioner of Education. When new teacher certification requirements were being drafted in Massachusetts in 1979, consideration was given to establishing a separate certificate. However, as explained by the Associate Commissioner, the State Board of Education decided not to establish a separate certificate for the following reasons:

> First, teachers of gifted and talented children are primarily teachers of an academic subject, or (on the elementary level) subjects, and are covered by subject matter certificates. Second, *those qualities which make a teacher especially successful with gifted children are not amendable to regulation:* it would be almost impossible to codify the particular attitudes, sensitivities, and concerns which define such a teacher. And third, *there is no set pattern in schools for teaching gifted and talented children.* To issue a certificate, you need to be able to define the role which the certificate covers, *and in the rich variety of programs across the state, there is an equally rich variety of teacher roles* (Case, 1984). [Emphasis added]

The reasons advanced for not creating a special certificate relate to the recognition that those qualities of a successful teacher are not amendable to regulation and that the roles of teachers vary from one local program to another. This statement reaffirms the State Board's decision to leave the matter of setting qualifications for programs for the gifted and talented to local control. In short, the absence of a special certificate does not mean that any teacher holding an elementary certificate is also qualified to teach gifted students. On the contrary, the qualifications of applicants for the position of teacher of the gifted and talented must be measured against requirements established by local boards for such positions. Clearly, these requirements go beyond the minimal requirements for an elementary teacher certificate which stipulates coursework in the field of elementary education. These requirements by no means address the unique needs of gifted elementary students. To further support this argument, Mr. Woodard offered several statements from the professional literature which clearly indicate that persons who work with gifted and talented students need special training and teaching abilities. The fact that the Senior Teacher had not sought out specialized training, nor expressed an interest in teaching in the gifted program prior to this reduction in force situation, nor visited the gifted and talented program while it was in session, were offered as examples of her lack of motivation to work in a program for the gifted and talented. While in no way demeaning the Senior Teacher's dedication as a professional nor her qualifications as a regular elementary classroom teacher, Mr. Woodard asserted that she had not demonstrated an interest in addressing the needs of gifted and talented children outside of a regular classroom setting. On the other hand, the Junior Teacher's motivation was indicated by her application for the position when originally posted, and her enrollment in training programs which were above and beyond the minimal number of credits specified in the job announcement. Her five years of successful operation of the gifted and talented program in Dedham were also cited as an example of interest, commitment, and the development of personal traits and teaching skills which are especially appropriate for working with gifted and talented students. Numerous examples of outstanding work completed by students during the last five years in the gifted program, under the Junior Teacher's supervision, provided further evidence of her qualifications.

OUTCOME AND CONCLUSIONS

On May 14, 1984, Lawrence T. Holden, Jr., the designated arbitrator for the American Arbitration Association rendered the following decision:

> The Dedham School Board did not violate the provisions of Articles XXXI,C of the collective bargaining agreement when it laid off for the 1983–84 school year [the Senior Teacher], a sixth grade teacher, and retained [the Junior Teacher], a teacher of fifth and sixth grade gifted and talented students.

There are several important lessons we can learn from this case which will enable us to protect the positions of teachers of the gifted and talented in those states not presently requiring teacher certification for this area of special education. First, the announcement or job description is a very important document in helping to establish the qualifications required of a teacher for the gifted and talented. These documents should be developed with great care and include explicit statements concerning both the training requirements for teachers of the gifted and talented and the types of teaching skills that will be involved in such positions. It would be a good idea to attach an addendum to such documents which includes information from the taxonomy described previously, along with the teaching behaviors included in earlier sections of this article. It is also wise to keep a record of persons who make application for the position. In this case, the Senior Teacher clearly did not demonstrate an interest in the position when it was originally posted. This fact was a strong part of Mr. Woodard's argument.

Descriptive statements regarding the special program should be maintained. These statements should point out all of the special activities involved in the program, along with the teacher's responsibilities in carrying out these activities. Whenever state-level documents exist, these publications should be officially accepted or adopted by local boards of education. It is especially important to reference statements in such state documents which indicate that programs for the gifted and talented are subject to local regulations and control. In many cases the application for state-level services and monies and the receipt thereof are a de facto indication of adherence to state policies and regulations.

A third conclusion relates to the adoption of a program model and the specification of teacher competencies within the context of any particular model or organized approach to providing services for gifted and talented students. In the Dedham case, the establishment of a program based on the Triad Model and the necessity of obtaining specialized training in the operation of this model were important ingredients for establishing the specialized qualifications of the Junior Teacher.

Finally, careful documentation of all program activities is an excellent way to highlight the specialized teaching requirements of persons who work with gifted and talented students. Examples of work completed by students, photographs and demonstrations of various activities and student projects, and regular feedback from students, parents, administrators, and classroom teachers will serve as powerful tools in establishing the specialized nature of gifted program activities and concomitant teacher characteristics, responsibilities, and behaviors. All of these factors, taken collectively, provided the rationale for a decision by the arbitrator appointed by the American Arbitration Association to uphold the uniqueness inherent in the position of teacher of the gifted and talented. Certainly this case, in and of itself, can be offered as a strong precedent for similar situations where reductions in force endanger the positions of persons who have taken special steps to develop their skills as teachers of the gifted and talented.

NOTE

1. In Massachusetts, Boards of Education are referred to as School Committees. However, I will use the term "Board of Education" because of its wider recognition throughout the country.

REFERENCES

Case, J. H. Letter to John V. Woodard, February 22, 1984.

Dedham Education Association. *Collective bargaining agreements between the Dedham Board of Education and the Dedham Education Association for the 1983–84 school year.*

Frank, R. (1979). *A resource guide for education of the gifted and talented.* Boston: Massachusetts Department of Education, Division of Curriculum and Instruction.

Holden, L. T. (1984). *Voluntary labor arbitration tribunal, Case No. 1139-1912-83.* [American Arbitration Association, 140 W. 51st St., New York, NY 10020].

Massachusetts Department of Education. (1978). *The education of gifted and talented: A position statement and proposed actions.* Boston: Division of Curriculum and Instruction, M. Bogert, Associate Commissioner and R. Frank, Project Director.

Massachusetts General Laws. (1983). *Selected general laws for school committees and school personnel.* Boston: Commonwealth of Massachusetts.

Reis, S. M., & Cellerino, M. V. (1983). Guiding gifted students through independent study. *Teaching Exceptional Children, 15,* 136–141.

Renzulli, J. S. (1983). Guiding the gifted in the pursuit of real problems: The transformed role of the teacher. *The Journal of Creative Behavior, 17,* 49–59.

Renzulli, J. S. (1977). *The enrichment triad model. A guide for developing defensible programs for the gifted and talented.* Mansfield Center, CT: Creative Learning Press.

Renzulli, J. S., & Reis, S. M. (in press). *A guide book for developing defensible programs for the gifted and talented: An action form approach.* Mansfield Center, CT: Creative Learning Press.

9

"Being a Teacher": Emotions and Optimal Experience While Teaching Gifted Children

Laurence J. Coleman

University of Tennessee

The emotions experienced by teachers while teaching is a relatively unexplored avenue of research. One teacher, Alex, was studied using phenomenological interviews and participant observation to understand the emotions he experienced while teaching in a special program for gifted and talented children. Data were analyzed using inductive procedures. Alex experienced a variety of emotions generated when the instructional dynamics of the lesson were congruent or incongruent with his professional practical knowledge. Most of his emotions were positive. A compelling emotional state, "being a teacher," was found to incorporate many of his feelings and was found repeatedly in his classes. Alex seemed to be

Editor's Note: From Coleman, L. J. (1994). "Being a teacher": Emotions and optimal experience while teaching gifted children. *Gifted Child Quarterly, 38*(3), 146-152. © 1994 National Association for Gifted Children. Reprinted with permission.

trying to recreate being a teacher as he taught. His emotional state was interpreted to be isomorphic to what Csikszentmihalyi (1990) calls "optimal experience." The findings suggest that the special class setting established conditions which increased the probability that Alex would be having an optimal experience.

Life in classrooms is familiar to almost everyone in American society. This familiarity is rooted in the sameness of the organization of classrooms over the past several generations, our experience as students, and our experience as consumers of the popular media. It appears that our familiarity leads to certainty about knowing what schools are like and insures the popular belief that one knows what teachers do and experience. Our confidence in knowing what is best for schools is seen in the statements of politicians and editorial writers who believe that anyone with a good liberal arts education can be an effective teacher.

It is this easy familiarity which makes schooling seem so ordinary and knowable. However, "the extraordinary and complex lurk just below the surface of the ordinary and common-place" (Clark, 1990, p. 334). This paper describes the experience of one teacher of gifted and talented children which suggests that while teaching some teachers might be having "optimal experiences" (Csikszentmihalyi, 1990).

I came to write this paper as a result of a project designed to study the experience of special education teachers (Coleman, 1989). One component of that project was to uncover the emotions teachers experienced while teaching in special settings. In the process of studying one teacher of the gifted, I came across an emotional state, "being a teacher," which seemed to have a powerful influence on teaching practice and significant implications for understanding teachers of the gifted. When I have shared this finding with other teachers, some have responded by nodding their heads and making remarks like, "yeah, I think I know what you mean" or "I have felt that way." The purpose of this paper is to explain being a teacher and to discuss the implications of this emotional state. I intend to show that what appeared to the observer as very good, but ordinary, lessons in a special program were in actuality extraordinary emotional experiences for the teacher. Relatively few researchers have looked at the ordinary emotional experience of teaching at all. Those researchers who have (Bolin, 1990; Butt, Raymond, & Yamagishi, 1989; Clandinin, 1986; Connelly & Clandinin, 1990) provide indirect evidence as they explore the metaphors, images, and stories of teachers. Wagner (1987) has studied how teachers' "self-imperated" thoughts, such as "I *must* . . . ," are connected to feelings of anxiety. In this paper I describe briefly emotional thoughts which emanate from classroom life in a special summer program for the gifted and explain in depth one extraordinary emotional state.

The Teacher, the Setting, and Professional Practical Knowledge

One teacher was studied as he taught philosophy in a special program for children who are gifted and talented. The fact that the teaching took place in a special program is an important part of the story. The teacher, Alex, had been teaching in this program for 7 years and had been teaching for 17 years. Alex had certifications in special education (K-12) and secondary English and had successfully taught children in self-contained settings, resource settings, and regular academic classes. In addition to his teaching experience, Alex had travelled around the world, was a skilled cook and mechanic, and wrote poetry. He had been teaching a philosophy course, the Theory of Knowledge, to high school gifted students for 10 years in an International Baccalaureate of North America program. Alex is an expert teacher who has earned awards for his teaching. His students have also earned national recognition. The course in the special program was regarded as a challenging experience by all who took it. Students who attended other summer programs for gifted and returned to this one told me that Alex's course was "superior" to anything else they had experienced.

Putting the Research to Use

The act of teaching is a volatile emotional experience. In the course of a day, emotions range from highs of excitement and thrill to lows of frustration and despair. Teachers could benefit from reflecting on the circumstances surrounding those feelings in order to understand better their own experience of teaching.

The program in which Alex taught was a residential summer program for gifted and talented children on a college campus. The curriculum was based on an enrichment model emphasizing academic and artistic studies. Students were identified on the basis of teacher and parent nomination. Most children also attended special education programs in their regular schools. The summer program had been in operation for 8 years.

Alex had a busy schedule. He taught four 90-minute classes every day. I gathered data in two 1-week courses in philosophy. The first course was titled The Nature of Reality; the second, The Nature of Time. Alex used a Socratic type discussion method as his instructional approach (Coleman, 1992a). In week one the enrollment was 11 and in week two, 9. Each course had a different group of students, ranging in age from 12 to 18 years, with a median of 14. His class was held in an old room containing discolored blackboards. 45 small movable desks, a loud air conditioner, and an uneven floor. No seats were assigned, but all sat in an oval so that everyone could be seen. On 3 days desks were moved to make the blackboard more visible and accessible.

This paper is built on the notion that teachers acquire through experience a body of skills and knowledge, professional practical knowledge (PPK), which functions as a gyroscope in the classroom. Teachers adjust what they do and say based upon their implicit sense of how the class should be proceeding. Alex's PPK contains various components; a complex network of thoughts connecting planning and action; multiple layers of PPK, much of which is partially hidden (Coleman, 1991); a cognitive map for conducting discussions (Coleman, 1992a); and emotional thoughts while teaching which are tied to his PPK (Coleman, 1992b). All of this occurs in the context of teaching students who are gifted and talented.

METHODS AND PROCEDURES

The methods used in this study are characteristic of qualitative research and are consistent with a growing body of research on how teachers experience being teachers (Butt et al., 1989; Clandinin, 1986). In this case study, participant observation, interviewing, and artifact collection were used to gather the data. The data were analyzed using inductive analysis, triangulation, and membership checks (Lincoln & Guba, 1985). For a fuller explanation of the methods and the assumptions underlying this study see Coleman (1993).

Data Collection

Field notes were taken in all classes and 15 hours of audiotape were collected. The field notes were transcribed with time notations.

Three kinds of interviews occurred. Each interview began with phenomenological questions (Giorgio, 1985). These questions were: What stands out in your mind about today's class? How do you feel it went today? What do you plan to do tomorrow? One kind of interview was a *self-interview*, administered by the teacher, alone, who spoke into a tape recorder during his first free time, lunch time, which occurred 90 minutes after he had taught the class. Another kind was the *daily* interview. It followed about 5 hours after class and lasted about 60 minutes. If they seemed appropriate to the interviewer, additional questions were infrequently added about specific incidents or practices in order to add clarity. The third type of interview was a summative interview, which occurred once at the end of each week of instruction. The questions used during those interviews emanated from previous interviews.

In addition to field notes and interviews, inspection of documents such as the teacher's notebook and student work provided data for analysis. In the notebook the teacher recorded his thoughts while planning classes and while teaching.

Data Analysis

These sources of data were analyzed to find expressions of emotion and feelings. My procedure was to listen to the self and daily interviews for expressions of feeling. The field notes for that day were reread for context and for signs of those emotions. Then the audiotapes with the time notations were reviewed to understand the context in greater depth and to listen for tone and speed of talking, as well as the words. Similar expressions of emotion were studied in order to clarify the meaning of the emotion and its context. Only those feelings which were shown to be repeated on different days and corroborated by two or more data sources are reported as common emotions (Goetz & LeCompte, 1984). Excerpts from the interviews were submitted to two persons to confirm the presence of expressions of emotional thoughts in the data.

A chronology of emotions was created for each day. Furthermore, the daily chronologies were compared to look for patterns among the emotions and across days. At this midpoint in my analysis I became concerned about how to represent Alex's many expressions of emotion. After wrestling with various thematic categories, for example, positive/negative feelings, internal versus external genesis, process related versus outcome related, and so forth, two things became apparent. The first was that my categories were not rooted enough in Alex's words and actions to be trustworthy, so I needed to return to the data. The second was that some broader, less usual pattern of emotions was present in the data that differed from, and combined with, other common expressions of emotion, so I needed to be able to describe that emotional state. Returning to the field notes and audiotapes to capture that pattern of emotional thoughts, I found a taxonomic framework that bound his feelings to the actual teaching situation which I named, using his words, "it [the class] is working." This expression functions as the anchor for his feelings because whenever Alex talked at any length about his emotions, his explanation invariably returned to how the discussion had been happening (it is working) at that time.

In essence, Alex had a standard for what constituted a good discussion which was part of his PPK. This standard was central to Alex's production of emotions. One hundred and twenty-four expressions of emotion were found to be bound to this theme. These emotions tended to group around his sense of success with the lesson. When his standard was met, it was working, and he experienced positive emotions. When the standard was almost met, "it was sort of working." Alex experienced negative emotions when the standard was not met, "it shouldn't work this way" (Coleman, 1992b). Beside these common expressions of feeling, another emotional state was discovered which seemed to incorporate a mixture of single feelings into a superordinate emotion. This paper is written to describe this broader emotional state, which Alex called being a teacher. As the analysis continued, Alex read a draft of this paper in order to verify my findings. He commented, "I recognize myself." In fact, he viewed my final conceptualization as "kind of neat" in the way it revealed to him his emotional thoughts. He agreed that I had identified an important part of his professional practice and welcomed the opportunity to reflect on his practice. On the following pages his words are presented in quotation marks.

Some of Alex's classes had a cycle of behavior and feeling which he called being a teacher. This emotion is very elusive, yet paradoxically, recurrent. Once I recognized the presence of this feeling, I was able to reenter the data and find instances of Alex being a teacher. In this section I will show that being a teacher emerges as an emotional state in the presence of more common feelings during a classroom discussion.

The idea that Alex has a sense of how he wants the class to work (his PPK) is crucial to understanding his feelings and the emergence of being a teacher. When the "flow of discussion" happens, Alex is experiencing many emotional thoughts. Table 1 reports his typical emotions associated with his statements about what was happening in the class. Being a teacher occurs during those times when these emotions are present, but experiencing these emotions does not mean he is being a teacher. Alex's actions and the emotions in this kind of situation combine to create a special kind of experience for him which is ordinary, yet goes beyond ordinary feelings. What makes the emotion so significant is that Alex strives to recreate this feeling every day, despite the fact he does not know when it will happen. To do so requires considerable effort on his part, yet he continues to do it.

Not only does being a teacher not occur whenever he is experiencing the emotions in Table 1, but being a teacher does not occur all the way through a class. During a class Alex's feelings are volatile. A class can start slow and change, or the opposite, start fast and change. In both situations Alex can recover. When the class is not working, he has a variety of moves he can make A *move* is his term for the strategies he implements to conduct a discussion (Coleman, 1992a). These moves begin when Alex recognizes that the class could work better. As he says, "If your great plan starts going sour, you better figure out a way to move off it." His move is to start it "going a little, and I kind of automatically start looking for the next step." One should realize that his recognition of the situation is not usually a conscious thought, so the move he makes is purposeful not deliberate. Often, "it just pops out. . . . Boom, it's there and I say it!" On less frequent occasions, he is thinking ahead and he "goes with it" as long as it works. All this changes when the discussion is going right. The feeling is different.

> When things are really clicking along, it's much more spontaneous. And when it is working . . . usually I feel like a flow, a flow of discussion. And the flow, if everyone's sort of engaged with it, then it's almost as if the stuff kind of grows organically out of what is going on.

The point is that there is a spontaneous organic quality to discussions that are working.

> I rarely pause to try and figure what to do. But a large part of the time it's more kind of an organic activity, you know, it just grows, [that's]

Table I   Common Emotions and Alex's Statements About What Is Happening

Statements of What Is Happening	Common Emotions
"the class is clicking along"	"hoping"
"students are speaking"	"excitement"
"ideas are bouncing"	"surprised"
"students are playing around"	"pleased"
"students are commenting on others' points"	"wondering"
"I keep the pot boiling"	"good feeling"
"students are revealing their feelings"	"gratified"
"students say nonstandard things"	"satisfied"

how I run a class. I don't spend a lot of time in class necessarily thinking about what I am going to do next, I can't.

When a discussion starts "to flow," his excitement keeps building and he gets caught up in the feeling of being a teacher. When I read instances of the emotion, I perceived a sensual quality to being a teacher. On those days, I usually detected that something special had happened in that class. A sequence which illustrates the *flow* of the discussion and being a teacher follows. I have chosen one class to illustrate the feeling which appeared on other days also.

The Flow and Being a Teacher: An Example

The class starts. It is 9:00 A.M. Everyone is exhausted, including him. "I'm feeling, kind of wondering what's going to get going." He wants them "to move out of that sort of morning fatigue syndrome and to be with it. . . ." He is having trouble. He becomes "a little angry" but "that rational side of" him recognizes the honesty of the situation "so there's that sort of mixture of feelings." (I do not see his anger.) He starts asking questions. In relating this situation he recalls "a generalized feeling that . . . no [student] did anything." He does not remember "the pattern of questions." He ventures a question about the reasons why we have time. Something about this question is appropriate for the class, and the flow experience begins. (*At this moment neither he nor I recognize what is about to happen.*)

They started [talking] and coming up with more. Wait a minute, I felt there was hope! (*laughs loudly*) When . . . [the] kids had trouble with it, I was able to redefine it, reexplain it, come up with an example that they could work with. And when they started working with it and I felt like, Ho! Ho! OK! Class is starting to move along and I'm feeling excited. OK!

Alex now senses the class can work. He continues, talking faster than before.

And it's kind of going up and down. . . . I'm kind of rising and falling with that. OK! Start to feel OK! It's starting to go up and down. (*He waves his arms as he talks.*) I feel myself moving with the surges of the class in a way.

The students are giving their ideas. "I'm starting to feel excited and feel as if more and more kids are clicking on that." The students are offering their reasons for why we have time.

And the reasons start to become personal through the examples . . . It's kind of like finding the right track when you get lost, that feeling of . . . I've finally found a way! And I'm trying to build [on it] by bringing in examples again.

Some more of the students move out of their lethargy and into the discussion.

There's a lot happening. . . . I'm feeling kind of a rush of ideas, that rush all right. . . . All right we didn't really come to a truthful conclusion on this, that's both a hope . . . and a feeling of satisfaction. . . . For the last 10 or 15 minutes somewhere in there I stop the class because we had hit all the points and I'm satisfied. . . . [I] feel good about my teaching.

An interesting part of this sequence of action and feeling is his expression of heightened awareness with terms such as *surges* and *rush*, and of a change in his awareness of the time. Apparently, loss of an awareness of time is one of the attributes of being a teacher.

It seemed again that the conversation took a while to get going. . . . The class seemed to warm up as we went along and then at one point I looked at my watch and it's a little after 10:00. . . . I kind of lost track of time. I was surprised.

When this happens to him, it "usually means to me that more has been happening than I had in some ways thought because I'm usually cognizant of what time it is so I can end on time." This alteration in his sense of time occurred because his attention became absorbed by several students' descriptions and the sensation of flow. Losing a sense of time "at least for me meant I was enjoying it and having a good time."

Alex is aware of this emotional experience, being a teacher. His recognition is evident not only from the daily interviews, but also from the final summative interview in which I asked him for the first time a direct question on the topic. This is an abbreviated version of his response.

I know when I am being a teacher when I observe in the class a general sense of excitement and engagement of what's going on. I don't mean everybody in the class is doing that either [although] I'd like that to be the case. Experience tells me that I really can't conceive of [them being excited and I'm not]. I mean if they're really excited about something, . . . I can't imagine not being excited myself. There's also a sense that the kids are beginning to listen to each other and to recognize they have valuable things to say . . . I'm looking for the kids to get excited. I'm looking for them to try and answer these difficult things in a way that I feel is sincere . . .

Note the mixture of feelings and the mutuality in his description. It reveals that being a teacher is a special, engrossing emotional state which incorporates a complex of feelings.

Being a Teacher and Optimal Experience

As I reread my notes and my analysis, I thought of the affinity of being a teacher with separate emotions such as feeling excitement, feeling good, feeling pleased, feeling satisfied, and feeling gratified. When Alex spoke of these feelings happening together in a class, I could see that teaching became a very positive experience for him. I also had the intuition that the manner in which he talked of these moments had a kind of transcendent quality to it. I speculated that Alex was trying to recreate the flow in a discussion because he found its associated feelings so rewarding. I found five instances over 10 classes in which the flow of discussion occurred. I was unable to fix the precise boundaries of each episode.

From our interviews I knew that being a teacher was very important to him and that he was most positive about teaching when describing that emotional state. While I was thinking about Alex's experience and what it might mean, I recalled a construct called flow (Csikszentmihalyi, 1990) which was the same word Alex used to describe when class discussion was going well. After finding the reference, I discovered that flow was shorthand for the construct of "optimal experiences" which is associated with "a sense of deep enjoyment that is so rewarding people feel that expending a great deal of energy is worthwhile simply to be able to feel it" (Csikszentmihalyi, 1990, p. 49). Alex was certainly a teacher who put a great deal of effort into his classes and experienced a rush of emotions at those times. This notion of optimal experience seemed to fit Alex's emotional state when he was being a teacher. According to Csikszentmihayli:

When people reflect on how it feels when their experience is most positive, they mention at *least one, and often all* [italics added], of the following. First, the experience usually occurs when we confront tasks we have a chance of completing. Second, we must be able to concentrate on what we are doing. Third and fourth, the concentration is usually possible because the task undertaken has clear goals and provides immediate feedback. Fifth, one acts with a deep but effortless involvement that removes from awareness the worries and frustrations of everyday life. Sixth, enjoyable experiences allow people to exercise a sense of control over their actions. Seventh, concern for the self disappears, yet paradoxically the sense of self emerges stronger after the flow experience is over. Finally, the sense of duration of time is altered; hours pass by in minutes, and minutes can stretch out to seem like hours. (1990, p. 49)

Reading this passage, I thought that Alex had mentioned many of the qualities which characterize optimal experience repeatedly in interviews. Furthermore, I knew that Alex had used the same term, *flow,* that Csikszentmihalyi had and that Alex was unaware of that research. Given these two points, I decided to return to the data to compare Alex's experience with the construct in order to confirm or disconfirm the idea that Alex's emotional state, being a teacher, was an example of optimal experience.

It is my contention that the existence and composition of Alex's PPK makes it likely that he has optimal experiences when he is teaching. His PPK enables him to create a new situation in the classroom, that is, a situation which exists in his mind, not in the unpredictable and very complex reality of the classroom (Doyle, 1986; Jackson, 1968). When Alex's PPK is imposed on this environment, the complexity and unpredictability is simplified in a manner which enables Alex to see the class as a series of activities which have properties that promote the possibility of optimal experience. (Other researchers have noted that teachers tend to think in terms of activities [Clark & Peterson, 1986].)

The import of activities is that they are similar to Csikszentmihalyi's notion of tasks. Alex can see that tasks can be completed because the tasks have relatively clear goals (something a class in philosophy does not), the activity provides immediate feedback, and concentration is possible. Thus while teaching, Alex can see where he is going, concentrate on achieving these goals, and get quick feedback on how his moves are working. Armed with this information he can make adjustments in his teaching (his moves) toward making the class work and recreating being a teacher.

The evidence is replete with examples which support these points. Alex's classes were a series of activities of varying size and complexity. The number and size of activities depend upon his plans. Many activities carry with them an expected pattern of behavior which can be met by his actions. Alex's classes can be ordered into a typology (Coleman, 1991) in which each type of class is associated with its own set of behaviors and outcomes. For example, "you're telling me" classes and "wrap-up" classes have their own patterns. Furthermore, every class can be segmented by the questions about the philosophical topic Alex asked the students to consider. The extent to which students get involved with the question can be judged by him before he moves to the next task, that is, question.

The data have many examples of his concentration. Alex has a large repertoire of moves (Coleman, 1992a). Certainly, staying on top of a 90-minute discussion is an exercise in concentration. Inherent in his practice are moves which illustrate his concentration. A frequent practice is to use earlier student comments, from either that day or that week, to keep the discussion working. He does this by mentioning the student by name, for example, "Billy's notion of time as a ladder with different distances between rungs might give us a clue." Another common move with many instances in each class is restatement, a "bringing the class together" move in which he summarizes what the class has said. The ability to recall and to interject the appropriate student comment is an obvious sign of Alex's ability to concentrate.

Csikszentmihalyi (1990) suggests that clear goals are needed for feedback. Alex's goals are not clear, but he has a well-developed sense of what should happen in the class. His goals are not evident in the sense that you and I would unmistakenly understand them, nor does he think in terms of behavioral objectives. Although Alex's long-term goals cannot provide him with immediate feedback in the sense that he knows his students have transferred what he wants them to learn outside the classroom, Alex does have a clear sense of his more immediate goal, having a good discussion. Thus Alex has a standard for providing himself with feedback. Many of his emotions seem tied to whether it (the class) is working, and their presence is an indication that he gets immediate feedback. To know something is working means to know what feedback one is seeking even in the midst of fuzzy goals such as "help them to philosophize" or "help them be better people." Interestingly, Alex's goals seem to be as clearly stated as most teachers' (Clark & Peterson, 1986).

As an observer, I could see what he was doing. I was able to see that he skillfully and apparently effortlessly moderated the discussion. To what extent he left behind the cares and anxieties of life (a characteristic of optimum experience) I am uncertain. In one of our interviews he mentioned that sometimes life outside the classroom in his regular teaching position could interfere, I have little evidence on this attribute.

Alex unquestionably saw himself as having some responsibility for directing what occurred in his class. Many of his instructional moves and his PPK are attempts to influence what was happening. The role of teacher implies the notion of instructional leader. Alex does have a personal sense of control, but it is not one he exercises by using brute force. Rather, it is exercised by guiding the course of the discussion. Alex was quite capable of exercising the direct approach to control the discussion, but more often he let go and allowed the class to direct itself. All in all, I suspect that his years of successful experience lead him to believe that even when a class is not proceeding as he wishes, he will be able to reclaim the situation.

I strongly believe that Alex's sense of self can disappear in the course of a lesson. Because he states that he is less "defensive and controlling" when he is being a teacher, I assume this is a sign of freeing himself from ordinary concerns. When the discussion is moving, "I'm not always sure whether I'm directing it or it is directing me." This statement suggests that he is able to loosen the influence of self. Also, his statements about "feeling gratified and satisfied" may mean that his sense of self is enhanced at the end of a lesson. On several occasions he mentioned that he felt he had "touched" the class in some way and that made

Table 2   Attributes of Optimal Experience in Alex's Teaching

Attribute	Presence
tasks can be completed	Yes
concentration is possible	Yes
task has clear goals	Yes
task provides immediate feedback	Yes
worries disappear in effortless involvement	Maybe
a sense of control over one's actions	Yes
self disappears and reemerges stronger	Maybe
sense of time is altered	Yes

him feel like he was doing his job. Thus, I think that his sense of self disappears and his sense of self as a teacher may be reaffirmed. I doubt that his sense of self is altered in the way outlined by the construct of optimal experience.

Alex made references on some days to his sense of time. On one day he said quite plainly that he "kind of lost track of time . . . [and] was surprised." On another occasion he remarked that losing a sense of time "meant I was enjoying it and having a good time." All in all it appears that he commonly experiences changes in his sense of time while teaching.

When the data are compared to the attributes of optimal experience, it became apparent that being a teacher had at least six of the eight attributes. The evidence is summarized in Table 2.

CONCLUSIONS AND IMPLICATIONS

One teacher was studied in great depth in order to learn about the emotional experience of teaching children who are gifted and talented. Many of his feelings were subsumed under an unexpected superordinate feeling, being a teacher. This feeling was described in detail using Alex's words. It was apparent that being a teacher was a compellingly powerful emotional state which appeared in 5 of 10 classes. The qualities of being a teacher were found to be similar to those of a construct called optimal experiences.

One may wonder whether other teachers of the gifted, or teachers in general, have optimal experiences or whether it is unique to Alex. My methodology does not permit such a generalization. Because I have mentioned my findings to other teachers of the gifted and talented and it seems to strike a responsive chord, I speculate that some teachers may have comparable experiences. Although I cannot determine the universality of the feeling, I can state that the specific context in which Alex was studied had an effect on him. He volunteered that being a teacher was experienced less frequently in his regular high school teaching assignment than in the summer program. Furthermore, he experienced being a teacher more frequently with gifted students.

From this I infer (a) that Alex is very committed to making a difference in the lives of his gifted students and his regular students and that his emotions are linked to that commitment; (b) that Alex experiences flow periodically as part of his professional practice in the special summer program, in the high school class with gifted children, and in the regular class; and (c) that the special environment creates some conditions which facilitate the emergence of optimal experience. The most obvious differences were: (a) classes were longer, 90 minutes versus 50 minutes in the special program; (b) classes were smaller; (c) all the children had picked the class from among other attractive alternatives in the special program; (d) the purpose of the special program was to learn while having fun with intellectual peers; (e) Alex created the content of his classes, free of a preestablished curriculum; and (f) Alex need not split his attention between his academic goals and managing misbehavior.

These factors may all be important, but my hunch, and Alex concurs, is that differences (c) through (f) and Alex's PPK interact in some way to increase the frequency of being a teacher. A missing element in this picture is information on what the gifted students were experiencing when Alex was having an optimal experience. This gap exists because my focus was on Alex and my recognition of the patterns which describe flow were not apparent at the time of the study. The only information I have are overheard positive comments as the students left the room.

Although the social context of a special program is likely to contribute to the emergence of a flow experience, I doubt that new teachers of the gifted in a specialized environment could have such experiences using the discussion method. New teachers have not yet established a base of PPK upon which to conduct discussions. I believe it is the imposition of Alex's PPK on the chaotic classroom which creates a framework within which he can set reachable clear goals, provide himself with immediate feedback, focus his attention, get a sense of control, and lose track of himself and of time in the teaching moment.

A problem with this paper is that the phrase *optimal experience* was not Alex's but mine. Being a teacher was found by continuously rereading the interviews and field notes until I saw repeated cycles of behavior and emotion. This observation led me to the conclusion that he was seeking to recapture good class discussions. It was later, by accident, that I recalled the idea of flow, one common link between Alex and Csikszentmihalyi. I am blurring the line between the theoretical construct of flow and Alex's use of the term.

If teaching gifted children in special settings increases the possibility of having an optimal experience, is it possible to help other teachers of gifted children have such experiences? My information is based on a single teacher's experience. I have no information on how to do it or whether it is a good idea to help others find this emotion. Only further study will enable us to know the transferability of the concept of optimal experience for understanding teachers' emotions.

The construct of optimal experience, and in this case being a teacher, may be useful for explaining in part a question about teachers of the gifted. Why do some teachers expend so much effort in a role or remain in a position which is associated with relatively low pay and frequent bashing in the popular media? If there are aspects of teaching that engender optimal experiences, then other teachers who have such experiences may be seeking to repeat them. Alex seems to be a person who does this. This usually unverbalized feeling may help him to sustain insulting comments such as "how come a bright guy like you is a teacher?" Being a teacher or other instances of optimal experience may help us understand the general passion for teaching we find in some highly competent teachers of the gifted.

Feelings and emotions are slippery things to grasp. By assuming the inseparability of person and context and by using a methodology which combined self-interviews, daily interviews, and summative interviews with participant observation, it was possible to tease out Alex's emotions. The redundancy in the data made the findings apparent in Alex's professional practice. Interestingly, the study also made his emotions apparent to him. I know that Alex does not often reflect on his feelings. He remarked on several occasions that "no one had ever asked" him about his feelings before I did. He was somewhat aware of his feelings but did not dwell on them. Emotions may be one of those things teachers do not talk about. Locked in their separate classrooms, teachers rarely get an opportunity to talk to others about their teaching. Furthermore, it may not be acceptable to talk about how one feels about an ordinary teaching situation. Perhaps the fact that there are no studies on the emotional experience of teaching gifted children, and so few studies of the emotional life of teachers in general, is an indicator of the low regard for emotions or the way in which emotions are typically dealt with in our society.

REFERENCES

Bolin, F. (1990). Helping student teachers think about teaching: Another look at Lou. *Journal of Teacher Education, 41,* 10–19.

Butt, R., Raymond, D., & Yamagishi, L. (1989). Autobiographic praxis: Studying the formation of teachers knowledge. *Journal of Curriculum Theorizing, 7,* 87–164.

Clandinin, D. (1986). *Classroom practice.* Philadelphia: Falmer.

Clark, C. (1990). What can you learn from applesauce? A case of qualitative inquiry in use. In E. W. Eisner & A. Peskin (Eds.), *Qualitative inquiry in education* (pp. 327–338). New York: Teachers College Press.

Clark, C., & Peterson, P. (1986). Teachers' thought processes. In M. C. Whittrock (Ed.), *Handbook of research on teaching* (pp. 255–296). New York: Macmillan.

Coleman, L. (1989, November). *Teacher cognition: The connection between plan and action in a special education teacher.* Paper presented at the Council for Exceptional Children. Teacher Education Division Conference, Memphis, TN.

Coleman, L. (1991). The invisible world of professional practical knowledge. *Journal for the Education of the Gifted, 14,* 151–165.

Coleman, L. (1992a). The cognitive map of a master teacher of the gifted conducting discussions with gifted students. *Exceptionality, 3,* 1–16.

Coleman, L. (1992b, January). *Finding the invisible knowledge of teachers of the gifted and the disabled.* Paper presented at the Qualitative Research in Education Conference, University of Georgia, Athens, GA.

Coleman, L. (1993). A method for studying professional practical knowledge of service providers. *Journal of Early Intervention, 17,* 1–9.

Connelly, F. M., & Clandinin, D. J. (1990). Stories of experience and narrative. *Educational Researcher, 19,* 2–14.

Csikszentmihalyi, M. (1990). *Flow: The psychology of optimal experience.* New York: Harper Row.

Doyle, W. (1986). Classroom organization and management. In M. C. Whittrock (Ed.), *Handbook of research on teaching* (pp. 432–463) New York: Macmillan.

Giorgio, A. (1985). *Phenomenology and psychological research.* Atlantic Highlands, NJ: Humanities Press.

Goetz, J., & LeCompte, M (1984). *Ethnography and qualitative design in educational research.* Orlando, FL: Academic Press.

Jackson, P. (1968). *Life in classrooms.* Chicago: Holt, Rinehart and Winston.

Lincoln, Y. S., & Guba, E. G. (1985). *Naturalistic inquiry.* Newbury Park, CA: Sage.

Wagner, A. (1987). Knots in teachers thinking. In J. Calderhead (Ed.), *Exploring teachers' thinking* (pp. 161–178). London: Cassell.

10

For the Good of Humankind: Matching the Budding Talent With a Curriculum of Conscience

Carolyn R. Cooper

For most of this century, educators have debated the types of differentiated curriculum highly able students require in order to realize their contribution to self and society (Gallagher et al., 1969; Marland, 1971; Milne, 1979; Passow, 1958, 1979, 1985; Renzulli, 1982; Tannenbaum, 1979; Tomlinson, 1995; Ward, 1961). Wherein lies the inspiration for the kind of human endeavor that talent development and, ultimately, creative expression engender? This paper traces the rationale for the development of unique talents to the eminent philosopher William James (1902) and suggests a relationship between this highly personal process and the maturity of one's ethos, or ethical worldview. Is one element of talent development,

---

Editor's Note: From Cooper, C. R. (1998). For the good of humankind: Matching the budding talent with a curriculum of conscience. *Gifted Child Quarterly, 42*(4), 238-244. © 1998 National Association for Gifted Children. Reprinted with permission.

ethical behavior, to benefit humankind? If so, what types of curricular opportunities do we need to provide bright, talented children and youth to stretch their current boundaries, to challenge them as they need to be challenged, and to stimulate them to use their creativity productively to make their world a better place?

A Harry Passow, honored in this special issue of *Gifted Child Quarterly*, conceptualized talent development (1985) a decade before the term became popular. A scholar of extraordinary vision, Passow knew that an individual's talent—be it artistic, academic, kinesthetic, charismatic, or other—was, indeed, an essential factor in giftedness, a construct he defined as "the potential for becoming either an outstanding producer or performer, not just a consumer, spectator, or amateur appreciator of ideas" (p. 25).

Passow (1985) made the following bold assertion about talent development:

What educators and psychologists recognize as giftedness in children is really potential giftedness, which denotes promise rather than fulfillment and probabilities rather than certainties about future accomplishments. How high these probabilities are in any given case depends on the match between a child's budding talents and the kinds of nurturance provided. (p. 24).

Thus, Passow at once relaxed to some degree the national conversation about stringent identification criteria and placed on the shoulders of gifted education leaders the onus of responsibility for determining the kinds of nurturance needed to develop a child's talent.

Further, Passow aligned giftedness with creativity (1985), laying the necessary groundwork for the talent development concept to be launched. He stated:

Because it denotes rare and valued human accomplishment, creativity should be conceptualized as interchangeable with giftedness. After all, giftedness is reflected in the ability to be an innovator of what is new and treasurable, not just a curator of what is old and treasured. (p. 26).

In addition to perceiving giftedness as a dynamic process of unfolding one's potential until a mature state had been achieved, Passow considered giftedness as unmistakably action-oriented.

Putting the Research to Use

What is it that enables some students to recognize others' needs and, more importantly, take positive action to address those needs? Is it a natural sensitivity to the human condition? A genuine concern for others' welfare? Or, as this article suggests, a mature ethos that, incorporating these two traits, prompts the individual to change the status quo for the good of humankind?

What stimulates the ethos is a personal philosophy one develops through firsthand involvement in complex, high quality, advanced level experiences grounded in real world, authentic curriculum. This personal philosophy, which reflects a magnanimous attitude of doing good for humankind just because it's right, prompts productive human behavior.

To realize Passow's vision of developing gifted and talented students' morality so they can carry out their special responsibilities to society effectively, opportunities for these students to demonstrate highly ethical behavior must become an integral component of a curriculum that promotes social consciousness at the highest level.

Passow was not alone in his position on the developmental nature of giftedness or in his insistence that students need special kinds of educational experiences in order to progress from the novice (amateur) stage to the expert (accomplished producer or performer) stage. A century earlier, for example, Galton (1869) had advanced the belief that great achievements required both intellect and enthusiasm. More recently, Renzulli (1978), in broadening the conception of giftedness, asserted that talent by itself was not sufficient to advance from what Passow called "promise" to fulfillment, or to transform "probabilities" into certain accomplishments. That a powerful affective factor plays a major role in an individual's developing his or her talent is a position that has been documented in the literature consistently (MacKinnon, 1965; Passow, 1979; Roe, 1952; Sumption, Norris, & Terman, 1950; Tannenbaum, 1979; Ward, 1961).

Talent development, as Passow conceptualized it, meant helping individuals identify and nurture their unique abilities and express, or apply, those talents creatively within a socially-valuable area (Kirschenbaum, this issue). Said another way, Passow saw talent development as a dynamic process of deliberately and thoughtfully matching a student's potential with opportunities designed for the distinct purpose of unfolding that potential creatively.

A fitting metaphor can be found in the unfolding of a rose bud. Given the proper food, water, environment, and encouragement, the bud gradually moves from its *en*-veloped, or closed, state to become a fully *de*-veloped blossom.

Unique among other roses, its appearance is singular. This blossom, for instance, may have long, flat petals where other blossoms may be shorter and curved; a dry velvety surface as contrasted with the moist texture of other roses; a blood-red hue, a shade darker than others on the same rose bush. No two will ever be alike. Likewise, many children and youth are buds of talent that will open, *if nurtured appropriately*, to become magnificent blossoms. Nor will two of these budding talents ever be identical, either.

The end point in this progression will be characterized by action—the talented individual will do something to express in a creative way the singular meaning the talent development journey has for him or her. Giving form to this meaning for the creative producer or the artist is a personal philosophy that, together with a highly-developed ethos, drives and shapes the individual's work.

PERSONAL PHILOSOPHY AND ETHICS

The philosopher William James (1907) believed that for individuals to be ethical, they must practice a personal philosophy derived from individual experience (Walters, 1997). How does a child develop the personal philosophy that will inform his or her creative work—his or her expression of talent? What types of personal experience contribute to the development of such a philosophy? The artist who advances from novice to expert meets with several phases of experience that become inextricably woven into a personal belief system: planning; experimentation; creation; peer response and criticism; modification; marketing; and approval or rejection by an appropriate audience. The cumulative effect of this experiential continuum will inform the artist's decisions concerning every detail of the expression of his or her talent. The philosophy that evolves is, indeed, personal in the strictest sense. Experiences unique to a given individual at a certain time and under certain circumstances have shaped it.

Wherein lies the inspiration for this type of human endeavor? Is this inspiration a pragmatic need, as is one's psychic survival (James, 1902)? Is religious experience its genesis, a tenet James advanced nearly a century ago? If so, what constitutes "religious experience" as James perceived it? Today this term would most likely be generalized as "spiritual experience," but the integrity of James's meaning would not necessarily be compromised. James implies that humankind is inherently good, and, as ethical beings, we bear a responsibility for lessening the burdens of our fellow humans. Certain individuals sense a "calling" to accept this responsibility willingly and enthusiastically. They know they are capable of being change agents, persons who initiate improvements for the benefit of others—indeed, for the good of humankind. Furthermore, these individuals perceive their gifts not as burdens, but as opportunities.

This call to action—this commitment to alleviate others' pain and suffering to the extent possible—can be detected even in primary-aged children. Ask the kindergartner who is adamant about preserving America's national symbol, the bald eagle. In this child's eyes are seriousness of purpose and a personal commitment to the change of the status quo. The child's work to this end belies his age. "Can a five-year-old really execute such an elaborate plan of action?" a teacher asks while listening to the child's breathless account of what he has accomplished to date and what still needs to be done.

This prompting by a higher order appears to inspire us to engage in human endeavor that is at once ethical and of benefit to others. Again, we see the strong action orientation that directs our talent and creativity toward creative production, perhaps the most personally-fulfilling expression of our talent. But although the inspiration to engage in ethical human endeavor appears to be fundamental to members of civilized society, at least, it must interact with—be put in motion by—a person's talent and creativity if others are to benefit from any more than merely our "good intentions."

The catalyst for positive action, I submit, is directly related to the degree to which one's own ethos is developed. Some individuals' moral development seems to occur early; their personal philosophy takes shape while they are young, to wit, our kindergarten environmental activist. Others require more time for their soul, or Self (Gregore, 1998), to define itself.

When the ethically developed Self is prepared to accept a call to responsibility, there is no choice but to translate the need into action. Students deeply troubled by the staggering statistics associated with child abuse in America, for example, work assiduously to respond to this social imperative with a seriousness of purpose and goals that border on idealism. To these youngsters, the concept that children are being willfully harmed is categorically unacceptable; abuse of living creatures is wrong and must not be allowed to occur. These students reflect a system of moral principles that will not permit them to ignore the injustices inflicted upon others. The personal philosophy shaping the action these youngsters have initiated is, I submit, one of conscience.

THE MATCH BETWEEN THE CHILD'S BUDDING TALENT AND NURTURANCE PROVIDED

In an ideal world, children's talents would unfold naturally as a function of growth and development. Each year, the talent, like the rose bud described earlier, would unfold ever so gradually, eventually opening into a magnificent gift that others could only envy. As each child was unique, so each child's talent would likewise be unique, capable of imitation but not duplication.

Unfortunately, for children at least, our world is far from ideal. Schools shortchange their brightest students. High ability children are not challenged in most classrooms; they suffer from the elimination of many forms of advanced or accelerated classes because it has become politically incorrect to separate students on the basis of ability (Reis, 1994). As a result, many a budding talent never unfolds, never develops, for lack of appropriate attention, instead, shrinking inside itself, where it withers and dies unfulfilled.

How high the probabilities of future accomplishments are in any given case, Passow (1985) explained, depends on the match between a child's budding talent and the kinds of nurturance provided. This budding talent needs to experience the process of purposeful, rigorous talent development in order for the youngster who possesses it to express his or her personal meaning (philosophy) through accomplishments valued in society. It is the need for this match that has fueled decades of discussion about differentiated curriculum and instruction for talented students. But, interpretations abound as to what differentiated curriculum and instruction mean in practice.

Long before the term *differentiation* was introduced, the Committee for the Twenty-third Yearbook of the National Society for the Study of Education pondered the issue of modifying bright students' curriculum and instruction. They observed in 1924 that "the biggest question and the most difficult of solution is this: 'How shall the superior powers [of capable children] be challenged, and how shall curriculum and schoolroom procedure be modified to meet more fully the rightful demands of superior endowments?'" (Whipple, 1991, pp. 63–64).

In the Fifty-seventh Yearbook of the same series, published some 30 years later, Passow (1958) reviewed various approaches to providing for gifted students and noted that particular modifications seemed to be of value for specific kinds of achievement (p. 201). This vision presaged the current recommendation we offer schools to develop a continuum of services that will accommodate various types and degrees of talent.

Arguably the preeminent theoretician in the area of differentiated curriculum is Ward (1961), who affirmed that gifted students needed recognizably different experiences, "in mathematics, the humanities, the natural and social sciences, and the fine arts of dance, drama, music, and painting" (p. 79). Further, he summarized the substance and process components of the differentiated curriculum to include "every significant kind of knowledge and human activity utilized as required by the individual in *life-long personal growth and contributory social interaction*" (p. 214, emphasis added).

Was not Ward promulgating James's (1907) theory about the need for a personal philosophy to transform thought into action? Clearly, Ward perceived gifted and talented students' needing to contribute to the social good; hence, a differentiated curriculum would be required to help them develop their own personal meanings (philosophy). Ward (1965) defined the goal, or outcome, of the appropriately differentiated curriculum for the gifted as "an optimally developed, continually becoming person, free and responsible universalized human mind and character, educated for social and cultural interaction" (p. 214). The theme of actualized behavior continued to be linked to talent and its purposeful development.

Building on Ward's seminal work on differential education for the gifted was the Marland Report, which appeared ten years later. A national study on gifted and talented students commissioned by the U.S. Congress, the Marland Report (1971) stated that, by virtue of their outstanding abilities, these youngsters "require differentiated educational programs and/or services beyond those normally provided by the regular school program *in order to realize their contribution to self and society*" (p. 2, emphasis added). Again, the ultimate goal of special programming for gifted and talented students appeared to be more than novel, advanced, or even esoteric curriculum for its own sake. Indeed, the goal was for students to contribute to the social good. Stunned by the Russians' launching of Sputnik in 1957, America was looking to its bright, talented youth to restore its position of power and prominence in the world. "The bids were high for brains in the early 1960s," Tannenbaum (1979) observed. Those with higher abilities, Tannenbaum averred, had more to contribute and were, therefore, under pressure not to bury their talents. A rekindled sense of social obligation was developing in America, a collective conscience that demanded creative solutions to new concerns of national security and the good of humankind.

In the years following the Marland Report (1971), volumes have been published on what constitutes appropriately differentiated curriculum for gifted and talented students, as well as the instructional artistry needed to implement that curriculum. And while seasoned practitioners in the field know that "differentiation" means something quite apart from merely "different," novice teachers of talented students often do not comprehend this critical distinction. The uninitiated teacher doesn't know that differentiation of curriculum and instruction is not just different. Preservice training for teachers [often] provides little or no guidance in developing curriculum for gifted and talented students (Olenchak, 1993).

By using curricular materials or instructional techniques that are simply different from what most students experience in the standard curriculum, many well-intentioned teachers believe they are differentiating both curriculum and instruction for their most capable students. What is lacking, of course, is the deliberate planning that the talent development process requires: the careful selection of high-quality, authentic learning experiences from the continuum of services a school must make available to challenge its talented youngsters to construct meaning: the decisions as to the content, process, and product expectations teachers will build into their curricula to accommodate the sophistication of their students' academic and artistic talents; the articulation of specific performance indicators for which students will be held accountable; and the on-going monitoring of students' social and emotional health as they engage in authentic curriculum with undeniably rigorous performance expectations. In short, the process of differentiation begins with a teacher making important decisions about accommodating his or her students' academic differences: what students will learn, how students will learn, and how students will demonstrate what they have learned (Tomlinson, 1995).

To be valid, the differentiated curriculum, as well as differentiated instruction, must be *qualitatively* different—different in kind, not amount—from the standard fare most students experience in the school setting. This requirement must not be misconstrued as endorsing elitism. We are not recommending that only bright, talented students experience high quality education. In fact, in the nearly three decades since the Principles of a Differentiated Curriculum for the Gifted and Talented (Gallagher et al., 1969) were developed, general education has gradually embraced several of these principles as good for all students. Interdisciplinary themes, independent study skills, real world problems, and higher-level thinking skills, for example, are now standard components of curriculum and instruction offered in general education classrooms across the nation. Many students today benefit from the type of qualitatively-different curriculum articulated originally for the gifted and talented (Renzulli, 1994).

With respect to how to incorporate these principles in the design of appropriate curriculum and instruction for bright, talented students, we should ask: What are the special ingredients of that match Passow (1985) admonished us to make between a child's budding talent and the nurturance the child needs in order to develop that talent? If we accept the premise of this discussion, a premise embedded in the corpus of gifted education literature, (i.e., gifted and talented students must be prepared for a life of responsible stewardship vis-à-vis humankind), then I believe our imperative is clear. We have a compelling obligation to structure learning experiences within a milieu that is at once inviting, genuinely stimulating, and conducive to learning at the highest level of which a given student is capable at a particular time. We must expose these bright, talented students to a panoply of extant knowledge in their respective fields of interest, be it ballet or botany, photography or pharmacology, rocketry or Russian history. Students must become thoroughly versed in the concepts, principles, precepts, and themes connecting these components in an organizational infrastructure. Detail of this magnitude is essential to knowing a discipline from within—of being *a part* of the discipline instead of being *apart from* it.

To the immersion of students in their chosen discipline we must add a second set of learning experiences. These center on the use of skills, tools, and techniques—primarily, those pertaining specifically to the discipline in which the student is immersed. Here, the student practices with the materials, processes, and equipment professionals use in the area of their expertise; begins to acquire and employ a working vocabulary of appropriate technical terms; poses fundamental questions about the discipline; and probes advanced-level resources to find the answers. The student also develops the dispositions needed to apply his/her knowledge within the context of services to humankind. Of paramount importance is the student's growth as a creative and critical thinker, involved deeply in the unique processes of the discipline he or she is studying.

Becoming ever more concerned with the essential elements of the discipline and equipped with firsthand practice in using the unique skills, materials, and processes that growth in the discipline requires, the student is ready to apply his or her knowledge to a real-life situation. It is at this stage of talent development that the student experiences his or her discipline in depth.

The aim is to *involve* students in the discipline, not just in the subject matter. If I grind glass, study the refraction of light waves through it, and make a pair of spectacles, I am involved in the discipline of optometry; if I simply read about the process, I am involved only in the subject matter. Thus, students need . . . to conduct genuine scientific inquiry, not simply experiments with known answers. *They need to do what people involved in a discipline actually do.* (Arnold, 1982, emphasis added)

During the process Arnold describes, research—not report writing, but research—is often a key component, and conducting a long-term investigation of a problem that to students is real is a valid approach to becoming a researcher. A five-year-old I met a decade ago told me he was planning to be a paleontologist, a word he could pronounce as easily as his one-syllable nickname. When I asked him why he'd chosen paleontology, Zak replied, matter-of-factly, "Because I've been studying dinosaurs all my life!" As a first-grader, he conducted a long-term investigation that—to him and many other scientists—was very real. His research was based on a clear question: Was the Loch Ness Monster a reptile or a dinosaur? Later, he sent me a copy of his research notes, findings to date, and conclusions. To me, this budding paleontologist was as genuine a researcher as a youngster his age could possibly be. His repertoire of information on dinosaurs was extensive; his research skills improved steadily; he scoured only the most reliable resources—even though his mom helped him read them; and his commitment to dinosaurs in general and to determining Nessie's origin, in particular, was nearly overwhelming. The research took him most of the year, a typical timeframe for long-term investigations of real-world problems.

The match between a child's budding talent and the kinds of nurturance provided? Surely, Passow (1985) envisioned a highly-advanced curriculum from which the student could construct his or her own personal meaning. This curriculum would purposefully address both the cognitive and affective factors of high achievement and the development of thinking skills. In addition, this curriculum would be implemented in a humanistic, socially conscious environment created to stimulate and support learning. In a 1991 interview, Passow urged program designers to "be concerned about feelings, attitudes, motivations, self-concept, values, and the personalities of individuals. Instructionally, we have to provide guidance and create an environment that stimulates and supports learning" (Kirschenbaum, this issue, p. 199).

A highly-moral, character-building curriculum need not be esoteric. However, it must be genuine, grounded in real world concerns, and it must impact on those with a vested interest in the work being done. Often, current events serve as the catalyst for such a curriculum. For instance, following the 1995 bombing of a federal building in Oklahoma City, students as far away as Connecticut on one coast and Alaska on the other connected, via computer on-line services, with students their age in that grieving city. Bright and talented youngsters want to lend a hand. They are empathic, caring, and concerned about others' welfare. Furthermore, they *know they have the ability to help.* Thus, it makes eminent sense that they should help whenever and however they can

(Cooper, 1995). It would not be unreasonable to expect that some of these children-to-children connections are still in place through deepened friendships. At a minimum, I would suggest these connections alleviated some children's sense of helplessness and offered them hope as a substitute for despair.

FOR THE GOOD OF HUMANKIND: THE CURRICULUM OF CONSCIENCE

From the descriptors advanced by researchers from Galton (1869) to Passow, we have a compelling directive: immerse the student in the discipline in which he or she is intensely interested, and provide access to "opportunities at advanced stages to move into more penetrating concentration upon issues" (Ward, 1979, p. 216) of the discipline the student is studying. In this way, the Self (Gregore, 1998) is maturing, preparing the student to accept the call to act on his or her own convictions, according to his or her own conscience.

Passion is the *sine qua non* of first-hand inquiry at advanced levels of learning. It fuels the mission that lies ahead: the unfolding of the talent already discovered. It helps the budding artist, poet, entomologist, and molecular biologist overcome inevitable obstacles creatively and graciously. In combination with an individual's maturing ethos, passion helps stretch the boundaries of previous personal achievement, providing incentive for excellence in every phase of the product. And, finally, passion sustains the flow of energy needed for that talent to fully develop—for that bud to mature into a magnificent blossom unlike any other on the planet.

Every Saturday morning, a Maryland high school student feeds the homeless on the steps of the city hall in Baltimore. For several hours on those mornings, she makes hundreds of sandwiches that she later distributes to those persons less fortunate than she. In South Carolina, a brave child with AIDS conducts seminars to raise other children's awareness about the disease. In St. Louis, a few years ago, primary-aged children organized and operated "Transcontinental Operation Diaper Drop," which shipped by freight train an entire carload of diapers and baby food they had worked three months to collect for needy infants displaced by Florida's Hurricane Andrew. Examples of individuals' contributing to the social good are multiplying daily. Students are becoming involved in making unselfish contributions to other people in their community (Lewis, 1992). Young people engage in social action not for personal rewards, but for the satisfaction of knowing they have helped make the world a better place in which to live. Again, this magnanimous attitude is a component of the personal philosophy of doing good for humankind just because it's right that seems to be an essential element of the mature ethos that prompts productive human endeavor.

Modifications to the roles that knowledge, students, teachers, and creativity play in talent development, in the becoming of actualized people (Ward, 1961), enable talented students to pursue their interests at a level and in a manner substantively different from how they would be learning—or not learning—if restricted to the standard curriculum offered to most students their age. Appropriate curriculum and instruction affords the student, the budding talent, the opportunity, specialized resources, and encouragement to experience life within his or her area(s) of intense personal interest.

Further, it is through this kind of high quality—religious, spiritual, moral, and ethical—experience that the student who is in the process of becoming, or actualizing, can develop a personal philosophy (James, 1907) that is rooted in social responsibility. Fueled by a passion for alleviating injustice, pain, and oppression, this personal philosophy may, indeed, lead to highly ethical behavior that benefits humankind. Passow firmly believed in developing gifted and talented students' morality so they could execute their special responsibilities to society effectively. I believe a curriculum of conscience is needed to make this happen.

REFERENCES

Arnold, J. (1982). Rhetoric and reform in middle schools. *Phi Delta Kappan, 63*(7), 453–456.

Cooper, C. R. (1995). Integrating gifted education into the total school curriculum. *The School Administrator, 4*(52), 8–15.

Gallagher, J. J., Kaplan, S. N., Passow, A. H., Renzulli, J. S., Sato, I. S., Sisk, D., & Wickless, J. (1969). *Principles of a differentiated curriculum for the gifted and talented.* Ventura, CA: National/State Leadership Training Institute on the Gifted and Talented.

Galton, F. (1869). *Hereditary genius: An inquiry into its laws and consequences.* London: Macmillan & Co.

Gregore, A. F. (1998). *The mind styles™ model: Theory, principles, and practice.* Columbia, CT: Gregore Associates, Inc.

James, W. (1902). *The varieties of religious experience.* New York: Longmans, Green, & Co.

James, W. (1907). *Pragmatism: A new name for old ways of thinking.* New York: Longmans, Green, & Co.

Lewis, B. A. (1992). *Kids with courage: True stories about young people making a difference.* Minneapolis, MN: Free Spirit.

MacKinnon, D. W. (1965). Personality and the realization of creative potential. *American Psychologist, 20*, 67.

Marland, S. P., Jr. (1971). *Education of the gifted and talented, 1.* Washington, DC: U.S. Government Printing Office.

Milne, B. G. (1979). Career education. In A. H. Passow (Ed.), *The gifted and the talented: Their education and development, the seventy-eighth yearbook of the National Society for the Study of Education, Part I* (pp. 97–103). Chicago: University of Chicago Press.

Olenchak, F. R. (1993). Teachers as role models of creative productivity: A longitudinal study in progress. (Research Brief, Vol. 8, pp. 37–44). Tuscaloosa: University of Alabama.

Passow, A. H. (1958). *Education for the gifted, the fifty-seventh yearbook of the National Society for the Study of Education, Part II.* Chicago: University of Chicago Press.

Passow, A. H. (1979). Educational policies, programs, and practices for the gifted and talented. In A. H. Passow (Ed.), *The gifted and the talented: Their education and development, the seventy-eighth yearbook of the National Society for the Study of Education, Part I* (pp. 97–103). Chicago: University of Chicago Press.

Passow, A. H. (1985). Intellectual development of the gifted. In F. R. Link (Ed.), *Essays on the intellect* (pp. 23–43). Alexandria, VA: Association for Supervision and Curriculum Development.

Reis, S. M. (1994). How schools are shortchanging the gifted. *Technology Review, 97*(3), 38–45.

Renzulli, J. S. (1978). What makes giftedness? Re-examining a definition. *Phi Delta Kappan, 60,* 180–184, 261.

Renzulli, J. S. (1982). What makes a problem real? Stalking the illusive meaning of qualitative differences in gifted education. *Gifted Child Quarterly, 26*(4), 147–156.

Renzulli, J. S. (1994). *Schools for talent development: A practical plan for total school improvement.* Mansfield Center, CT: Creative Learning Press.

Roe, A. (1952). *The making of a scientist.* New York: Dodd, Mead.

Sumption, M. B., Norris, D., & Terman, L. M. (1950). Special education for the gifted child. In N. B. Henry (Ed.), *The education of exceptional children, the forty-ninth yearbook of the National Society for the Study of Education, Part II.* Chicago: University of Chicago Press.

Tannenbaum, A. J. (1979). Pre-Sputnik to Post-Watergate concern about the gifted. In A. H. Passow (Ed.), *The gifted and the talented: Their education and development, the seventy-eighth yearbook of the National Society for the Study of Education, Part I.* Chicago: University of Chicago Press.

Tomlinson, C. A. (1995). *How to differentiate instruction in mixed-ability classrooms.* Alexandria, VA: Association for Supervision and Curriculum Development.

Walters, M. E. (1997). William James (1842–1910) and the varieties of human abilities. *Gifted Education Press Quarterly, 11*(2), 12.

Ward, V. S. (1961). *Educating the gifted: An axiomatic approach.* Columbus, OH: Charles E. Merrill.

Ward, V. S. (1965). *Differential education for the gifted: Theory and application.* Paper presented at the annual conference of the Council for Exceptional Children, Portland, OR.

Ward, V. S. (1979). The Governor's School of North Carolina. In A. H. Passow (Ed.), *The gifted and the talented: Their education and development, the seventy-eighth yearbook of the National Society for the Study of Education, Part I.* Chicago: University of Chicago Press.

Whipple, G. M. (1991). *The twenty-third yearbook of the National Society for the Study of Education, Part I. Report of the society's committee on the education of gifted children.* (ERIC Document Reproduction Service No. ED 196 204) (Original work published 1924)

11

Will the Gifted Child Movement Be Alive and Well in 1990?

Joseph S. Renzulli

The beginning of a new decade, like graduation ceremonies, elections, and other "passages," is a time when we are likely to reflect upon some of the collective wisdom of the past. At these times, we attempt to chart new courses that will guide us through the uncertainties that are the only universal characteristic of the future. The decade beginning now is an especially important time for such reflection because we are in the midst of enjoying the strongest amount of acceptance and public support that has ever been accorded to the gifted child movement in America. The question that is continually being raised, however, is whether the movement will grow and prosper, or whether it will once again fade into obscurity as has happened so many times in the past. The answer to this question is obviously very complex, and yet at the same time it seems that the entire future of the field revolves around one "big" issue and its related creative challenges for program development. Oversimplifications of important

Editor's Note: From Renzulli, J. S. (1980). Will the gifted child movement be alive and well in 1990? *Gifted Child Quarterly, 24*(1), 3–9. © 1980 National Association for Gifted Children. Reprinted with permission.

issues are always dangerous; but perhaps by bringing the larger issue into focus around a single problem the thoughts presented here will help to establish a common target towards which many people can take aim in the decade ahead.

What is this big and important issue? Simply stated, the field of education for the gifted and talented must develop as strong and as defensible a rationale for the practices it advocates as has been developed for those things that it is against. Perhaps an analogy will help to clarify both the issue and the reason for its importance.

During the 1930's and 1940's the Progressive Education Association was the biggest and strongest educational force in the United States. Today it is virtually unknown. Why did this pioneering attempt to reform American education, this revolution in educational thought inspired by John Dewey, fade into oblivion? Most historians attribute the demise to the fact that the progressives knew more about what they were against than what they stood for. Like educators of the gifted, this innovative group was against the content-centered, memory-oriented curriculum. They were against schools that were more subject-centered than child-centered, schools that were lock-step in even the smallest detail, and a curriculum that was based on a philosophy of functionalism rather than humanism. To be certain, many of the ideas of the progressives were integrated into the mainstream of American education, but the movement bogged down and lost its punch as a major reformation because it failed to follow through on its criticisms with a solid and positive course of action. A similar analogy could also be presented using the open education movement of the 1960's.

Let us now turn our attention to the present day gifted child movement. First, most educators of the gifted would agree on the types of educational practices we are against. Second, many of the things we stand for (e.g., more emphasis on cognitive and affective process development) have been integrated, or at least accepted, by persons in general education. Finally, in spite of several years of increased activity within the field, very little attention has been given to the development of systems, theories, or models that can be used as defensible rationales for the day-to-day activities that we advocate for gifted youngsters.[1]

At this point I feel certain that the practical-minded reader is ready to give up on this article! Why, he or she might ask, is the writer making a pitch for more of "that theory stuff" when what I need are some Monday-morning activities to use with my gifted students? The answer to this question is a difficult one, and having been a teacher of the gifted, I can readily identify with the urgency of learning (usually quickly) how to "do something" to keep a dozen or so active minds busy for two and one-half hours. But therein lies the dilemma. Suppose that I were to complete this article by carefully describing four or five of my favorite no-fail activities for gifted youngsters. This approach would certainly have popular appeal, but I fear that it would also be a disservice to the reader unless it was accompanied by a defensible rationale for why such activities are being recommended for gifted youngsters. Unless the teacher of the gifted or program director can stand before the board of education or curriculum council and answer what I have described elsewhere as "those haunting questions" (Renzulli, 1977), we may be in danger of winning the battle but losing the war. The most frequently raised haunting question is familiar to almost all people working in this field: "Isn't what you are doing for the gifted good for all youngsters?" If we deal only with Monday-morning realities and do not give equal attention to the development of systems, theories, and models, we may never be able to answer this question in a defensible manner.

Let us examine one example of how the development of systems and theories can help us to win the war. Another haunting question that both critics and people within the field are beginning to raise relates to evaluation. How, they ask, do we know that our programs are having any payoff or that one approach to gifted education has certain advantages over another? The sad but true fact is that we can't really develop respectable evaluation designs when our programs are little more than patchwork collections of random practices and activities. Researchers and evaluators can only obtain effective results (and hopefully gain maximum support for programs) when they are testing a model or a comprehensive and integrated approach to programming. Then the program director can stand before the board of education and say, "Our program is based on (this or that) model, and within this framework, our evaluation data reveals (thus and so)."

Before going on to some specific needs related to the development of rationale, there are two final concerns about the general issue that should be mentioned. First, I am not advocating esoteric systems, theories, or models. Any theory that is not rich in examples and suggestions for practical application is as valueless to an applied science or field of study as are specific activities without an accompanying rationale. I believe that "practical theory" is the best of both worlds, because the two approaches (theory and practice) working together side-by-side can provide actual learning activities that will help to validate the theories and models, and provide a framework within which numerous creative people can contribute practical applications of a given theory or model.

Second, if the field is to advance, we need competitive and even conflicting theories so that we may test one against the other in a never-ending search for better ways of serving gifted and talented youth. There is an old saying in science about the accepted theories of today being tomorrow's outmoded ideas. Just as Einstein's work largely disproved many of Newton's "laws" of physics, so also must we challenge conventional wisdom and existing ways of doing things. This challenging attitude is exactly what we advocate for gifted youth. Perhaps the time is long overdue for us to begin practicing what we preach. In order for our field to advance we need to create systems, theories, and models that will serve as the vehicle for a great in-house dialogue directed toward providing a true meaning for our most frequently used (and abused) concept; "qualitative differentiation."

FOUR RELATED ISSUES

Following is a discussion of four areas in which there is a need for the development of more defensible systems, theories, and models. The four issues that follow are particularly interesting because of past or present efforts and because they may stimulate a little of the controversy that is needed in our field.

The Identification of the Gifted and "Gifted Hypocrisy"

Although most people will not admit it, up to this point in our history we have continued to view giftedness as an absolute concept—something that exists in and by itself, without relation to anything else. For this reason, most of our identification efforts are directed toward uncovering the magic piece of evidence that will tell us if a child is "really gifted." The absolute conception causes us to act as if giftedness is something that "you have" or "you don't have," and consequently, we still think in terms of a child being "in" or "not in" a program. Any mistakes in the selection (or rejection) process, according to the absolutist, are attributed to deficiencies in identification instruments rather than to giftedness being a relative or situational concept.

Although there is a great deal of platform rhetoric about multiple talents and multiple criteria for identification, the sad fact remains that most students participating in special programs are preselected for time periods of at least one year, and in most cases the major criterion for selection is a predetermined cut-off score of 125 or 130 on an intelligence test.[2] One need only survey the identification procedures for a cross section of special programs or review several states' guidelines to affirm the continued reliance upon high test scores.

Our reliance upon intelligence test scores has resulted in pupil selection on an all-or-nothing basis. Students are either "in" or "out" of a program for an entire year and seldom are nonselected students given an opportunity for special services even when very valid indications of superior potential arise. This approach is roughly analogous to selecting students on the basis of hair or eye color because it assumes that giftedness is some sort of absolute and pre-determined condition rather than a set of behaviors that emerge when certain traits interact with one another in relation to a particular topic, area of interest, or specific talent.

A large amount of accumulated research (Renzulli, 1978) clearly indicates that the type of gifted behavior displayed by creative and productive persons is always the result of interaction among three clusters of traits; above average ability, task commitment, and creativity. Outstanding accomplishments occur when these interacting traits are brought to bear on one or a combination of specific performance areas (i.e., the numerous ways and means through which human beings express themselves in real life situations). Research and plain old common sense tell us that gifted behavior is both topical and temporal in nature. That is, such behavior emerges in relation to a sincere area of interest and it operates at maximum efficiency during given periods of time. It is at such times as this—when a strong interest emerges and the child is unquestionably eager to put forth maximum creative effort—that supplementary services and resources should be made available to the child. It goes without saying that an important part of overall programming is the encouragement (indeed, the creation) of task commitment and creativity. But if we restrict our efforts for such encouragement to students who have been preselected (on the basis of test scores) for a special program, we may fail to "turn on" the child who has the greatest potential for benefiting from interest development and creativity producing activities.[3] Gifted behavior emerges as a result of certain youngsters (generally of above average ability) taking advantage of opportunities that are made available to them. We can serve gifted students more effectively if we (1) expand the number and variety of opportunities, (2) make the opportunities available to more students, (3) do not require every child to follow through on every activity, and (4) provide supplementary services at the time and in the areas where a child shows the eagerness to follow through. In other words, our identification procedures should place as much emphasis on the ways in which children interact with experiences (i.e., action or performance information) as they do on the ways in which children respond to structured questions or ratings (i.e., status or psychometric information).

Before discussing the characteristics of a more relative concept of giftedness and our need to think in terms of "gifted behavior" rather than "being gifted," consider one other reason why giftedness has traditionally been viewed as an absolute concept. There are in fact certain abilities that are more pervasive and enduring than others and it is precisely these abilities that have resulted in our rather narrow conception of giftedness. Essentially, these abilities include being a good test-taker and/or lesson-learner in a traditional learning situation. In most cases, good test-takers are also good lesson-learners, although there are many examples of youngsters who "go to school well" but who do not "show up" well on intelligence, aptitude, or achievement tests. There are also many cases of youngsters who score well on tests but who, for one reason or another, do not achieve well in traditional learning situations. Let us assume for a moment that being a good test-taker or lesson-learner is a certain type of "giftedness." These types of giftedness should obviously be respected and provided for to whatever extent possible in the school program. In fact, it is these types of giftedness that are most easily provided for through modifications and adaptations in the regular curriculum. Any child (regardless of test scores) who can cover regular curriculum material in a more compact and streamlined fashion should be given the opportunity to do so provided, of course, that it does not present the child with undue stress or emotional problems. If there is one important area in which regular classroom teachers might be legally actionable for negligence, it is in their lack of providing youngsters with appropriate modifications in the coverage of regular curricular materials.

If we consider test-taking and lesson-learning ability as certain types of giftedness, there are at least three important considerations that must be kept in mind. First, being a good test-taker or lesson-learner does not necessarily guarantee that a child will display gifted behavior in the creative and productive sense of that term. Creative and productive endeavors are the result of combining particular abilities in certain areas (including but not restricted to general intelligence) with task commitment and creativity. A second consideration is that one need not necessarily be a good test-taker or lesson-learner in order to display creative and productive behavior which emanates from high levels of task commitment and creativity. Our limited conception of giftedness, however, has often precluded entrance into special programs or supplementary services to good test-taking and lesson-learning ability and therefore highly creative youngsters or youngsters who have displayed unusual amounts of motivation to pursue topics or talent areas have been systematically excluded from special programs.

Our third consideration is simply that no one is "born with" task commitment or creativity. Rather, these are clusters of abilities that we should seek to develop in all students. Obviously, good test-takers and lesson-learners have high potential for benefiting from experiences designed to develop creativity and task commitment, but once again, these abilities are no guarantee of success nor should they preclude youngsters who do not have the test taking and lesson-learning abilities. In a certain sense, activities that are conscientiously and systematically designed to develop task commitment and creativity could be viewed as the situations or occasions whereby we can spot examples of gifted behavior. In other words, performance in these situations should become part of our identification procedure, and the entire identification process should be built around a "revolving door" concept that allows children to flow into and out of the special program as the need arises.

The main difference between this approach and the traditional method of having the same students in the program for the entire year is that there is a specific *raison d'etre* for a child (or small group of children working on a common problem) to be in the program for a given period of time. The period of time may be a few weeks or several months, the major determining factor being the amount of time necessary for completing the project or solving a particular problem. In a certain sense, this approach means that a child "earns the right" to obtain special services by showing some or all of the "necessary ingredients" of giftedness (that is, above-average ability, task commitment, and creativity). The concept of "earning the right" to obtain special services will obviously be a controversial one, but this approach will certainly help to overcome some of the very valid criticism that has recently been expressed by parents about the identification process (see especially Weiler, 1978). This approach also helps to insure continuous involvement on the part of the regular classroom teacher. In the traditional approach (in which the child is preselected and placed in the program for an entire year), the regular and special programs frequently operate as two separate entities and it is not uncommon for the regular classroom teacher "to forget" about advanced expressions of ability once children have been placed in the gifted program. The revolving-door approach, on the other hand, requires the regular classroom teacher to be constantly on the look-out for signs of interest, creativity, task commitment, and advanced expressions of ability. In addition to becoming a more sensitive "talent spotter," the regular classroom teacher can become more involved by providing certain types of enrichment experiences that will become useful as the situations or occasions for spotting children who should be "fed into" the resource room. The resource room becomes a place where extensions of the regular curriculum and more advanced levels of involvement can occur.

This approach can also help to overcome one of the main deficiencies of special programs that are organized around the resource room or itinerant teacher model. Most resource room teachers are not resources—they are teachers in the traditional sense of the term. In far too many instances when I have visited resource rooms, the teacher is teaching predetermined, prescribed lessons to the entire group. The content of the lessons may be different from the content of the regular curriculum, and the atmosphere may be a little more relaxed, but otherwise, the learning or instructional model is exactly the same as the type of teaching that goes on in any good classroom. If resource teachers want to become real resources to gifted and talented children, then they must drastically reduce the amount of time that they spend instructing students and "teaching lessons." A real resource person serves an individual student (or small group of students working on a common project) in much the same way that a graduate advisor serves a doctoral student working on a research project. The teacher helps the student to focus or frame the area of interest into a researchable problem; suggests where the student can find appropriate methodologies for pursuing the problem like a professional inquirer; helps the youngster to obtain appropriate resources (persons, equipment, reference materials, financial support); provides critical feedback, editorial assistance, encouragement, and a shoulder to cry on; and helps the child find appropriate outlets and audiences for his or her creative work.

But how, you may ask, can the revolving-door approach help to accomplish these types of behaviors on the part of resource room teachers? The answer to this question lies in the greater emphasis that this approach places on the individual child, the child's particular area of interest, and his or her commitment to work on a certain problem. In other words, the *raison d'etre* that caused us to send children to the resource room becomes the basis for the supplementary services that are provided when they are working under the direction of the resource teacher. The revolving-door approach, in a certain sense, "forces" the resource teacher to deal with the individual child and the specific reason that the child was sent to the resource room.

This approach also will help us in matters of accountability and program evaluation. If we know the specific reason why a given child was sent to the resource room, and if we have some documentation about the specific services that were provided, then we can review the youngster's work and make determinations about growth in relation to the objectives set forth for the individual student.

By way of summary, the revolving-door approach can help to overcome many of the problems and criticisms that have been associated with programs for the gifted and talented. This is especially true for relatively affluent school districts where large numbers of parents feel that their children are gifted. This approach allows us to serve more students, to avoid the IQ cut-off score game, to place the rationale for advanced level services on characteristics that are unequivocally supported by the research literature, and to shift the emphasis of special programs from lesson-oriented, whole group activities to the development of individual strengths and interests.

Curriculum Hocus-Pocus

A second area in which we need to examine the rationale underlying special programs is concerned with the so-called "process models" that form the most sacred part of the litany in the area of education for the gifted and talented. Bloom's *Taxonomy of Educational Objectives* (Bloom, et al., 1956) and Guilford's *Structure-of-the-Intellect* (Guilford, 1967) model are almost universally offered as the rationale for special programs. If we examine these models carefully, however, two almost obvious conclusions emerge. First, the models point out mental processes that should be developed in all children. Indeed, when Bloom referred to his taxonomy as a classification of "higher mental processes," he was merely calling attention to the distinction between these processes (which are common to all humans) and the lower processes of sensation and perception (which humans share with other members of the animal family). One of the reasons we cannot defend programs for the gifted by simply saying that focus should be placed on the upper end of Bloom's continuum (analysis, synthesis, and evaluation) is that the taxonomy is a hierarchical structure—one cannot engage in advanced levels of analysis or creativity unless one has dealt with advanced levels of knowledge and comprehension (the two lowest levels in the taxonomy). Contrary to what the prophets of process would have us believe, knowledge is important, and for the person who is going to make a significant breakthrough in his or her field, knowledge of methodology (Bloom's level 1.20) is perhaps the most important skill that one can possess. Failure to understand this hierarchical arrangement has undoubtedly resulted in gifted education's over-reliance on the cute games and situational-specific training activities that purport to develop creativity and other thinking skills. Suffice it to say that there is a vast difference between the types of mental growth that result from a thirty-minute exercise in creative ways to paste macaroni on oatmeal boxes and the kind of disciplined inquiry and task commitment that sparked the work of Marie Curie, Rudyard Kipling, Martin Luther King, or anyone else that history has recognized as a truly gifted person. Our major theory development need in this regard is to learn how situational training activities can be used as stepping stones to more advanced kinds of inquiry rather than as ends in and of themselves.

A second conclusion that becomes apparent if we carefully examine the process models is the large amount of rigidity that such models place on learning activities. In their seemingly noble goal of focusing on particular processes (rather than content), such activities tend to fractionate learning into the highly structured kinds of experiences that we criticized in the content-centered curriculum. So now, rather than filling kids' heads with isolated facts and figures, we are filling each "cell" of the Guilford model with isolated processes according to a structured and predetermined lesson plan. Reliance upon the process models has undoubtedly resulted from a popular but completely unsupported belief that the gifted person is "process oriented." The reality, however, is that authors, inventors, designers, and anyone else engaged in the creative aspects of art or science attack a problem because they are attempting to produce a new and imaginative product. In the act of writing the story or designing the new piece of machinery certain processes undoubtedly are used and further developed. But gifted persons are highly product oriented—processes are the paths rather than the goals of their creative efforts. Unless we view process activities in this manner, there is a danger of trying to ram them down students' throats in much the same way that we force-fed youngsters with facts and figures.

My concern about a preoccupation with process models started to emerge a few years ago when I worked on a curriculum development project (for the gifted) that involved several scholars from the academic disciplines. When we tried to "sell" these scholars on the Taxonomy and the Structure-of-the-Intellect models they flatly stated these approaches where a kind of phony educationese or "curriculum hocus-pocus." They accepted the processes as psychological phenomena and even agreed that certain kinds of elementary training activities could be built around the models. But when it came to our target population—gifted persons—they said that these models simply were not reflections of the ways in which first-hand inquirers pursued knowledge in their respective fields. If we are to overcome our naiveté in this regard, perhaps the starting point should be a careful study of the ways in which creative people attack real problems within the various fields of knowledge.

Some additional curriculum hocus-pocus has also resulted from the almost obsessive concern that many educators of the gifted have had for speed and efficiency in learning. Although we do know that brighter students can cover curricular material faster and more precisely than those of lesser ability, our knowledge about the contributions of other important factors such as task commitment, individual interests, and learning styles is far less sophisticated. Our lack of understanding about these factors has frequently resulted in quantitative rather than qualitative approaches to educating the gifted. In other words, we have simply dealt with the gifted by speeding up the traditional approach to learning.

Let us briefly analyze a typical learning situation. Almost all traditional learning experiences are characterized by the step-by-step pursuit of curricular material that is planned and administered by the teacher. Students engage in predetermined exercises with generally prescribed procedures for problem solving and generally agreed upon standards of acceptability for success. Thus, the curriculum from the early grades through most college-level courses consists of one long progression of exercises after another, and the student is cast mainly in the role of a "doer of exercises." Are we really doing anything that is qualitatively different when we merely accelerate students or the rate at which we expose them to a never-ending diet of prescribed exercises? Simply removing youngsters from one exercise-learning situation and placing them in another similar situation (albeit at a more advanced level) does not change the role of the learner. Unless appropriate modifications are made in the ways in which advanced material is taught, I fail to see how an accelerated learning experience differs qualitatively from the regular curriculum. Providing highly able youngsters with opportunities to learn at advanced rates of speed is certainly an important objective of special education for the gifted, but what is equally certain is that the great accomplishments of mankind have always resulted when bold and adventuresome persons have dared to go beyond predetermined and step-by-step progressions through traditional material. The "stuff" out of which greatness is made can only result from experiences in real discovery, inquiry, and creativity rather than presented exercises in these important processes. It is for this reason that I am somewhat skeptical when people tell me they are "writing curriculum" for the gifted, even if the curricular material is in a nontraditional area or related to an esoteric topic or process. If the epistemology of the learning experience remains the same (i.e., the role of the learner and the ways in which he or she pursues knowledge), then I believe that writing curriculum for the gifted is yet another example of self-deluding hocus pocus. "Writing curriculum" implies more prescribed and presented exercises rather than starting with the child and his or her interests, and then providing the conditions, resources, and guidance that will result in first-hand investigative activity and real creativity. We will only make a break-through in our quest for qualitative differentiation when we learn how to "de-exercise" at least a portion of the school experience for gifted and talented youth.

THE TEACHER OF THE GIFTED AND AMERICAN PIE

One of the more fortunate developments in the last few years has been a greater emphasis on identifying those characteristics and behaviors that help to define the so-called "teacher of the gifted." There are at least two groups of persons to whom we refer in discussing the "teacher of the gifted." The first group is obviously specialists—those individuals who have, by job designation, been assigned to work with gifted students at particular times and under particular circumstances.

The second group consists of regular classroom teachers when they are dealing with a child in whom we are trying to promote gifted behavior. It is sad but true that in the foreseeable future most gifted youngsters will spend most of their time in regular classrooms, and in the majority of school districts, they may not have access to any supplementary services or specialists in gifted education. It is in these situations that we must attempt to provide at least some of the services as those proposed in special or "pull-out" programs. There is no magic in being a specialist who is assigned to work with gifted children. Certain of the teaching behaviors employed by such specialists can also be used very effectively by regular classroom teachers, provided of course such teachers learn the competencies and have the time and resources to bring them to bear within their classrooms.

Let us now turn our attention to the question of what some of the special competencies of teachers of the gifted and talented are. On several occasions I have asked people in the field to list the most important characteristics of teachers of the gifted. The resultant lists can best be described as pure "American Pie"!

That is, such lists always contain very general and highly idealistic truisms with which very few people would disagree. Items that always show up high on such listings are: flexible, democratic, considerate of individual differences, open-minded, has a sense of humor, sensitive to the affective needs of students, varies the learning environment, etc.[4] (Just for the fun of it—if you were asked to list the characteristics of teachers of the gifted, would not the above items appear relatively high on your list?)

This is not to suggest that these traits are not characteristics of teachers of the gifted. Let us assume, however, that you are the parent of a so-called average (or even below average) child. Does this mean that your child's teacher can be *in*flexible? *un*democratic? *in*considerate of individual differences? *closed*-minded? *lacking* in a sense of humor? *in*sensitive to affective needs? does *not* vary the learning environment? etc.? I would hesitate to tell the board of education in my home town that these are the kinds of things we seek in teachers of the gifted but not in other members of our teaching faculty.

An even bigger problem with the "American Pie" lists is that the items are too general or highly inferential to be of any practical value so far as teacher training is concerned. The "American Pie" list is really a list of personality variables, perhaps far less subject to modification (through teacher training) than specific teaching behaviors which relate more directly to the instructional process. We should, quite obviously, attempt to select teachers on the bases of these characteristics and to do whatever training we can to promote them further. But once again, we should select and train *all* teachers with these characteristics in mind.

If we are ever going to make progress in defining the characteristics of the teacher of the gifted, I think it is important for us to get serious about specific teaching behaviors that promote specific kinds of learning and especially creative/productive behavior. To be certain, we can train all (or almost all) teachers to be more flexible, to ask higher level questions, and to teach lessons that promote creativity and affective development. At the same time, however, there are certain teaching behaviors that should be brought to bear upon youngsters who have transcended the role of merely being lesson-learners (at whatever advanced levels they are learning lessons), and it is these behaviors that are *most* crucial in helping youngsters develop their true creative and productive abilities.

Evaluation and the Absurdity of the Hard Data Mystique

A final area in which we need to give more attention to the development of a defensible rationale is program evaluation. Because of the relatively unique objectives of programs for the gifted and talented (Renzulli, 1975), the traditional models, instruments, and procedures that have been used to evaluate programs in other areas of education are largely inappropriate for evaluating programs that serve gifted and talented youth. In recent years there has been a great deal of concern about the specification of objectives in terms of observable and measurable student behaviors. Many evaluators have looked upon the "behavioral objectives models" as a panacea for conducting evaluation studies. The nature of gifted programs, however, and their concern for developing more complex behaviors and more comprehensive types of creative products may make this model too cumbersome to be practically applied to programs for the gifted and talented.

The rigid behavioral objectives model is mainly inappropriate for programs that serve gifted youngsters because it forces us to focus primarily upon those behaviors that are most easily measured, but also the most trivial. Such a situation may well result in the tail wagging the dog—that is, our programs may tend to focus on lower level (basic skill) objectives because of the neatness and precision with which they can be measured. Michael Scriven, the single-most influential person writing on educational evaluation today, has pointed out that "putting pressures on [a person] to formulate his goals, to keep to them, and to express them in testable terms may enormously alter his product in ways that are certainly not always desirable" (Scriven, 1967, p. 55). Other writers (Stake, 1973, pp. 196–199) have pointed out that the errors of testing increase markedly when we move from highly specific areas of performance to items which tend to measure more complex processes and youngsters' attempts to strive toward more unreached human potential.

Although the testing industry has provided us with a vast array of instruments for measuring the mastery of basic skills and general achievement, there has thus far been an absence of technology when it comes to evaluating the more complex types of learning and the creative accomplishments that oftentimes characterize programs for the gifted and talented. The constant call for "hard data" has undoubtedly been the reason for limited technology and the development of alternative evaluation models that can better serve the types of programs advocated by persons in this field. On the one hand, persons are [in effect] saying, "Go forth educators of the gifted and develop in this special population of students the upper levels of their most creative and productive behavior!" At the same time, however, the persons who offer us this creative challenge frequently also request that we show the results of our efforts in terms of some nice, neat scores on a standardized test. Unfortunately, the complexity of our objectives and the neatness and precision of the evaluation data requested do not go together. Tests simply do not exist to tell us the amount of growth that takes place when a youngster's work is instrumental in changing a state law, stopping the construction of an environmentally unsafe interstate highway, producing an award-winning film, publishing a special-topic newspaper, or bringing about the erection of a monument at a place with important historical significance. These types of creative products are the right and proper types of data upon which our evaluations should focus. They may not be as precise and objective as scores on a standardized test; however, if we are to make any important breakthroughs in evaluation, the products of children must be viewed as data. Our evaluations of such data may be more imprecise than test-score data; however, it is far better to have imprecise information about the right type of objective than precise information about the wrong objective.

What is most surprising about the hard data mystique is that very few persons calling for such objective data would question the more comprehensive types of objectives that we advocate for gifted youngsters. Using these objectives as our starting point, the first and biggest job in evaluation is to convince persons receiving evaluation reports (state departments of education, boards of education) that our special efforts require—indeed, demand—new evaluation models.

Although I can only speculate about some of the major characteristics of such models, one certainty is that we must develop better means for assessing the quality of all types of students' products. Such assessment will require that we seek the advice of specialists within particular fields (architects, furniture designers, choreographers, etc.). Through their knowledge, appreciation, special insights, and "connoisseurship" we may be able to learn about benchmarks of quality that will assist us in program evaluation.

NOTES

1. Six notable exceptions to the lack of theory and system development can be found in the work of Ward (1961), Stanley (1974), Feldhusen & Kolloff (1978), Treffinger (1975), Renzulli (1977), and Renzulli and Smith (1979).

2. Indeed, the well-known Pegnato and Birch study (1965) validated multiple criteria approaches to identification by comparing the alternative approaches with individual IQ test scores. In other words, a child was judged to be "really gifted" only if he or she met this ultimate criterion on a single measure. This being the case, one wonders why we should bother with alternative criteria and merely use individual IQ scores! Alternatives to the type of research design used by Pegnato and Birch can be found in Renzulli and Smith (1977) and Jenkins (1979).

3. Space does not permit a detailed discussion of how interest and creativity development activities are related to developing gifted behavior. The reader is referred to sections on Type I and Type II Enrichment in Renzulli, J. S., *The Enrichment Triad Model: A Guide for Developing Defensible Programs for the Gifted and Talented.* Mansfield Center, CT: Creative Learning Press, 1977.

4. Some of these lists of characteristics have been used for research studies and can be found in the literature. See for example, *Instructor*, May, 1977, p. 20.

REFERENCES

Bloom, B. S. (Ed.). *Taxonomy of educational objectives, handbook I: The cognitive domain.* New York: David McKay Co., 1956.

Do you have to be gifted to teach the gifted? *Instructor*, 1977, May, 20.

Feldhusen, J. F., & Kolloff, M. B. A three-stage model for gifted education. *G/C/T*, 1978, 4, 3–5; 53–57.

Guilford, J. P. *The nature of human intelligence.* New York: McGraw-Hill, 1967.

Jenkins, R. C. W. The identification of gifted and talented students through peer nomination (Doctoral dissertation, University of Connecticut, 1978). *Dissertation Abstracts International*, 1979, 40. (University Microfilms No. 7914161, 167-A)

Pegnato, C. W., & Birch, J. W. Locating gifted children in junior high schools: Comparison of methods. In W. B. Barbe & J. S. Renzulli (Eds.), *Psychology and education of the gifted: Selected readings.* New York: Irvington Press, 1975.

Renzulli, J. S. *A guidebook for evaluating programs for the gifted and talented.* Ventura, CA: Ventura County Superintendent of Schools, 1975.

Renzulli, J. S. *The enrichment triad model: A guide for developing defensible programs for the gifted and talented.* Mansfield Center, CT: Creative Learning Press, 1977.

Renzulli, J. S. What makes giftedness: Reexamining a definition. *Phi Delta Kappan*, 1978, 60, 180–184.

Renzulli, J. S., & Smith, L. H. Two approaches to identification of gifted students. *Exceptional Children*, 1977, 44, 512–518.

Renzulli, J. S., & Smith, L. H. *A guidebook for developing individualized educational programs (IEP) for the gifted and talented.* Mansfield Center, CT: Creative Learning Press, 1979.

Scriven, M. *Perspectives on curriculum evaluation.* AERA monograph series on curriculum evaluation, No. 1. Chicago: Rand McNally, 1967.

Stake, R. E. Measuring what learners learn. In E. R. House (Ed.), *School evaluation: The politics and process.* Berkeley, CA: McCutchan, 1973.

Stanley, J. C., Keating, D. P., & Fox, L. H. (Eds.). *Mathematical talent: Discovery, description, and development.* Baltimore: Johns Hopkins University Press, 1974.

Treffinger, D. J. Teaching for self-directed learning: A priority for the gifted and talented. *Gifted Child Quarterly*, 1975, 19, 46–59.

Ward, V. S. *Educating the gifted: An axiomatic approach.* Columbus, OH: Charles E. Merrill, Inc., 1965.

Weiler, D. The alpha children: California's brave new world for the gifted. *Phi Delta Kappan*, 1978, 60, 185–187.

Index

Note: References to tables or figures are indicated by *italic type* and the addition of "*t*" or "*f*," respectively.

**CORWIN
PRESS**

The Corwin Press logo—a raven striding across an open book—represents the union of courage and learning. Corwin Press is committed to improving education for all learners by publishing books and other professional development resources for those serving the field of K–12 education. By providing practical, hands-on materials, Corwin Press continues to carry out the promise of its motto: **"Helping Educators Do Their Work Better."**

Lightning Source UK Ltd.
Milton Keynes UK
UKHW031820200421
382322UK00006B/101

9 781412 904377